Successful pricing creates value for customers and provides valuable strategic insights and guidelines, w manager can relate to.

Roger Best, Emeritus Professor of Marketing, University of Oregon, USA

With a wide variety of contributions from pricing experts and a thorough – yet detailed – list of topics, this latest book from Liozu and Hinterhuber will be an invaluable resource for those who are looking to increase their pricing knowledge and improve their company's profitability. This book addresses many of the important questions stemming from the renewed importance of the pricing discipline today.

Kevin Mitchell, President, The Professional Pricing Society

It is critical for pricing organizations to adopt a rigorous, investment-oriented culture around their efforts to build new capabilities. This book brings an important contribution to the pricing profession so that they can better compete for investment funds.

Andres Reiner, President and CEO, PROS Holdings

Measuring the impact of pricing projects and the pricing function is THE key to driving firm performance via pricing. Once calculated, the Executive Suite can see sustainable and immediate payback and justify investing in the tools, processes, and people to realize this value. This book by Stephan Liozu and Andreas Hinterhuber provides a framework and best practices on how to do this and is recommended reading for any pricing professional.

Todd Snelgrove, Global Manager, Value, SKF

Not a moment too soon! *The ROI of Pricing* is a timely and exciting contribution to our understanding of a pressing business issue – the ability to systematically justify and show the impact of pricing decisions. The authors tackle this issue with contributions from expert practitioners and leading academics and successfully manage to provide acute and critical insights with depth and rigour. As a niche area that contributes directly to the bottom line, this book is a must read for anyone managing pricing decisions or anyone with an interest in understanding the power of pricing!

Dr Ben Lowe, Kent Business School, University of Kent, UK

Finally! A practical and intelligent explanation of pricing! This book describes the downstream consequences when firms get their pricing strategies right, as well as when they get them wrong. With detailed explanations and real-life examples, this book clearly explains the complexity of pricing. The reader will find everything they need to know about pricing strategies to enter new markets, beat their competitors, and ensure that they don't unwittingly cannibalize their own products.

Dr Richard Pech, Associate Professor of Management,
La Trobe University, Melbourne Australia

The ROI of Pricing provides an excellent overview of contemporary research and practitioner thinking about the financial impact of strategic pricing. It provides evidence-based guidelines for how to evaluate such investments in pricing capability and motivate the expense within your organization by quantifying the returns.

Niklas L. Hallberg PhD, Senior Lecturer of Strategic Management,
Lund University, Sweden

With today's macroeconomic and competitive market pressures, general managers push their business functions to deeper clarifications of the value that they contribute and the costs that they incur. As all this information culminates in the price decision, the logical next step is to quantify the contributions and costs of the pricing function itself. *The ROI of Pricing* brings together relevant insights in this topic and is therefore a must read for managers that want to stay ahead of competition. Readers will discover that pricing as the final step in the value creation process can be a major source of tomorrow's competitive advantage.

Paul Ingenbleek, Wageningen University, The Netherlands

As a practitioner in the "real" world trying to implement best-practice pricing in global organizations, I have several times seen the paradox hindering organizations to move from cost-plus to value-based pricing. On one hand, everyone see the rationale and agree that it makes sense, whereas, on the other hand, it is very difficult to get the organization to make the effort, or to get decision-makers to support the steps needed to make the transition. I believe this book will be a great help in this process, by giving compelling examples and evidence in a clear-cut and motivating way.

Berndt Berndtsson, Marketing Processes Director, Sweden

THE ROI OF PRICING

As with executives and managers in so many other business functions, pricing specialists are being challenged more and more to substantiate the added value of their activities. Pricing is a core function of every business and needs not only to contribute positively to short- and long-term results but also to document its impact on the bottom line. A fundamental part of this is the pricing return on investment (ROI) calculations.

This book, edited by globally renowned thought leaders Stephan Liozu and Andreas Hinterhuber, is the first to outline contemporary theories and best practices of documenting pricing ROI and make the case for pricing investments. It provides proven methods, practices and theories on how to calculate the impact of pricing activities on performance. Marketing ROI is now a common concept: this collection aims to do the same for pricing.

Liozu and Hinterhuber introduce the concept of pricing ROI, documenting and quantifying the return on pricing activities and on the pricing function, which itself is of increasing relevance today and in the future, in times of budget constraints. Twenty world-class specialists explore the concept of pricing ROI from both a theoretical perspective and a managerial perspective to shed much-needed light on how to measure and increase pricing ROI.

This ground-breaking book will enlighten students and specialists of marketing and sales, pricing managers and executives alike.

Stephan M. Liozu is the Founder of Value Innoruption Advisors, based in the USA.

Andreas Hinterhuber is a Partner of Hinterhuber & Partners, based in Austria.

THE ROI OF PRICING

Measuring the impact and making the business case

Edited by
Stephan M. Liozu and Andreas Hinterhuber

Routledge
Taylor & Francis Group

LONDON AND NEW YORK

First published 2014
by Routledge
2 Park Square, Milton Park, Abingdon, Oxon OX14 4RN

and by Routledge
711 Third Avenue, New York, NY 10017

Routledge is an imprint of the Taylor & Francis Group, an informa business

British Library Cataloguing in Publication Data
A catalogue record for this book is available from the British Library

Library of Congress Cataloging in Publication Data
The ROI of pricing : measuring the impact and making the business case / edited by Stephan M. Liozu and Andreas Hinterhuber.
    pages cm
  1. Pricing. I. Liozu, Stephan. II. Hinterhuber, Andreas.
  HF5416.5.R647 2014
  658.8'16—dc23   2013027391

ISBN: 978-0-415-83379-0 (hbk)
ISBN: 978-0-415-73071-6 (pbk)
ISBN: 978-0-203-36266-2 (ebk)

Typeset in Bembo
by Keystroke, Station Road, Codsall, Wolverhampton

MIX
Paper from
responsible sources
FSC   FSC° C013056
www.fsc.org

Printed and bound in Great Britain by
TJ International Ltd, Padstow, Cornwall

CONTENTS

LIST OF ILLUSTRATIONS

Figures

Tables

Box

NOTES ON CONTRIBUTORS

Book editors

Stephan M. Liozu is the Founder of Value Innoruption Advisors (www.stephan liozu.com), a consultancy specialized in disruptive approaches to value, pricing and innovation management. He holds a PhD in Management from and is an Adjunct Professor and a Visiting Scholar at Case Western Reserve University, Weatherhead School of Management, Ohio. His dissertation explores the organizational journey towards pricing excellence with a special focus on strategic and organizational pricing capabilities. He has published papers in *MIT Sloan Management Review*, *Industrial Marketing Management*, *Journal of Strategic Marketing*, *Journal of Business Strategy*, *Journal of Revenue & Pricing Management*, as well as the *Journal of Professional Pricing*. He resides in Sewickley, Pennsylvania, USA.

Andreas Hinterhuber is a Partner of Hinterhuber & Partners (www.hinterhuber. com), a consultancy specialized in strategy, pricing and leadership. He is also a Visiting Professor at the USI Lugano and at Bolzano University and was acting Chair of the Department of International Management at the Katholische Universität Eichstaett-Ingolstadt (Germany). Previously he was a Marketing Executive with Bayer AG, where he was responsible for the largest product group with worldwide responsibilities. His papers have been published in *MIT Sloan Management Review*, *Industrial Marketing Management*, *Long Range Planning*, *International Journal of Innovation Management* and other leading international journals. He lives in Innsbruck, Austria.

Book contributors

Ed Arnold is Vice President of Product Development at LeveragePoint Innovations and also a founder of LeveragePoint, the only cloud-based solution for value-based pricing, and currently leads product development and marketing. In addition, he is responsible for LeveragePoint's successful adoption at multiple leading B2B companies, as well as establishing LeveragePoint's market presence. Previously, Ed held key management roles in software and management consulting firms such as Communispace, the Monitor Group and Diamond Technology.

Carmen Balan is Professor PhD at the Faculty of Marketing of the Bucharest University of Economic Studies in Romania. Her teaching assignments encompass areas of marketing management and marketing research. Her research interests focus on the marketing mix and particularly on distribution.

Roger J. Best PhD is Emeritus Professor of Marketing at the University of Oregon and author of *Market-Based Management* (Prentice Hall, 6th edition, 2012), the best-selling textbook on calculating marketing ROI. He has worked extensively with Peter Vomocil in the area of Marketing Performance Metrics and Profitable Growth.

Mathias Chenal is a 2010 graduate of CPE Lyon Engineering School and the University of Birmingham with a Master's Degree in Chemical Engineering with Business Management. In 2011 he obtained a Specialized Master's Degree in Technology and Innovation Management from EM Lyon Business School. He is currently working as a project manager in the innovation field and is responsible for implementing innovation processes and managing innovative projects. His main topics of interest are strategic innovation and pricing as part of the innovation process. He achieved the CPP (Certified Pricing Professional) designation from the Professional Pricing Society in September 2012.

Jeffery Collins PhD serves as Director of Value Engineering at the PROS. He developed PROS Value Engineering practice which supports prospective customers' efforts to identify and quantify potential value from a pricing software investment. Jeffery works with existing customers to quantify the realized value of their pricing software investment.

Stefano Denicolai is an Assistant Professor at the Department of Business and Economics of the University of Pavia in Italy, where he is a Professor of Innovation Management and Vice-Director of the PhD Program in Economics and Management. He is also a Visiting Scholar at the 'Science Technology Research Policy' [SPRU], University of Sussex, UK. His research interests focus on Corporate Strategy, Business Modeling, Innovation, Startups and Entrepreneurship.

David Dvorin is a Senior Operating Executive at Welsh, Carson, Anderson & Stowe (WCAS). At WCAS, David is responsible for identifying and implementing pricing improvement initiatives across the firm's portfolio. Before joining WCAS, he was Vice President, Global Strategic Pricing at Thermo Fisher Scientific, where he led the development and implementation of strategic pricing tools and methodologies.

David has over ten years of pricing experience, having previously worked as the Director of Pricing at American Greetings and as an Engagement Manager at McKinsey & Company. David received a BS from the University of Michigan and a Master's Degree in Public Policy from the John F. Kennedy School of Government at Harvard University. David lives in Pittsburgh, Pennsylvania, USA.

Doug Fuehne runs the Strategic Consulting team for the PROS, which is responsible for consulting, best practice implementation, presales solution development and industry thought leadership. Previously, he ran the Professional Services team and the Science Solutions teams at the PROS. Prior to his work at the PROS, Doug consulted across multiple diverse industries in pricing and supply chain design, focusing on science- and process-based solutions.

Jered Haedt is a Chief Scientist and Managing Partner of The Pricing Cloud. He has diversified experience in analytics and strategy, specializing in econometrics and strategic business intelligence platforms. His experience provides significant and comprehensive utilization of complex application of theory in data-sparse environments and adaptive modeling. Whether Jered is implementing a global monitoring database for predictive failure analyses or implementing advanced product and margin analytics, his projects consistently return high ROI.

Kostis Indounas is an Assistant Professor of Marketing at the Athens University of Economics and Business, Athens, from where he received his PhD. His works have appeared in international conferences and academic journals such as *Industrial Marketing Management, Journal of Service Management, Journal of Business and Industrial Marketing, Business Horizons, Journal of Retailing and Consumer Services, European Journal of Marketing* and *Journal of Services Marketing*, among others. His teaching and research interests are in the areas of pricing, services marketing, marketing for non-profit organizations and new product development. He is a member of the European Marketing Academy and the Academy of Marketing in the UK.

Vernon Lennon is Principal and CEO of The Pricing Cloud. A seasoned pricing professional and business consultant, Vernon has vast strategic and scientific pricing experience in over ten different industries. As Principal and CEO of The Pricing Cloud, he has been driving the newly formed discipline of Strategic and Scientific Pricing across multiple organizations. Vernon holds an MBA in Finance from Southern New Hampshire University and a BS in Resource Economics from the University of New Hampshire.

Federica Merli is a Manager working with Mediterranean Shipping Company, based in Charleston, South Carolina. She holds a Master's Degree in business from the University of Pavia, Italy. She has been working in the fashion industry as Project Manager for the start-up company 'Moi Multiple' in Italy and as Research Assistant at the University of Pavia, Italy.

Kevin Mitchell is President of the Professional Pricing Society. He is also the Publisher of *The Pricing Advisor* newsletter and the *Journal of Professional Pricing*. His previous experience includes marketing and finance roles at Colgate-Palmolive and General Electric. He has a BA in Economics and English from Duke University and a MBA in Marketing from the William E. Simon Graduate School of Business at the University of Rochester, New York. He lives in Atlanta, Georgia, USA.

Antonio Ruggiero is COO and Managing Partner of The Pricing Cloud. He has been involved with the design and implementation of pricing optimization software for more than ten years. Antonio's focus has been providing Business Intelligence, Business Analytics and Business Optimizations to solve business challenges with particular emphasis on enterprise software solutions. Antonio has published articles on pricing and revenue management, is a frequent speaker at conferences and has patents pending on using competitive information in pricing solutions. He holds a MSc in Mathematics from the University of Toronto and a MSc in Physics from Guelph-Waterloo Physics Program, University of Guelph, Ontario.

Robert Smith is the Director of Corporate Pricing for Eastman Chemical Company. He serves as the leader of Eastman Chemical's Pricing Council, a cross-business and functional team dedicated to improving margin performance and pricing processes. Robert is a native of Hendersonville, North Carolina, and received a BS degree in Chemical Engineering from the Georgia Institute of Technology and a MBA from the University of Tennessee. He is a member of the Professional Pricing Society (PPS) and has been a presenter at PPS, the Vendavo User Summit, and the Institute for the Study of Business Markets (ISBM). He co-authored with Dr George Cressman the article 'Share Wars', which was published in *Marketing Management* and the *Journal of Professional Pricing*. He was also a contributor to the book *Value Merchants* by James Anderson, Nirmalya Kumar and James Narus and has been quoted in various articles on pricing.

Navdeep Sodhi is a Managing Director at Sodhi Pricing. He specializes in pricing consultancy that helps companies improve revenues and earnings. His experience as practitioner and consultant spans several global industries: airlines, B2B manufacturing, building products, chemicals, electronics and outsourced services. Navdeep's approach to price improvement is presented in his book *Six Sigma Pricing: Improving Pricing Operations to Increase Profits* (Financial Times Press, 2008) and was first introduced in a seminal *Harvard Business Review* article (2005). He has published other articles on pricing strategy and execution in reputed publications such as *Quality Digest* and *Journal of Professional Pricing*. Navdeep is a teaching fellow at the University of Minnesota's executive program and teaches a pricing seminar at the University of Saint Thomas, Minnesota.

Linda Trevenen is Director of Marketing Excellence & Market Intelligence for Philips Home Healthcare Solutions (HHS). She has been working for Philips

Healthcare Solutions since 2005. Linda is currently leading the transformation at Philips Respironics from a product and technology focus to an outside-in strategy via a customer-centric mindset. She is tasked with improving HHS customers' experience across the enterprise, driving faster innovations that solve meaningful problems in the care cycle and elevating marketing competencies among all marketers across HHS. She earned her CPP (Certified Pricing Professional) in 2009 and speaks annually at Georgetown University on segmentation to MBA students.

Peter J. Vomocil MBA, from the University of Oregon, is a customer and marketing strategy consultant. He has worked extensively with Roger Best in the area of Marketing Performance Metrics and Profitable Growth.

Craig Zawada serves as Chief Visionary Officer at the PROS, a leading provider of pricing and revenue management software. Prior to joining the PROS, Craig was a partner and co-leader of the Pricing Strategy Practice at McKinsey & Company. He also co-authored both the first and second editions of the book *The Price Advantage*, as well as articles in the *Harvard Business Review* and many other publications. He resides in Kimberley, British Columbia.

INTRODUCTION: PRICING – FROM FINANCE BACK TO FINANCE

The coming of age of pricing ROI

Stephan M. Liozu and Andreas Hinterhuber

Pricing managers, marketing managers, product managers, marketing planners and other marketing personnel are increasingly challenged to substantiate the value added of the pricing function and of pricing activities. Pricing is a core function of every business which not only needs to contribute positively to short- and long-term results, but also to document its impact to the bottom line. This book aims to provide guidance.

A short history: With strong roots in economics and finance, pricing has evolved to include core concepts from marketing, operations research, production, consumer psychology and statistics. Pricing today, next to general management, is probably the broadest discipline, both for practitioners as well as academics, touching virtually every function of a company. With this, also the research in pricing has progressed: today, concepts such as "pricing capabilities" (Dutta et al. 2002), "CEO championing of pricing" (Liozu and Hinterhuber 2013a) and "innovation in pricing" (Hinterhuber and Liozu 2012) have firmly entered the mainstream.

What next? Pricing today and in the future will need to speak the language of finance. With this, pricing will have made a full-circle turn. Instruments to measure the contribution of the pricing function and of pricing activities to company profitability are largely lacking. In this respect the marketing function and marketing activities certainly provide illuminating reference points. Until only a few years ago marketing, even in the best managed companies, was an expense. General Electric may provide an example. In 2008 a reporter of a marketing magazine asked Beth Comstock, Chief Marketing Officer of General Electric about the specific approach the company used to determine the return on marketing expenses. Her answer: "I would say that we haven't figured it out yet." Today this answer would be unthinkable and would put the company at a serious risk of lawsuits from shareholders demanding accountability on multibillion marketing investments.

Thanks to substantial academic research in this area (Ataman et al. 2010; Mela et al. 1997, 1998; Pauwels et al. 2002; Slotegraaf and Pauwels 2008), the concept of marketing return on investment, especially an understanding of the financial return of price promotions, is well established nowadays.

Pricing today, like marketing in the past, is called to substantiate its contribution to the bottom line. In a first step, we have witnessed a wave of studies documenting the financial consequences of alternative pricing strategies. In the future we expect to witness a rising interest in the concept of pricing return on investment, i.e. a calculation that quantifies the financial return of the pricing function or of pricing activities.

The financial consequences of alternative pricing strategies

The pricing literature studies the relationship between pricing approach and firm performance: Monroe (1990, p.24), for example, argues: "[. . .] the profit potential for having a value-oriented pricing strategy that works is far greater than with any other pricing approach." Similarly, Cannon and Morgan (1990, p.25) recommend perceived value pricing if profit maximization is the objective: "Perceived value pricing enables a company to select an optimal price/volume combination." Cost-based pricing approaches, conversely, lead to sub-optimal profitability (Backman 1953; Myers et al. 2002).

Ingenbleek et al. (2003) find that value-informed pricing has the overall strongest positive effect on product performance. More recently, we have launched a stream of research linking pricing to firm performance (Liozu and Hinterhuber 2013a). In a large quantitative study with 1,812 respondents, we find a positive and strong link between value-based pricing and firm performance, whereas the relationship between competition-based pricing and firm performance is negative and significant (Liozu and Hinterhuber 2013b). In sum, we now know that value-based pricing strategies increase profits.

Towards a concept of pricing ROI

From the macro-domain of performance consequences of pricing strategies we aim to move to the micro-domain of performance consequences of the pricing function or of pricing activities, i.e. to the pricing ROI. In this respect the well-established concept of marketing ROI provides a fruitful starting point. In the current literature we find two main approaches to measure marketing ROI: Best (2012) and Lenskold (2003). Both approaches can be modified to quantify the pricing ROI as shown in Table 0.1.

The objectives of this book

It is our intent to advance the theory and practice of pricing ROI, i.e. of documenting the causal relationship between pricing activities or the pricing function itself and performance. Specifically, this book:

TABLE 0.1 Approaches to marketing ROI

	Best (2012)	*Lenskold (2003)*
Formula	Marketing ROI (%) = $$\frac{\text{Net marketing contribution}}{\text{Marketing and sales expenses}}$$	Marketing ROI (%) = $$\text{NPV of incremental margin} - \frac{\text{Marketing investment}}{\text{Marketing investment}}$$
Whereas	Net marketing contribution = gross profit (*sales* − *COGS*) − marketing and sales expenses	NPV of incremental margin = net present value of incremental margins related to marketing investment
	Marketing and sales expenses = all fixed expenses related to marketing and sales activities	Marketing investment = cost of marketing investment (e.g. cost of campaign, promotional activity, etc.)
Key strength	Aggregate measure capable of analyzing the contribution of the *overall* marketing function	Narrow measure capable of analyzing the contributions of *specific* marketing activities to profitability
Open questions	Causal relationship of "Net marketing contribution" to "Marketing and sales expenses"; managerial relevance	Definition of "Incremental margin" versus baseline scenario.

- provides a summary of current research on the impact of pricing;
- reports own research on tools firms currently use to measure pricing ROI;
- highlights how to calculate pricing ROI;
- illustrates the calculation of pricing ROI through case studies.

The structure of the book

This book consists of 15 chapters from academia, practitioners and consultants in the field of value and pricing management. These 15 chapters, shown in Table 0.2, have been grouped into three major categories: pricing strategy, pricing tactics and pricing organization. Most chapters propose a definition or an approach for the measurement of pricing ROI while others focus on making the business case for pricing investments.

Pricing strategy

The first five chapters focus on pricing at the strategic level. Roger Best and Peter Vomocil propose an essay on how value-based pricing improves pricing ROI. Andreas Hinterhuber addresses one of the most neglected subjects in pricing

TABLE 0.2 Chapter presentation and classification

Chapter number	Authors	Short title	Focus			Measurement of pricing ROI	Key findings and contributions
			Empirical	Conceptual	Literature review		
1	Best and Vomocil	Value-based Pricing ROI	X			X	Value-based pricing improves pricing ROI.
2	Hinterhuber	Cannibalization	X		X	X	When and why cannibalization increases/decreases profits.
3	Balan	Return on price promotions		X	X	(X)	Negative long-term return on price promotions.
4	Denicolai and Merli	Pricing in start-ups	X				Pricing contributes to performance of start-ups.
5	Liozu	The case for value-based pricing		X			Uses incremental approach in making the case.
6	Ruggiero and Haedt	Evaluating pricing actions		X		X	Sources of data and statistical measurement of effects are key.
7	Trevenen	VOC and product launch	X				Conjoint analysis can deliver pricing impact and avoid failure.
8	Liozu and Chenal	Power of quick wins	X				Use quick wins to document ROI and build confidence.

#	Author	Title				Description
9	Sodhi	Stepwise price measurement		X	X	Avoid roadblocks to measurement.
10	Indounas	Break-even analysis	X		X	Breakeven analysis versus cost-based pricing in shipyard field.
11	Dvorin and Lennon	Expected ROI and resource allocation		X	X	Use ROI analysis to allocate resources among divisions.
12	Arnold	The case for organizational collaboration	X		X	The ROI and payback of collaborative value-based pricing tool.
13	Zawada, Collins and Fuehne	Pricing software investments		X	X	Using the right metrics to measure ROI of pricing software.
14	Smith	Interview with pricing expert	X			Measurement discipline is critical.
15	Liozu	ROI of pricing; state of profession	X		X	Firms do not formally measure ROI or have lack of success.

discussions, i.e. cannibalization evaluation and how it might increase or decrease profits. Carmen Balan focuses on the impact of price promotions while Stefano Denicolai and Federica Merli propose a framework on how pricing contributes to the performance of start-up companies. Finally, Stephan Liozu proposes an essay on what main issues pricing professionals face in making the case for value-based pricing.

Pricing tactics

This section of the book starts with a very practical paper from Antonio Ruggiero and Jered Haedt on where to find the right data for the measurement of pricing actions as well as on how to statistically calculate the incremental effect. Linda Trevenen makes the case for greater use of conjoint analysis to improve payback and avoid product failures. Stephan Liozu and Mathias Chenal propose the results of an informal controlled experiment and how quick wins can help make the case for greater investments and increase team confidence. Navdeep Sodhi also proposes a case study and an approach to avoid measurement roadblocks for pricing ROI. Finally, Kostis Indounas illustrates the need to calculate breakeven analysis to support pricing decisions instead on the traditional cost-based pricing approach used in the shipyard industry.

Pricing organization

This section also offers five papers. David Dvorin and Vernon Lennon propose a framework to prioritize pricing projects across multiple divisions using the ROI of pricing calculation. Ed Arnold presents the results of a qualitative inquiry with several customers who have adopted value-based pricing collaborative cloud platforms and discusses the ROI of their implementation. Craig Zawada, Jeff Collins and Doug Fuehne list all relevant metrics to calculate the ROI of pricing software. We then present a unique interview with Robert Smith, one of the best pricing experts in the world. Robert discussed best practices on making the case for pricing investments and for a greater discipline in measuring the impact of pricing. Stephan Liozu then presents the state of the profession with the findings from a unique survey conducted among 313 pricing professionals. He highlights the current practices of the profession and the future areas for improvement.

This book is a unique compilation of concepts, methods and case studies related to the calculation of pricing ROI and to making the case for pricing investments. It is a first attempt to propose a holistic approach for these topics and is dedicated to the advancement of the pricing profession. We hope to generate a dialog among pricing professionals and to bring the tools necessary to help document the great impact they have on their organization's bottom line.

References

Ataman, M. B., Van Heerde, H. J. and Mela, C. F. (2010) The long-term effect of marketing strategy on brand sales. *Journal of Marketing Research*, 47 (5), pp. 866–882.

Backman, J. (1953) *Price practices and policies*. New York, NY: Ronald Press.

Best, R. (2012) *Market-based management: Strategies for growing customer value and profitability* (6th ed.). Upper Saddle River, NJ: Prentice Hall.

Cannon, H. M. and Morgan, F. W. (1990) A strategic pricing framework. *Journal of Services Marketing*, 4 (2), pp. 19–30.

Dutta, S., Bergen, M., Levy, D., Ritson, M. and Zbaracki, M. (2002) Pricing as a strategic capability. *MIT Sloan Management Review*, 43 (3), pp. 61–66.

Hinterhuber, A. and Liozu, S. (2012) Innovation in pricing. In: A. Hinterhuber and S. Liozu (Eds) *Innovation in pricing: Contemporary theories and best practices*. New York, NY: Routledge, pp. 1–12.

Ingenbleek, P., Debruyne, M., Frambach, R. T. and Verhallen, T. M. M. (2003) Successful new product pricing practices: A contingency approach. *Marketing Letters*, 14 (4), pp. 289–305.

Lenskold, J. (2003) *Marketing ROI: The path to campaign, customer, and corporate profitability*. New York, NY: McGraw-Hill Professional.

Liozu, S. and Hinterhuber, A. (2013a) CEO championing of pricing, pricing capabilities and firm performance in industrial firms. *Industrial Marketing Management*, 42 (4), pp. 633–643.

Liozu, S. and Hinterhuber, A. (2013b) Pricing orientation, pricing capabilities, and firm performance. *Management Decision*, 51 (3), pp. 594–614.

Mela, C. F., Gupta, S. and Lehmann, D. R. (1997) The long-term impact of promotion and advertising on consumer brand choice. *Journal of Marketing Research*, 34 (2), pp. 248–261.

Mela, C. F., Gupta, S. and Jedidi, K. (1998) Assessing long-term promotional influences on market structure. *International Journal of Research in Marketing*, 15 (2), pp. 89–107.

Monroe, K. B. (1990) *Pricing: Making profitable decisions*. New York, NY: McGraw-Hill Pub. Co.

Myers, M. B., Cavusgil, S. T. and Diamantopoulos, A. (2002) Antecedents and actions of export pricing strategy: A conceptual framework and research propositions. *European Journal of Marketing*, 36 (1/2), pp. 159–188.

Pauwels, K., Hanssens, D. M. and Siddarth, S. (2002) The long-term effects of price promotions on category incidence, brand choice, and purchase quantity. *Journal of Marketing Research*, 39 (4), pp. 421–439.

Slotegraaf, R. J. and Pauwels, K. (2008) The impact of brand equity and innovation on the long-term effectiveness of promotions. *Journal of Marketing Research*, 45 (3), pp. 293–306.

1

VALUE-BASED PRICING ROI

Roger J. Best and Peter J. Vomocil

Pricing arguably has the most dramatic and immediate impact on sales and profits. Yet, it is one of the most mismanaged areas of marketing management. Sixty percent of businesses default to using cost-based pricing—a pricing strategy wherein price is determined by a business's cost and margin requirements—with no real idea of the value their product, whether positive or negative (Cressman Jr. 1999; Noble and Gruca 1999). Since cost-based pricing ignores market intelligence, it often results in overpricing which lowers volume and profits; or in underpricing, which lowers gross profits despite higher volume. For example, a media tablet with a unit cost of $350 would require a price of $700 at a desired margin of 50 percent, as shown in Figure 1.1. At a desired margin of 30 percent, the cost-based price would be $500.

A different approach would be to adopt a market-based price—a price based on the needs of target customers, competitors' product positions, and the strength of a business's product, service, or brand advantage. Based on an understanding of customers' willingness to pay at ten different price points (Retrevo 2009), a market-based price of $600 would be more desirable since it produces a higher level of gross profit. The market-based price of $600 is close to the average selling price of the iPad when launched in 2010.

We can take it one step further and employ a value-based pricing strategy—charging a price that creates a meaningful difference between a fair-market price and a price for a certain level of performance. Value-based pricing requires an understanding of the value that a customer derives from a product, and how it compares to competing offerings. In this chapter, we will explore three value-based pricing methods and examine the corresponding Pricing ROI for each method.

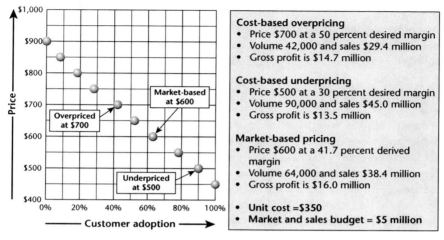

FIGURE 1.1 Cost-based pricing vs. market-based pricing: media tablets

Value-based pricing and net marketing contribution

There are several aspects of a successful value-based pricing strategy. The most important factor is that target customers perceive value that is clearly superior over competing products. Customer value is the difference between a product's fair price and the selling price. Superior value can be based on a meaningful advantage in actual or perceived performance; total cost of ownership; and preferences for certain price-performance combinations. Each of these sources of customer value will be demonstrated in the remainder of this chapter as we examine three different value-based pricing methods.

Before we discuss Pricing ROI, we need to discuss the foundation of the Pricing ROI equation. Net Marketing Contribution (NMC) is a fundamental measure of marketing profitability. We will use NMC as a core element of the Pricing ROI calculation. It is defined simply as the contribution to profits after deducting marketing and sales expenses (Best 2013).

FIGURE 1.2 How value-based pricing impacts net market contribution

Regardless of how superior value is created, it has the potential to impact each area of performance in the NMC equation, as shown in Figure 1.2. Each of these potential impacts on NMC can contribute to a larger numerator in the Pricing ROI equation when a value-based pricing strategy is successful.

Value-based Pricing ROI

Pricing ROI is a measure of the performance of pricing decisions and enables marketers to compare investments in various pricing opportunities. In order to accurately measure the Pricing ROI of a value-based price change, we need to capture the investment required to execute a new pricing strategy, in addition to measuring the impact on marketing profits. We propose to measure Pricing ROI based on the difference in NMC before and after a value-based price change strategy, divided by the investment needed to create, communicate, and deliver the value-based pricing strategy.

This can be expressed as:

$$\textbf{Pricing ROI} = \frac{\text{NMC (after)} - \text{NMC (before)}}{\text{Investment in Pricing Strategy}} \times 100\%$$

For example, the tablet in Figure 1.1 that is overpriced at $700 would produce a NMC of $9.7 million as shown below:

$$
\begin{aligned}
\textbf{NMC} &= \text{volume sold} \times \text{net price} \times \% \text{ margin} \\
&\quad - \text{marketing and sales expenses} \\
&= 42{,}000 \times \$700 \times 50\% - \$5 \text{ million} \\
&= \$14.7 \text{ million} - \$5 \text{ million} \\
&= \$9.7 \text{ million}
\end{aligned}
$$

With an investment of $500,000 for market intelligence and additions to the marketing budget to communicate the new market-based price of $600, the following NMC is produced:

$$
\begin{aligned}
\textbf{NMC} &= \text{volume} \times \text{net price} \times \% \text{ margin} - \text{marketing and sales expenses} \\
&\quad - \text{pricing strategy expense} \\
&= 64{,}000 \times \$600 \times 41.7\% - \$5 \text{ million} - \$300{,}000 \\
&= \$16 \text{ million} - \$5.3 \text{ million} \\
&= \$10.7 \text{ million}
\end{aligned}
$$

Pricing ROI is subsequently computed as shown below. With an incremental gain of $1 million in NMC that required an investment of $300,000, the Pricing ROI for this pricing strategy was 333 percent.

$$\textbf{Pricing ROI} = \frac{\text{NMC (after)} - \text{NMC (before)}}{\text{Investment in pricing strategy}} \times 100\%$$

$$= \frac{\$10.7 \text{ million} - \$9.7 \text{ million}}{\$300,000} \times 100\%$$

$$= \frac{\$1 \text{ million}}{\$300,000} \times 100\%$$

$$= 333\%$$

Investing in value-based pricing

Potential gains in marketing performance and profits are only possible with a true investment in the value-based pricing strategy. Value-based pricing requires time and investment to create, communicate, and deliver value that is meaningful to target customers. However, businesses often resist investing in pricing strategies because they are accustomed to simply changing a price and passively observing the resulting changes in performance. Let's looks at the requisite investment in pricing for these three steps in building a value-based pricing strategy.

Creating value

For customer value to be meaningful it needs to be based on a superior and sustainable performance advantage that is valued by target customers. For most businesses, this means some level of customer research to determine the sources of advantage. For example, a producer of gas chromatographs found that its $50,000 product has a lifespan of five years, while their competitor's similarly priced product has a lifespan of four years. On an annualized basis, the competitor's customer pays $12,500 more. In this case there was an investment in competitive benchmarking to uncover a meaningful source of advantage.

The business also found that their gas chromatograph had superior performance, but the product was difficult to use. The difficulty of product use diminished the perceived value and had to be addressed in order to improve the customer experience. In this case an investment in customer intelligence and product engineering created a complete product that offered a higher value to target customers.

Communicating value

Simply because a business creates superior customer value does not mean target customers will understand their value advantage. Marketing communication is often needed to illustrate how a product creates a superior value and how that value is an advantage to the customer.

In many value-based pricing situations, sales training and new sales collateral will also need to be created. The sales force may need to be trained how to communicate the benefit of the customer value, thereby justifying the higher price of the product. This investment in the value-based pricing strategy is critical and the strategy will most likely fail without it, despite any value created.

Delivering value

In order for the value-based pricing strategy to achieve the desired sales and profit objectives, the customer must recognize the value created and be willing to pay a premium for that superior value. This requires an additional investment in customer intelligence to determine the value realized and the strength of the customer's commitment to the business's product due to their value advantage.

Figure 1.3 illustrates two examples of communicating and delivering customer value. The recreation of an AirCap advertisement positions a typical customer application against a competing product to illustrate how AirCap could save a customer $0.65 per shipment. The Kyocera advertisement challenges customers to understand their total cost of purchase, by utilizing the Kyocera TCO Tracker website (http://usa.kyoceradocumentsolutions.com/americas/jsp/Kyocera/tcotracker.jsp) to estimate the savings they would achieve over an average printer life using a Kyocera printer.

Let's now look at three value-based pricing methodologies, namely, price performance, total cost of ownership, and trade-off. In the following section, we will discuss each method and the corresponding Pricing ROI in detail.

AirCap: Packaging Material	**Kyocera: Printer**

AirCap vs. Corrugated Inserts

A manufacturer using corrugated inserts switched to AirCap and obtained the per shipment savings shown below.

Item	Corrugated Packaging	AirCap Packaging
Carton	$.55	$.55
Packaging	$.80	$1.05
Labor	$.83	$.13
Freight	$2.60	$2.40
Total Cost	$4.78	$4.13

Savings using AirCap........................$.65

FIGURE 1.3 Demonstrating and communicating customer value

Value-based pricing method #1: price performance

Performance drives price, although not all potential customers will pay more for increased performance. As a result, there is a price–performance relationship that can be measured and managed to create a value-added price position. The question, of course, is whether the investment required to create a value-based price will yield a meaningful Pricing ROI.

The performance of competing products can be measured in a variety of ways. One recognized performance rating system is created by *Consumer Reports*. *Consumer Reports* rates products on a five-category scale that ranges from poor to excellent for different aspects of performance. We can utilize this data to create a performance index with scores on a zero to 100-point scale. A score of 50 would be considered average, while scores above 50 would be above average on overall performance.

The product performance ratings for ten digital cameras and their associated retail prices are shown in Figure 1.4. The ten digital cameras in this example range from 50 to 90 points, with an average of 72. Retail prices range from $130 to $300 with an average price of $206.

What is a fair price?

When these ten digital cameras are graphed based on performance and price we can see some obvious variance in this relationship, as shown in Figure 1.4. For example, the four digital cameras rated at 70 in performance vary in price from $130 to $230. The "Fair Price Line" in Figure 1.4 is a least-squares regression estimate of the relationship between price and performance (Gale 1994; learn much more at www.cval.com). The Fair Price Line represents the price one would expect to pay for a product based on performance. All Fair Price Lines run through the average of price and performance. For example, the Canon A580 is priced at $180 with a performance rating of 80. The fair price would be $226 for this level of performance.

Digital cameras	No.	Performance rating	Product price	Fair price	Customer value
Casio EX-29	1	79	$150	$202	$52
Casio EX-280	2	50	$180	$155	($25)
Canon A580	**3**	**80**	**$180**	**$226**	**$46**
Canon SD870	4	80	$280	$226	($54)
Canon SD790	5	90	$300	$250	($50)
Fuji J10	6	70	$130	$202	$72
Kodak M1033	7	75	$200	$214	$14
Kodak V1073	8	60	$230	$179	($51)
Nikon P60	9	70	$230	$202	($28)
Pentax M50	10	70	$180	$202	$22
Average		72	$206	$206	$0

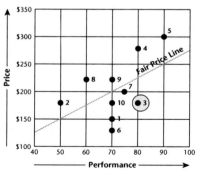

FIGURE 1.4 Price performance, fair value, and customer value—digital cameras

What is the customer value?

Customer value is the difference between a product's fair price and the selling price. For example, the Canon A580 has a positive customer value of $46 with a fair price of $226 and a selling price of $180 as shown below:

$$\text{Customer value (Canon A580)} = \text{fair price} - \text{selling price}$$
$$= \$226 - \$180$$
$$= \$46$$

The five digital cameras above the Fair Price Line all have negative customer values, as their selling prices exceed their fair price based on performance. Manufacturers with a negative customer value are overpriced for their level of product performance. The five digital cameras below the Fair Price Line each have a positive customer value that ranges from $22 for the Pentax M50 to $72 for the Fuji J10.

We do not have sufficient information to estimate the actual Pricing ROI for this Canon value pricing strategy. However, to illustrate a value-based Pricing ROI we offer the following example.

As shown in Figure 1.5, a value-based price of $190 is $10 higher than the current selling price of $180. While this price increase lowers the customer value by $10, the resulting customer value of $33 is still sufficiently large to be meaningful in attracting potential customers.

At this new price of $190—and assuming volume is unchanged—the product sales and gross profits each increase by $8 million. The marketing and sales budget also increases by $3 million in order to communicate the price performance and value of the product. The result of this pricing strategy is a $5 million increase in NMC. When this incremental gain in marketing profits is divided by the $3 million invested in the value-based pricing strategy, the resulting Pricing ROI is 167 percent.

Performance (millions)	Current pricing	Value-based pricing	Change
Selling price	$180	$190	$10
Customer value	$43	$33	($10)
Volume sold (units)	1.0	1.0	0.0
Net price	$144	$152	$8
Sales	$144	$152	$8
Unit cost	$100	$100	$0
Unit margin	$44	$52	$8
Gross profit	$44	$52	$8
Marketing and sales budget	$20	$23	$3
Net marketing contribution	$24	$29	$5

Value-based Pricing ROI

$$= \frac{\text{NMC (post)} - \text{NMC (pre)}}{\text{price strategy investment}} \times 100\%$$

$$= \frac{\$29 \text{ million} - \$24 \text{ million}}{\$3 \text{ million}} \times 100\%$$

$$= 167\%$$

FIGURE 1.5 Price-performance value-based Pricing ROI

Value drivers and value creation

In the digital camera example, we presented an overall measure of performance, which masked important individual sources of value creation and value reduction. The overall performance score can be disaggregated into more definitive sources of performance. Figure 1.6 illustrates an example of competing industrial products rated on four aspects of performance, service quality, and company reputation (Sullivan 2008). These influences on overall performance are weighted to further delineate the importance of different aspects of performance.

In this example, competitors C, F, and H offer the best customer values, while competitors A, E, and G offer the poorest values. Competitor A is high-priced and would have to work to improve areas of performance to offer a fair value. Competitor B could work on improving below-average areas of performance to build a positive value and could then raise their price to $125. However, this strategy would require a determination that the value-based Pricing ROI warrants this investment.

Value-based pricing method #2: total cost of ownership

For many consumer, industrial, and hi-tech products, price is only one considera-tion in the total cost of ownership (Forbis and Mehta 1981; Snelgrove 2012). For

Performance drivers	Weight	A	B	C	D	E	F	G	H	AVG.
Product performance										
* Reliability	20%	75	45	50	80	35	80	85	60	64
* Throughput	20%	80	67	50	85	40	75	80	65	68
* Product life	20%	60	50	35	80	30	60	85	65	58
* Maintenance	10%	50	40	40	75	30	60	75	55	53
Service quality	20%	30	55	40	80	25	65	75	55	53
Company reputation	10%	67	50	35	70	20	75	75	50	55
Overall performance	100%	61	52	43	80	31	70	80	60	60
Price		$165	$120	$65	$155	$95	$120	$200	$95	$127

Industrial product

Product	Performance rating	Product price	Fair price	Customer value
A	61	$166	$130	($36)
B	52	$120	$112	($8)
C	43	$65	$95	$30
D	80	$155	$166	$11
E	31	$95	$72	($23)
F	70	$120	$147	$27
G	80	$200	$166	($34)
H	60	$95	$128	$33
Average	60	$127	$130	$0

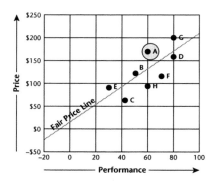

FIGURE 1.6 Price-performance value pricing with performance drivers

example, the average selling price of a Subaru Forrester is $20,051 (Sullivan 2008), but the cost to own this vehicle over its five-year life is significantly higher when all the costs of ownership are considered. These expenses include the cost of fuel, maintenance, repairs, insurance, taxes and fees, and depreciation (Edmonds.com 2011). These additional costs result in a total cost to own of $41,901 over five years, as shown in Figure 1.7. The resale value of this car after five years is $10,714. Taking into consideration the price paid, resale value, and cost to own yields a total cost of ownership of $51,238.

A comparable SUV like the Toyota RAV4 has a selling price of $24,084 and higher total cost of ownership equal to $45,273. However, the RAV4 also has a higher resale value. When all factors are considered, the total cost of ownership is $55,697. The difference of $4,459 is the value Subaru offers customers considering the two SUVs. Subaru could raise the price of the Forrester by $1,000 to capture more of this value for the company and would still offer a positive customer value of $3,459.

Next, consider an automotive component that has a list price of $10.00 and sells for $8.00 after normal discounts. Shown in Figure 1.8 is the total cost of purchase for the company's product and a competing product. In this industry, purchasing agents will not accept premium-priced products without justification. This is where an investment in a Total Cost of Ownership Pricing starts. If the company believes its product can save the customer money, they need to prove it.

While both products have a net price of $8.00, the total cost of purchase for the competitor's product and the company's product when fully installed and tested are $14.50 and $11.00 respectively. This is largely due to a lower installation cost, but there are other customer savings as well. These individual savings produce an overall customer savings of $3.50 per unit installed. This results in a savings of $3.5 million per year for every million units installed.

Subaru Forrester

Cost of ownership	Purchase	5-year expenses
Price paid	$20,051	
Fuel		$13,950
Maintenance		$5,466
Insurance		$7,565
Repairs		$1,472
Taxes and fees		$2,133
Financing		$1,978
Depreciation		$9,337
Resale value	($10,714)	
Ownership costs		$41,901
Total cost to own	$41,901	
Cost of ownership	$51,238	

Toyota RAV4

Cost of ownership	Purchase	5-year expenses
Price paid	$24,084	
Fuel		$13,371
Maintenance		$4,291
Insurance		$11,314
Repairs		$887
Taxes and fees		$2,665
Financing		$2,321
Depreciation		$10,424
Resale value	($13,660)	
Ownership costs		$45,273
Total cost to own	$45,273	
Cost of ownership	$55,697	

FIGURE 1.7 Total cost of ownership—automobiles

Note: Both 4 door SUV 2.5L 4 cylinder

Total cost of ownership (per unit)	Benchmark competitor	Company	Customer savings	Total cost of ownership (per unit)	Benchmark competitor	Company	Customer savings
List price	$10.00	$10.00	$0.00	List price	$10.00	$11.50	$0.00
Discounts	($2.00)	($2.00)	$0.00	Discounts	($2.00)	($2.00)	$0.00
Net price	**$8.00**	**$8.00**	**$0.00**	**Net price**	**$8.00**	**$9.50**	**$0.00**
Ownership costs				**Ownership costs**			
Shipping and handling	$1.00	$0.50	$0.50	Shipping and handling	$1.00	$0.50	$0.50
Installation cost	$4.50	$2.00	$2.50	Installation cost	$4.50	$2.00	$2.50
Quality control	$0.50	$0.20	$0.30	Quality control	$0.50	$0.20	$0.30
Re-work	$0.50	$0.30	$0.20	Re-work	$0.50	$0.30	$0.20
Ownership costs	**$6.50**	**$3.00**	**$3.50**	**Ownership costs**	**$6.50**	**$3.00**	**$3.50**
Total cost of ownership	**$14.50**	**$11.00**	**$3.50**	**Total cost of ownership**	**$14.50**	**$12.50**	**$2.00**

FIGURE 1.8 Customer total cost of ownership—automotive component product

Performance (millions)	Current pricing	Value-based pricing	Change
List price	$10.00	$11.50	$1.50
Selling price	$8.00	$9.50	$1.50
Customer value	$3.50	$2.00	($1.50)
Volume sold (units)	1.0	1.0	0.0
Sales	$8.0	$9.50	$1.50
Unit cost	$6.00	$6.00	$0.00
Unit margin	$2.00	$3.50	$1.50
Gross profit	$2.00	$3.50	$1.50
Marketing and sales budget	$1.00	$1.65	$0.65
Net marketing contribution	**$1.00**	**$1.85**	**$0.85**

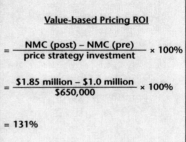

Value-based Pricing ROI

$$= \frac{\text{NMC (post)} - \text{NMC (pre)}}{\text{price strategy investment}} \times 100\%$$

$$= \frac{\$1.85 \text{ million} - \$1.0 \text{ million}}{\$650,000} \times 100\%$$

$$= 131\%$$

FIGURE 1.9 Total cost of ownership value-based Pricing ROI

To capture more value for the company, the list price could be increased to $11.50 with a net price of $9.50, a $1.50 price premium. The customer savings at this price would still be $2.00 per unit installed and $2 million per year. With this value proposition the business would expect to maintain their current volume of one million units but would hope to increase their share of the automotive component manufacturing business (Nagle and Hogan 2006; Smith and Nagle 2005).

The investment in this case included production engineering tests and sales force training on how to sell using value-based pricing. The incremental investment in this example was $500,000 and the incremental gain in NMC was $1 million as shown in Figure 1.9. This produced a value-based Pricing ROI of 131 percent.

Value-based pricing method #3: trade-off analysis

Not all customers will want the same combination of performance and price. A "price buyer" will use price as their primary value driver and then seek the best performance based on various different types of performance (Morton and Devine 1985). Using trade-off analysis (conjoint analysis) we can see how customers trade-off different levels of price with different levels of performance (Axelrod and Frendberg 1990; Green and Srinivasan 1990; Page and Rosenbaum 1987; Wittink and Cattin 1989).

A "quality buyer" treats price as an important factor, but prioritizes desired levels of quality and performance ahead of price. Among quality buyers there can be many variations in customer needs for performance. This creates different price-performance segments, each with different value drivers. Using trade-off value-based pricing we can determine the degree to which price and value segments exist (Gale and Swire 2006).

Let's consider the market for fiber cement siding. The product is guaranteed to last 30 years and is resistant to fire, dry rot, and bug infestation. While the retail price at $1.00 per square foot was acceptable to most customers, 30 percent would pay considerably more for a higher quality paint finish and higher quality trim items. This led to the following product positioning considerations:

- **Retail price**: $1.00, $2.00, $3.00
- **Paint finish**: None, Primed, Color Plus
- **Finish trim**: None, Limited, Full

From these nine factors there are 81 possible combinations. By utilizing a Latin-square design, the number can be systematically reduced to a representative subset of nine combinations. In Figure 1.10 we show how these nine combinations were ranked in order of buyer preference for a "price buyer." When these preferences are processed they can be represented by the customer preference curves shown in the lower left of the figure. As shown, price was the most important factor and accounted for 75 percent of the price buyer choice variance. The other 25 percent went to paint finish.

Price buyer value index

For the "price segment," the company's current positioning is the most attractive product offering of the three shown in Figure 1.11. This yields the highest value index for price buyers (1.83) as shown below. This is computed using the preference curve values for the price buyer and the positioning shown in Figure 1.11. Also shown in Figure 1.11, the other two strategies produced a lower value index. The premium strategy for the price segment has the lowest value index (1.17).

$$\begin{aligned} \textbf{Value index } (current) &= \textbf{paint finish } (none) + \textbf{finish trim } (none) \\ &\quad + \textbf{price } (\$1.00 \text{ per sq. ft.}) \\ &= 0.33 + 0.50 + 1.00 \\ &= \textbf{1.83} \end{aligned}$$

Quality buyer value index

Quality buyers ranked the same nine combinations differently. Notice how differently they ranked their first three preferences for the product bundles presented in Figure 1.10. They placed more importance on paint finish (43 percent) and finish

FIGURE 1.10
Customer segment price–performance preferences

Option A	**3**
Paint finish	None
Finish trim	None
Price per sq. ft.	$1.00

Option B	**5**
Paint finish	Primed
Finish trim	None
Price per sq. ft.	$2.00

Option C	**7**
Paint finish	Color
Finish trim	None
Price per sq. ft.	$3.00

Option D	**9**
Paint finish	None
Finish trim	Limited
Price per sq. ft.	$3.00

Option E	**2**
Paint finish	Primed
Finish trim	Limited
Price per sq. ft.	$1.00

Option F	**4**
Paint finish	Color
Finish trim	Limited
Price per sq. ft.	$2.00

Option G	**6**
Paint finish	None
Finish trim	Full
Price per sq. ft.	$2.00

Option H	**8**
Paint finish	Primed
Finish trim	Full
Price per sq. ft.	$3.00

Option I	**1**
Paint finish	Color
Finish trim	Full
Price per sq. ft.	$1.00

Product bundles	Price segment	Quality segment
A	3	8
B	5	7
C	7	6
D	9	9
E	2	4
F	4	2
G	6	5
H	8	3
I	1	1

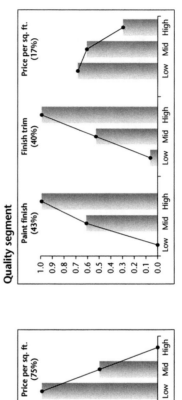

Price segment

Paint finish (25%) — Finish trim (0%) — Price per sq. ft. (75%)

Quality segment

Paint finish (43%) — Finish trim (40%) — Price per sq. ft. (17%)

Prime segment

Features	Current	Plus	Premium
Paint finish	**None**	Primed	Color finish
Finish trim	**None**	Basic trim	Full trim
Price per sq. ft.	**$1.00**	$2.00	$3.00
Value index	1.83	1.50	1.17

Quality segment

Features	Current	Plus	Premium
Paint finish	None	Primed	**Color finish**
Finish trim	None	Basic trim	**Full trim**
Price per sq. ft.	$1.00	$2.00	**$3.00**
Value index	0.77	1.77	**2.31**

FIGURE 1.11 Trade-off value-based pricing strategy and value index

trim (40 percent). Price accounted for only 17 percent of the product preferences. For this segment of customers (30 percent) the premium product offering provided the highest value index (2.31). The current product offering is the least attractive to quality buyers with a value index of 0.77.

Trade-off value-based Pricing ROI

The company has used the current strategy for the past ten years with the results shown in Figure 1.12. The trade-off value-based pricing strategy would retain the current offering for price buyers (70 percent of their customers) but would offer a second value-based strategy as an option for quality buyers. As shown in Figure 1.12, sales would grow from $600 million to $870 million. More importantly, gross profits would grow from $200 million to $320 million. Clearly, these are impressive performance gains.

But what about marketing and sales expenses? As shown, these expenses would have to increase to adequately communicate the new value proposition. This value-based pricing strategy would require new communications channels, new messaging, and more frequent communications to adequately reach and influence the buyers

Performance (millions)	Current pricing	Value-based price segment	Pricing quality segment	Strategy total	Change
Served market	100%	70%	30%	100%	0%
Selling price	$1.00	$1.00	$2.50	$1.45	$0.45
Customer value index	1.63	1.83	2.31	1.97	0.34
Net Price (*)	$0.60	$0.60	$1.50	$0.87	$0.27
Volume sold (units)	1,000	700	300	1,000	300
Sales	$600	$420	$450	$870	$270
Unit cost	$0.40	$0.40	$0.90	$0.55	$0.15
Unit margin	$0.20	$0.20	$0.60	$0.32	$0.12
Gross profit	$200	$140	$180	$320	$120
Marketing and sales budget	$90	$60	$75	$135	$45
Net marketing contribution	$110	$80	$105	$185	$75

(*) Net price after retailer discount

Non-marketing and sales investment ($million)	
Product R&D	$1
Plant and equipment	$10
Total	$11

Pricing ROI

$$= \frac{\$185 \text{ million} - \$110 \text{ million}}{\$45 \text{ million} + \$11 \text{ million}} \times 100\%$$

$$= 134\%$$

FIGURE 1.12 Market segmentation and value-based Pricing ROI

in the quality segment. This would result in an increase in the marketing and sales budget from $90 million to $135 million, as shown in Figure 1.12.

The company would also have to invest $1 million in product and process R&D (research and development) and $10 million in new plant and equipment to manufacture these new product features. Thus, the total investment would be significant at $56 million. Given a potential incremental gain in NMC of $75 million, this strategy produces a Pricing ROI of 134 percent as shown in Figure 1.12.

Managerial summary

We have highlighted three value-based pricing methods that have the potential to produce higher levels of marketing profits, measured as NMC. For each application, current marketing performance can be measured with respect to price, customer value, margin, marketing and sales expenses, and NMC. With this data we can use the following steps to select the appropriate value-based price method and measure the resulting Pricing ROI.

Step 1: Method selection

Determine which value-based pricing method is appropriate for your product or service. Selecting the right method for your product-market is discussed in the next section (Guidelines for managers).

Step 2: Customer value

Using the value-based pricing method selected in Step 1, determine the degree to which your product has a positive customer value. If there is negligible or negative customer value, then there is no room for improving prices. The focus should not be on price but how to improve performance and value.

Step 3: Value pricing

If you have a considerable value advantage, the next step is to determine how much you can increase price and still maintain an attractive customer value. This is shown in Figure 1.13 for each of the value-based pricing methods.

Step 4: Investment

Next, determine if the unit cost will change and how much additional marketing and sales budget is needed to communicate your value advantage to target customers.

Performance (millions)	Price-performance Cost-based Value-based		Total cost of ownership Cost-based Value-based		Trade-off analysis Cost-based Value-based	
Application	Digital cameras		Automotive component		Building materials	
Strategy	Current	Value-based	Current	Value-based	Current	Value-based
Customer value	$43	$33	$3.50	$2.00	1.63	1.97
Net price	$144	$152	$8.00	$9.50	$0.60	$0.87
Percent margin	30.6%	34.2%	25.0%	36.7%	33.3%	36.8%
Marketing and sales	$20	$23	$1.00	$1.65	$90	$135
Net marketing contribution	$24	$29	$1.00	$1.85	$110	$185
Investment		$3.0		$0.65		$55.0
Pricing ROI		167%		131%		134%

FIGURE 1.13 Summary of value-based Pricing ROI applications

Step 5: Profit impact

With Steps 3 and 4 completed, estimate the proposed strategy NMC. If the difference is sufficiently large, this strategy should be seriously considered. If the gain is negligible or negative, the strategy lacks the profit potential to make the investment risk tolerable.

Step 6: Pricing ROI

Pricing ROI is a good index for evaluating investment risk. Divide the change in NMC by the investment in marketing and sales expenses to measure Pricing ROI. In the applications summarized in Figure 1.13, the Pricing ROIs ranged from 131 percent to 167 percent. These ROIs would have to be compared with other opportunities to determine if they are sufficiently attractive to pursue.

Guidelines for managers

Recognizing that most managers use cost-based pricing, we are hopeful that the value-based pricing methods presented offer an incentive for managers to re-evaluate their products with respect to value pricing. In this section we will present guidelines and resources to aid in the planning and execution of the value-based pricing methods we have examined in this chapter.

Price-performance value-based pricing

Price-performance value-based pricing requires ten or more competing products that vary in price and performance. If there is little product differentiation in price and performance, this method will not work. Some applications where this value-based pricing method works best are summarized below.

- **Consumer**: Cars, appliances, electronics, home and garden, babies and kids, services and health

- **Business**: Office equipment, earth-moving equipment, cutting tools, small motors, industrial adhesives, and chain saws

To get started we recommend using price-performance value mapping (Tool 4.2) as shown in Figure 1.14. Using this resource, you can modify the example data to see how the customer value changes with changes in price and performance. You can also enter and save your own data and perform your own value-based pricing analysis. For a more in-depth experience we recommend creating a table like the one shown in Figure 1.6.

Then have your sales force and/or management team rate your performance and nine competitors on each criterion to create an overall performance index. Use the average results to create a value map to get a consensus view of your customer value and competitive position. If promising, the next step would be to collect the same data from a sample of 30 customers and perform the same analysis. It is also very useful to see how much agreement or disagreement there is between company and customer perceptions of performance.

Total cost of ownership value-based pricing

This value-based pricing method is best used in situations where the ownership costs are equal to or greater than the purchase price. This is often the case for products that have a multi-year life like a car or machinery. These products have a variety of ownership costs that are often less obvious to sellers as shown in Figure 1.15. Some areas of application are shown below:

- **Consumer**: Cars, printers, computers, solar energy systems, household paint, siding and roofs, major appliances, gas BBQs, water heaters
- **Business**: Turbines, electronic instruments, medical diagnostic equipment, large earth moving machines, industrial machinery, food processing equipment, robotic equipment, conveyor systems

Value pricing method considerations	Price-performance	Value based pricing methods Total cost of ownership	Trade-off analysis
Type of data required	Price and performance	Price and cost to own	Price-performance levels
Minimum data requirements	10 or more products	One competing product	Price and performance
Application example	Flat screen TVs	Farm machinery	Airlines
Customer value metric	Dollars	Dollars	Numerical index
Measures price importance	No	% Total cost to own	% Price use in choice
Identifies value-drivers	No	Yes	Yes
Competitor position	Yes	Yes	Yes
Value pricing tools (*)	4.2 Price-performance value mapping	8.1 Value in-use pricing	8.3 Performance-based value pricing

(*) These resources can be accessed at www.MBM-Best.com

FIGURE 1.14 Manager guidelines for value-based pricing tools

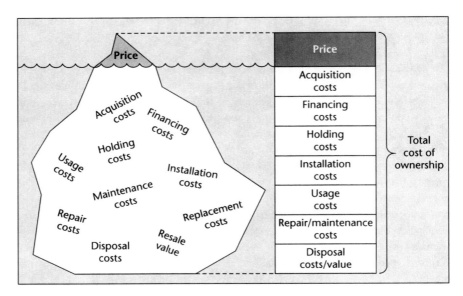

FIGURE 1.15 Ownership costs are often less visible

To get started with this value-based pricing method, we recommend using value in-use pricing (Tool 8.1), as shown in Figure 1.14. Using your best estimates, input the price for a company product and identify areas of customer ownership costs. Next, estimate your product life and the ownership costs for each product (see Figure 1.7). Then repeat this step for a benchmark competitor. Then evaluate your customer value as presented in Step 2 in the previous section.

This exercise will provide a feel for this value-based pricing method and how it can uncover sources of competitive advantage and opportunities to communicate how your products create customer value in the form of customer savings.

To take this application a step further, identify a customer you have a strong relationship with and ask to setup a side-by-side analysis of the two products. Customers may see costs of ownership that you did not consider as well as assess those costs for the two products differently. Adding more customer applications will further enhance and expand your understanding of your product's customer value and opportunities to improve pricing.

Trade-off value-based pricing

This value-based pricing method is best used for products and services that have few key performance drivers (2 or 3) and price. Trade-off analysis requires customers to make trade-offs between price and different levels of performance and is powerful for understanding how important price is relative to performance. As a result, this method is also excellent for discovering market segments.

3M is a perfect company for trade-off value-based pricing tools. 3M's roughly 20,000 products are mostly value-added products that command a premium price based on some aspect of superior performance. Obviously, price buyers are going to like the 3M performance but may not be willing to pay for it. Other consumer and business applications are summarized below:

- **Consumer**: Services such as airlines, banks, hotels, golf courses, restaurants, gas stations, toothpaste, household consumables, vacation packages, schooling, etc.
- **Business**: Industrial adhesives, electronic controls, security systems, electronic components, plastics, silicone and epoxy applications, graphic design, financial services, etc.

To get started we recommend using the performance-based value pricing tool (Tool 8.3), as shown in Figure 1.14. Start with your own analysis following the instructions presented. Interpret the results to determine if this tool provides some new insights to customer value and pricing. The next step would be to have your management team and sales force rank the same nine choice options, then compare and discuss the results. A lot can be learned with just this inside-company application. Obviously, if your team sees value in doing this, the next step is to include customers in the ranking of these choice options.

Future research considerations

Recognizing the value-based pricing methods and Pricing ROI examples presented, it is important to look forward to additional research to extend our knowledge and application of these pricing methods. Three areas of research that would add to our knowledge in this area are presented.

Total cost of purchase vs. total cost of ownership

Past research on the total cost of ownership has looked at this as a transaction. This would be appropriate for single transactions. Southwest Airlines demonstrates and communicates its total cost of purchase with advertisements that show the price and added costs of a competing ticket to the same destination as shown in Figure 1.16. Value-based pricing focused on single transactions should be referred to as the **total cost of purchase**.

Total cost of ownership should be used when ownership costs occur over several years, such as in the purchase and use of cars as presented in Figure 1.7. Because these ownership costs occur over time, we should utilize a net present value approach to determining the total cost of ownership.

For example, in Figure 1.17 are two gas chromatographs, one priced at $50,000, the other at $55,000. However, the competing product has a four-year life and the company's product has a five-year life. Using a 15 percent discount rate, the company product is a better buy with a customer value of $5,028 in today's dollars.

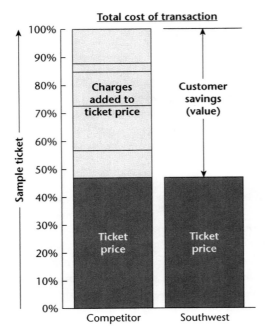

FIGURE 1.16 Total cost of purchase

Product life (years)	Price	1	2	3	4	5
Competitor (4-year product life)	$50,000	$12,500	$12,500	$12,500	$12,500	
Company (5-year product life)	$55,000	$11,000	$11,000	$11,000	$11,000	$11,000
Discount rate	15%					
Present value factor		0.870	0.756	0.658	0.572	0.497
Competitor present value	$41,902	$10,870	$9,452	$8,219	$7,147	$6,215
Company present value	$36,874	$9,565	$8,318	$7,233	$6,289	$5,469
Customer savings	$5,028					

FIGURE 1.17 Total cost of ownership

Total cost of ownership as net present value has not been presented as a method for assessing customer value. Issues that would need to be addressed are: 1) What types of products lend themselves to this method? 2) What is the appropriate discount rate? 3) How should investment in marketing communications be incorporated into this method to allow businesses to communicate their value advantage story? 4) How should Pricing ROI be calculated?

Value advantage and cost of marketing and sales

A business with a value advantage should find it easier to attract new customers and retain existing customers when the value is clearly communicated to consumers. Product A in Figure 1.18 should have a higher level of customer retention than

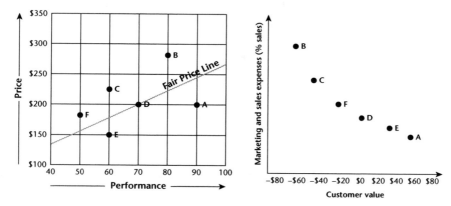

FIGURE 1.18 Customer value and marketing and sales expenses

Product C. That means that Product C has to spend more on marketing and sales to acquire new customers to replace lost customers to maintain the same level of sales. This would suggest that Product A has a lower cost of marketing and sales as a percent of sales.

Likewise, Product A is more likely to have a higher Net Promoter Score than Product C since Product A offers a greater customer value. This means customers of Product A are more likely to tell people about Product A than customers of Product C. This should lower Product A's new customer acquisition expenses. In Figure 1.18 we present this hypothesis as an area for future research. If proved to be true, products with a value advantage are even more profitable in the long run due to higher levels of marketing productivity.

Emotional value and value-based pricing

The Converse Chuck Taylor sneaker was conceived as a basketball shoe that provided performance advantages that competing shoes did not have. But, the Chuck Taylor is now a symbol of status and fashion that has even greater value to both athletes and non-athletes, as shown in Figure 1.19. Current value pricing methods do not capture this aspect of "Emotional Value."

While consumers can readily list rational purchase considerations, customers also weigh emotional factors (Aaker 1997) such as perceived safety, belongingness (group identity), and status (does the product enhance my image to others?). For products that offer a desired emotional value, the value is underestimated using the current methods of value pricing. Future research should focus on how this aspect of customer value can be included in customer value measurement and value-based pricing.

FIGURE 1.19 Converse is more than an athletic shoe

Summary comments

In this chapter, we explored three value-based pricing methods and examined the corresponding Pricing ROI for each method. Since most businesses employ cost-based pricing or some form of reactive pricing, there are significant opportunities for companies to evaluate alternate pricing methods when developing pricing strategies.

The first step in executing any value-based pricing strategy is to understand value drivers. The next steps can be much more expensive and can involve product and packaging redesign, new marketing communications, and sales force trainings to create, communicate, and deliver your premium price value proposition. These are all elements of an investment in the value pricing strategy that need to be considered in determining your value-based Pricing ROI.

Value-based pricing strategies require pricing intelligence and courage because the investment stakes are high. But, if analyzed with adequate pricing intelligence, a business can easily estimate the Pricing ROI based on projected gains in marketing profits and required investment. We measure the numerator of the Pricing ROI equation as the incremental gain in NMC that the value-based pricing strategy produced over the current pricing strategy. This delta in NMC is then divided by the investment required to accomplish these outcomes, resulting in a measure of value-based Pricing ROI.

References

Aaker, J. (1997) Dimensions of brand personality. *Journal of Marketing Research* (August), pp. 347–356.

Axelrod, J. and Frendberg, N. (1990) Conjoint analysis. *Marketing Research* (June), pp. 28–35.

Best, R. J. (2013) Marketing metrics and marketing profitability. In: R. Best, *Market-based management: Strategies for growing customer value and profitability* (6th ed.). Upper Saddle River, NJ: Prentice Hall, pp. 59–69.

Cressman Jr., G. (1999) Commentary on industrial pricing: Theory and managerial practice. *Marketing Science*, 18 (3), pp. 455–457.

Edmunds.com, Inc. (2011) Total cost of ownership (TCO). Retrieved August 30, 2012 from www.edmunds.com/tco.html

Forbis, J. and Mehta, N. (1981) Value-based strategies for industrial products. *Business Horizons* (May), pp. 32–42.

Gale, B. (1994) *Managing customer value*. New York: Free Press.

Gale, B. and Swire, D. (2006) A value-based marketing & pricing (October 2006). Customer Value, Inc. Retrieved August 30, 2012 from www.cval.com/pdfs/VBMarketingAnd Pricing.pdf

Green, P. and Srinivasan, V. (1990) Conjoint analysis in marketing research. *Journal of Marketing* (October), pp. 3–19.

Morton, J. and Devine, H. (1985) How to diagnose what buyers really want. *Business Marketing* (October), pp. 70–83.

Nagle, T. T. and Hogan, J. E. (2006) *The strategy and tactics of pricing*. Upper Saddle River, NJ: Prentice Hall, pp. 27–44.

Noble, P. and Gruca, T. (1999) Industrial pricing: Theory and managerial practice. *Marketing Science*, 18 (3), pp. 435–454.

Page, A. and Rosenbaum, H. (1987) Redesigning product lines with conjoint analysis. *Journal of Product Management*, 4 (2), pp. 120–137.

Retrevo. (2009) Step aside Apple fans, Apple needs to sell tablets to the PC crowd. *Retrevo Blog* (February 23, 2009). Retrieved December 2010 from www.retrevo.com/content/blog/apple-tablets-pc-users

Satmetrix. Net Promoter Score. Retrieved April 30, 2012 from www.netpromoter.com

Smith, G. and Nagle, T. (2005) Question of value. *Marketing Management* (July–August), pp. 39–43.

Snelgrove, T. (2012) Value pricing when you understand your customers: Total cost of ownership – past, present and future. *Journal of Revenue and Pricing Management*, 11, pp. 76–80.

Sullivan, E. (2008) Value pricing. *Marketing News* (January 15), p. 8.

Wittink, D. R. and Cattin, P. (1989) Commercial use of conjoint analysis. *Journal of Marketing*, 52 (3), pp. 19–96.

2

CANNIBALIZATION – FIVE EASY PIECES

Andreas Hinterhuber

Introduction

Cannibalization occurs when products in a portfolio take market share from each other instead of from competitor brands. Cannibalization is relevant in two contexts: new product introductions and price promotions. In its most common form, cannibalization refers to the loss of sales on an existing product item when a new item is introduced (Mason and Milne 1994). While this is the most common form, cannibalization is relevant also in conjunction with price promotions. Here, cannibalization refers to the loss of sales on an un-promoted item in a product line as a result of the price promotion.

Academic research has not yet dedicated substantial attention to this phenomenon: Mason and Milne find 'surprisingly little research in this area' (1994, p.164). Similarly, Lomax et al. speak about a 'very real threat' and, at the same time, 'very little empirical work' in this area (1997, p.27). Cannibalization is indeed a very relevant problem of management practice. Figure 2.1 reproduces a slide from an investor presentation of a large, global chemical company to shareholders (Berschauer 2005): new product sales are presented as if they were entirely incremental to existing product sales.

This is, obviously, impossible. New product sales will, to a large degree, cannibalize sales of existing products. Given the substantial costs and failure rates of new product development, it is a very real possibility that the profitability of new product introductions, after taking cannibalization into account, is negative. Managers are thus well advised to anticipate cannibalization in their analysis of decisions on new product introductions and price promotions. Based on my own, cursory analysis of new product introduction practices at large companies globally, it seems that most B2B companies essentially ignore cannibalization, whereas many B2C companies have developed quite sophisticated models in this respect.

In sum: the analysis of cannibalization effects in the context of price promotions is directly related to analysis of the pricing ROI of a specific pricing activity, i.e.

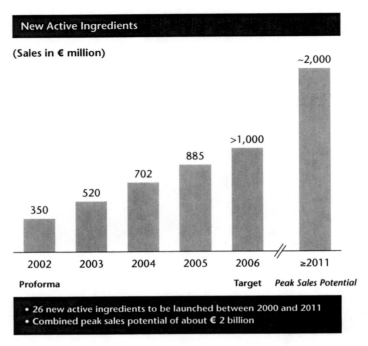

New Active Ingredients

(Sales in € million)

FIGURE 2.1 Cannibalization – in practice largely ignored

price promotion. The analysis of cannibalization effects in the context of new product launches is relevant in the context of calculating marketing ROI and may be of particular interest also in the context of pricing ROI analysis when the profit impact of alternative new product pricing decisions with corresponding differing cannibalization rates is analysed.

In the following, I will discuss five easy pieces of cannibalization. These cases are drawn from current academic research, own research and own consulting practice with large, global companies. For all cases, I will discuss implications and key learnings, which will be relevant for practising managers in both industrial as well as consumer-goods companies. For researchers, these case studies point towards future opportunities to develop models and theories to better understand cannibalization and its contingency effects.

Piece #1: cannibalization in a flat market

In cases where all new demand comes from either competitive or own products (i.e. no market expansion/no acquisition of new customers), the critical cannibalization rate provides the threshold that indicates the allowable level of cannibalization. More formally: the critical cannibalization rate is cannibalization rate which leaves gross margins of not launching the new product and launching the new product constant. Consider the following case study from the pharmaceutical industry.

The brand has an average selling price of 100 € and a contribution margin of 80 per cent. In order to respond to low-cost competitors, the company is considering launching an own generic product at a price of 20 € with a contribution margin of 35 per cent. Assume that the company forecasts unit sales for the new product at 50 per cent of unit sales of the current premium product. The company anticipates that demand will come either from competitors or from own products. In these cases, managers need to understand the allowable rate of cannibalization of the new product, i.e. the maximum per cent share of new product sales that can come at the expense of current product sales under the constraint that total profitability will not decline. Figure 2.2 highlights total sales and contribution margins as a function of the cannibalization rate.

It is fairly obvious that sales and margins are at their highest levels if cannibalization is 0 per cent. In this case all new product sales are incremental. This is indicated with the upward arrow in the left part of the figure. Furthermore, under the assumption that new product sales come from either company or competitor products (zero market expansion), it is intuitive that at 100 per cent cannibalization the number of units sold after the new product launch is the same as before.

Consequently, since new product sales occur at lower prices than existing product sales, total turnover after the new product launch is, at 100 per cent cannibalization, below current turnover. This is indicated with the downward arrow in the right part of the figure. Finally, since new product sales occur at lower margins, margins at 100 per cent cannibalization are proportionally lower than turnover at this point. With increasing cannibalization, margins decline faster than turnover.

We can thus calculate two critical cannibalization rates: one at which turnover after the new product launch is equal to current turnover and one at which contribution margin is at the same level. In practice, the critical cannibalization rate is calculated on the contribution margin. In this case, the rate is at 9 per cent. In the

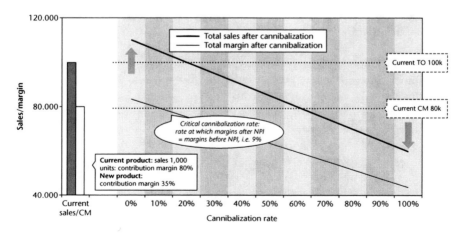

FIGURE 2.2 The critical cannibalization rate as cut-off rate

figure this is the point where current contribution margin intersects the lower downward sloping line representing contribution margins as a function of the cannibalization rate.

Calculating the critical cannibalization rate

If CM_E denotes the contribution margin from existing product sales, if S_E denotes the turnover from existing products and if CM_N and S_N represent the contribution margin and the turnover from the new product, then the critical cannibalization rate can be calculated as follows:

$$CM_E \times S_E - \text{Cannibalized margin} + S_N \times CM_N > CM_E \times S_E$$

$$\text{Cannibalized margin} < S_N \times CM_N$$

$$S_N \times CM_E < S_N \times CM_N$$

$$\text{Critical cannibalization rate } (\%) < CM_N / CM_E$$

In other words, the critical cannibalization rate is the result of dividing the absolute contribution margin of the new product by the absolute contribution margin of the current products. The higher the critical cannibalization rate, the better: higher critical cannibalization rates indicate higher permissible cannibalization and require lower incremental sales. An example further illustrates this point.

To launch or not to launch a low-cost airline?

Imagine a full-service airline (such as Lufthansa) debating to launch an own low-cost, no-frills airline – a big decision, given the ongoing success of low-cost airlines in Europe.

Considerations:

- unit margins on the new low-cost airline are lower.
- some customers who would have paid for the 'full service' will now migrate to the new low-cost offer by Lufthansa.
- the key question is thus: what is the critical cannibalization rate, above which it becomes uneconomical to launch the new service?

What do we need to know?

- demand if low-cost airline is not launched: 100,000
- unit margin of full-service airline: 50 €/seat
- demand for low-cost airline   10,000
- unit margin for low-cost airline   30 €/seat

	Without new product		With new product launch					
			0% cannibalization		100% cannibalization		Critical cannibalization	
	Existing product	New product	Existing product	New product	Existing product	New product	Existing product	New product
Sales (quantity)	100.000	–	100.000	10.000	90.000	10.000	94.000	10.000
Margin (per unit)	50	–	50	30	50	30	50	30
	5.000.000		5.000.000	300.000	4.500.000	300.000	4.700.000	300.000
MARGIN (TOTAL)	5.000.000		5.300.000		4.800.000		5.000.000	

FIGURE 2.3 The decision to launch a low-cost product under different cannibalization rates

Figure 2.3 compares total company profits under three different rates of cannibalization: 0 per cent, 100 per cent and the critical cannibalization rate (60 per cent).

In this example, the critical cannibalization rate is 60 per cent, i.e. the result of dividing the absolute contribution margin of the new product (30 €) by the contribution margin of the company's existing product (50 €). Conceptually, the critical cannibalization rate is thus similar to the weighted average cost of capital (WACC). Both concepts do not allow to forecast future events (actual cannibalization or future income streams), but both concepts provide managerially useful cut-off points which allow us to understand under which conditions pricing or investment decisions increase profitability. In our example, if cannibalization is below 60 per cent – or, expressed equivalently, if incremental demand exceeds 40 per cent of new product sales (i.e. 4,000 units) – then the introduction of the low-cost product increases overall company profitability.

Piece #1: key considerations

Under conditions of zero market expansion (all demand comes from either competitors or the company) and with a stable baseline, the critical cannibalization rate (CM_N/CM_E) provides the cut-off rate below which lower margin, new product introductions increase overall company profitability. Higher critical cannibalization rates are better and allow for more room for errors.

Piece #2: cannibalization with market expansion

In an expanding market, a portion of the demand for the new, low-margin product comes from non-customers. Cannibalization rates above the critical rate can thus be tolerated. The case of Unilever in Brazil illuminates this point.

In 1996, the company faces stagnating growth prospects in its Brazilian market, then composed of middle-income cities located mainly in the South, and considers entering the low-income market in the Northeast. Income disparity between the Northeast and the company's currently served market is substantial. Entering the low-income market is a risky decision. In the worst case, this move will be interpreted by customers and investors alike as a tangible admission that growth can be achieved only with lower prices and margins. The memories of 'Marlboro Friday' come to mind. This is the day when Philip Morris unexpectedly cuts the price of Marlboro by 20 per cent to fight off private label and generic cigarette brands. On that day in April 1993, shares of Philip Morris fall by 23 per cent. While the company's market share grows quickly as a result, profitability drops immediately and substantially. It takes the company more than a decade to again reach previous levels of profitability. Since then, the Marlboro price cut is the marketing blunder 'of the century' (Isaacson and Silk 1997, p.1).

On the other hand, the low-income segment can also unlock new growth opportunities, pre-empt competitors and, in the best case, build marketing capabilities for low-income markets deployable in other countries across the globe. In any case, cannibalization is a very real threat.

At that time, the weighted contribution margin of Unilever's product portfolio is approximately US $ 0.36 on weighted ex company sales of US $ 2.20 per unit. To effectively compete in the low-income market, the company designs a product that is radically different from its current product offering. The new product has a completely new brand name (instead of being a new item in an existing product line), a new packaging (sachet instead of cartons), new distributors, a new formulation and, finally, a substantially lower price: US $ 1.50, with margins of US $ 0.20 per unit.

The critical cannibalization rate is thus 56 per cent. The management team of Unilever does not see this rate as problematic, since the product is positioned to tap into new markets. Actual cannibalization rate of Unilever's product range is 44 per cent one year after launch (Guimaraes and Chandon 2007). Critically, the new low-cost product causes the overall market in the Northeast to expand by 40 per cent.

Most importantly, this product launch is probably the moment in the history of Unilever where its capabilities to successfully and profitably serve low-income markets originate. As a result, today Unilever is the company with the largest share of sales originating from emerging markets (52 per cent), far ahead of key competitors such as Procter & Gamble or Nestlé (both around 30 per cent). Unilever today is, in the words of the company's CEO, 'the emerging markets company' (Polman 2010) and the launch of ALA in Brazil is probably the moment where it all started – this is Unilever's Big Bang.

Piece #2: key considerations

The critical cannibalization rate is less relevant if the new low-cost product causes the overall market to expand. Calculating the critical cannibalization rate provides guidance; much more important is, however, the process of segmentation and product positioning to ensure that the new low-cost offer taps into segments of non-customers that expand overall consumption.

Piece #3: cannibalization with market expansion and a changing baseline

So far we assume a stable baseline, i.e. not launching the new product will leave sales unaffected. This assumption can be questioned. In many instances, not launching the new product will lead to shrinking sales; launching the product will lead to both cannibalization and market expansion. The conceptually most demanding case is thus a changing baseline and market expansion.

The launch of the Toyota RX 300, the first crossover SUV, provides an interesting case in point (Van Heerde et al. 2010). Since this car is a crossover between a SUV and a sedan, Toyota anticipates that the RX 300 will lead to cannibalization of the company's SUV range (the 450 and 470) as well as the company's luxury sedans (the Lexus). The authors use a time-varying vector error-correction (VEC) model to decompose the demand for the RX 300 into cannibalization, brand switching and market expansion.

The demand decomposition about one year after launch reveals the following sources of demand for the new product (Van Heerde et al. 2010, p.1035):

- cannibalization: 26 per cent
- brand switching: 37 per cent
- market expansion: 36 per cent

Toyota's management views this product launch as 'hugely successful' – cannibalization is quite small and substantially lower than brand switching. Furthermore, Toyota's management considers that, without the RX 300 introduction, 15 per cent of Toyota's luxury sedan owners would have switched anyway to competing brands. Thus, taking into account a reduced baseline, the actual cannibalization becomes much smaller (approximately 13 per cent) of total demand.

These considerations show that cannibalization is – especially if markets expand and baseline sales are not stable, but negative – desirable. In 2007, shortly after the launch of the iPhone, a journalist asks Steve Jobs about cannibalization concerns between the iPhone and the iPod touch. His answer: 'If anyone is going to cannibalize us, I want it to be us. I don't want it to be a competitor' (Graham and Baig 2007).

The model discussed here does not allow forecasting of actual cannibalization for radical new product introductions prior to launch. But this case study shows that multivariate time-series models (such as the VEC model) can be used ex-post to decompose new product demand. Augmented by data from expert interviews and customer feedback on, e.g. the similarity between the new product and existing products, these models will allow us, to a degree, to forecast likely cannibalization rates for new product introductions. Together with data on anticipated market expansion, these calculations can then be used to improve new product launch decisions.

Finally, advertising is an important element of the marketing mix which mitigates the effect of cannibalization. Advertising elasticities are generally substantially lower than price elasticities. Demand decomposition models also allow a simulation of marketing mix elements – in the case of the RX 300, this model predicts that quadrupling investments into advertising would have eliminated cannibalization (Van Heerde et al. 2010). This relationship and the profitability of any such move are of course highly context specific; this study reminds us that, in addition to market segmentation, advertising spending at least mitigates cannibalization.

Piece #3: key considerations

Cannibalization is desirable if the new product is likely to cause the overall market to expand and if the baseline is negative (i.e. customers defect if no product is launched). Decomposing likely demand for the new product into brand switching, cannibalization and market expansion increases the quality and profitability of new product launches. Advertising spending reduces and can even completely eliminate cannibalization.

Piece #4: price promotions and cannibalization – the Coca Cola case

We turn now to the evaluation of price promotions. Also in this context cannibalization effects are real, but under-researched. For retailers, trade promotion is 'the biggest, most complex, and most controversial dilemma facing the industry today' (Orler 1998). Similarly, the efficiency of trade promotions is the number one concern for manufacturers (Hilarides 1999).

In addition to the well documented adverse effects of price promotions on consumers – education of consumers to buy on deal (Mela et al. 1998b), reduction of consumer reference prices and increase of customer price sensitivity (Mela et al. 1998a) – price promotions also have adverse effects on competitors: price promotions lead to competitive escalation and an increased risk of price wars (Van Heerde et al. 2008). Furthermore, price promotions have a negative impact on the company, since they typically erode brand equity (Mela et al. 1997). Price promotions, finally, are subject to retailer abuse (Drèze and Bell 2003): a) forward buying and sale of discounted products beyond intended promotional period with a corresponding negative impact on brand equity; b) opportunism and limited pass-through of price reduction with retailers pocketing part of the difference between promoted and regular prices; and c) diversion of excess inventory to other retailers at lower prices. Retailer abuse of price promotions is a concern with detrimental effects on manufacturer profitability.

These adverse effects raise the question: Are price promotions ever profitable? Conclusive answers are probably elusive – for a review of recent studies see Slotegraaf and Pauwels (2008). The following case study illuminates the impact of cannibalization on manufacturer profits in the context of price promotions.

Let us assume that Coca Cola evaluates the opportunity of an upcoming price promotion by analysing historical data on the effect of price promotions on product sales. In this example, all data are disguised and I use the name Coca Cola as a substitute for an existing fast moving consumer goods company. Let us assume the products analysed are Coca Cola (red), the flagship product, and Coca Cola Diet/Zero, its closest substitutes.

These data reveal that price promotions on the company's flagship product lead to an immediate uplift in sales (upper part of Figure 2.4). With a promotional price elasticity of 2–4, a 10 per cent price reduction leads to an immediate volume gain of about 30 per cent and, in this case, also an immediate margin gain. After taking into account fixed promotional expenses, the price promotion delivers a positive pricing ROI – *before* cannibalization:

$$\text{Pricing ROI} = \text{(incremental margin } - \text{ promotion expenses)/promotion expenses}$$
$$= (2{,}238 - 1{,}878)/1{,}878 = 19\%$$

In order to understand the effects of cannibalization we need to analyze the effect of a price promotion of Coca Cola (red) on sales of Coca Cola Diet/Zero. Two steps are necessary. We first analyse the baseline sales of Coca Cola Diet/Zero, i.e. the sales when no promotion on any product takes place. We then analyse sales of the latter products when the focal product is promoted. Data in this case study reveal that the sales loss due to cannibalization is larger than the revenue gain due to price promotions (lower part of Figure 2.4). Cannibalized sales are computed at full price levels, while volume gains of course occur at lower, promotional prices.

The net effect in this case (right part of Figure 2.4) reveals a small incremental margin due to the price promotion which is more than counterbalanced by a substantial margin loss as a result of cannibalization. Here, after taking cannibalization into account, the price promotion is unprofitable and the pricing ROI is negative.

Piece #4: key considerations

Price promotions lead to an immediate volume gain and may increase contribution margins of the focal product. If this product is part of a product family, cannibalization effects are likely. By comparing the incremental margin from price promotions with the margin loss due to cannibalization, the overall profitability of price promotions can be calculated. Frequently, the net effect and thus the pricing return on investment are negative.

Piece #5: price promotions and cannibalization – general findings

We can generalize these findings. In a recent study summarizing over 100 cross-pack cannibalization effects in 12 product categories in three countries, Dawes (2012) finds the following: first, cannibalization is real and occurs in about 74 per cent of promotions; second, with four items in a product line and one on promotion, the

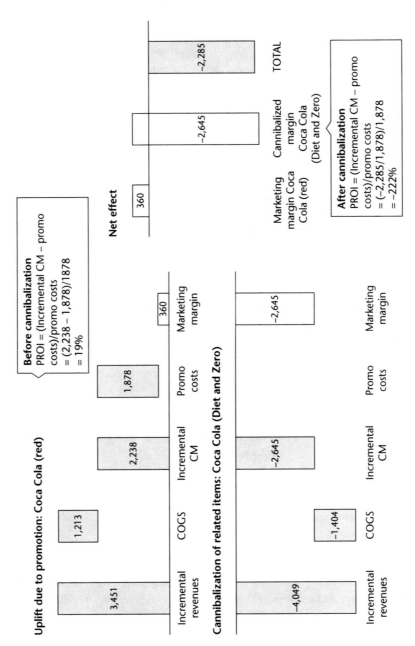

FIGURE 2.4 Pricing ROI, price promotions and cannibalization

average volume uplift of a 20 per cent price promotion is +72 per cent (price elasticity 3,6), whereas the average volume downlift on the unpromoted pack sizes is −5 per cent each (−16 per cent in total). Thirty-four per cent of the gross extra revenue (and about 42 per cent of the extra volume) following the price promotion is thus lost due to reduced sales of other pack sizes. The net effect of a 20 per cent price promotion is +5 per cent volume gain for the product line.

This important study makes it clear that, for retailers and manufacturers alike, cannibalization effects across pack sizes render price promotions prohibitively expensive. Unless contribution margins are close to 100 per cent (a virtual impossibility for retailers and manufacturers alike), price promotions produce a negative pricing ROI.

Dawes (2012) also offers substantive findings on factors influencing cannibalization rates. Pack sizes selling at lower absolute prices lead to lower cannibalization than more expensive items. This finding confirms the intuition: promotions on expensive items cannibalize less expensive items in the product line much more than a price promotion on the least expensive item cannibalizes other, more expensive products. Further, less cannibalization occurs for top-selling items than for slow-selling items. Finally, different packaging formats reduce cannibalization. This finding confirms intuitive reasoning: segmentation and fences between market segments are important elements to reduce cannibalization.

Piece #5: key considerations

Broad empirical research suggests that, after considering pack size cannibalization, a price promotion of 20 per cent increases revenues for all items in the product line by 5 per cent. The pricing ROI for price promotions is thus negative, for both retailers and manufacturers alike. Cannibalization effects by far outweigh revenue increase of the promoted pack size. Factors leading to reduced cannibalization effects are: price promotion on low-price pack sizes (and not on mid-range or expensive items), price promotions on top-selling items (and not on slow-moving items) and price promotions on items that have a different packaging format.

Implications for practice and for research

For practising managers, these case studies – our five easy pieces – offer the following suggestions for managing cannibalization in the context of new product launches and price promotions. First, since new product demand can only originate from other items in the company's product portfolio, from competitor brands or from market expansion, calculating critical cannibalization rates is essential in the context of new product introductions. Higher critical cannibalization rates are better. Actual cannibalization rates need to be monitored post-launch in order to ensure that they are below the critical rate. Second, in an expanding market, this critical cannibalization rate is less relevant and higher cannibalization can be tolerated, as long as effective market segmentation and a distinct product positioning, i.e. fences, ensure that the new product addresses previously untapped markets and thus expands the overall market. Third, in an expanding market and with negative baseline sales (customers defect to competitors in the absence of new products), cannibalization is desirable. Decomposing likely demand for the new product into brand switching, cannibalization and market expansion increases the quality and profitability of new product launches. Advertising spending reduces and can even completely eliminate cannibalization. Fourth, cannibalization is a key concern in the context of price promotions. Price promotions lead to an immediate volume gain and may increase contribution margins of the focal product. If this product is part of a product family, cannibalization effects are very likely. By comparing the incremental margin from price promotions with the margin loss due to cannibalization, the overall profitability of price promotions can be calculated. Frequently, the net effect and thus the pricing ROI are negative. Fifth and finally, recent empirical research (Dawes 2012) suggests that, after considering pack size cannibalization, a price promotion of 20 per cent increases revenues for all items in the product line by 5 per cent. The pricing ROI for price promotions is thus negative, for both retailers and manufacturers alike. Cannibalization effects by far outweigh revenue increase of the promoted pack size. Factors leading to reduced cannibalization effects are: price promotion on low-price pack sizes (and not on mid-range or expensive items), price promotions on top-selling items (and not on slow-moving items) and price promotions on items that have a different packaging format.

This discussion also suggests potentially fruitful research avenues for researchers. In the context of new product introductions, further research into demand decomposition models appears fruitful, especially if these models can be augmented to predict cannibalization or market expansion. Further research on the effectiveness of price promotions is also warranted (Dawes 2012). Of particular interest are further studies on contingency effects of cannibalization, both in the context of price promotions as well as in the context of new product launches.

References

Berschauer, F. (2005) *Bayer CropScience – Creating value through innovation*. Investor presentation, Credit Suisse Agro Conference, Lyon.

Dawes, J. G. (2012) Brand-pack size cannibalization arising from temporary price promotions. *Journal of Retailing*, 88 (3), pp. 343–355.

Drèze, X. and Bell, D. R. (2003) Creating win-win trade promotions: Theory and empirical analysis of scan-back trade deals. *Marketing Science*, 22 (1), pp. 16–39.

Graham, J. and Baig, E. (2007) Q&A with Jobs: "That's what happens in technology." *USA Today* (September 5), http://usatoday30.usatoday.com/tech/products/2007-09-05-jobs-qanda_N.htm

Guimaraes, P. and Chandon, P. (2007) *Unilever in Brazil 1997–2007: Marketing strategies for low-income consumers*. Insead case, #504-009-1.

Hilarides, B. (1999) What makes a trade promotion successful. *Frozen Food*, 47 (12), p. 48.

Isaacson, B. and Silk, A. (1997) *Philip Morris: Marlboro friday (A)*. Harvard Business School Case, # 9-596-001.

Lomax, W., Hammond, K., East, R. and Clemente, M. (1997) The measurement of cannibalization. *Journal of Product and Brand Management*, 6 (1), pp. 27–39.

Mason, C. H. and Milne, G. R. (1994) An approach for identifying cannibalization within product line extensions and multi-brand strategies. *Journal of Business Research*, 31 (2), pp. 163–170.

Mela, C. F., Gupta, S. and Lehmann, D. R. (1997) The long-term impact of promotion and advertising on consumer brand choice. *Journal of Marketing Research*, 34 (2), pp. 248–261.

Mela, C. F., Gupta, S. and Jedidi, K. (1998a) Assessing long-term promotional influences on market structure. *International Journal of Research in Marketing*, 15 (2), pp. 89–107.

Mela, C. F., Jedidi, K. and Bowman, D. (1998b) The long-term impact of promotions on consumer stockpiling behavior. *Journal of Marketing Research*, 35 (2), pp. 250–262.

Orler, V. (1998) The trade promotion quagmire. *Supermarket Business* (June).

Polman, P. (2010) Investor presentation. Sanford C. Bernstein, Strategic Decisions Conference, 20 January.

Slotegraaf, R. J. and Pauwels, K. (2008) The impact of brand equity and innovation on the long-term effectiveness of promotions. *Journal of Marketing Research*, 45 (3), pp. 293–306.

Van Heerde, H., Gijsbrechts, E. and Pauwels, K. (2008) Winners and losers in a major price war. *Journal of Marketing Research*, 45 (5), pp. 499–518.

Van Heerde, H., Srinivasan, S. and Dekimpe, M. (2010) Estimating cannibalization rates for pioneering innovations. *Marketing Science*, 29 (6), pp. 1024–1039.

3

IS THERE A LONG-TERM RETURN ON PRICE PROMOTIONS?

Carmen Balan

Introduction

In the turmoil of the recent economic crisis, the use of price promotions became a common practice for many marketers, with the aim to stimulate demand in the short run. The question is whether companies have evaluated the long-term impact of such marketing tools.

Price promotions are defined as temporary price discounts offered to a customer (Blattberg et al. 1995, p.G122). At the beginning of the 1990s, promotions represented 65 per cent of the typical marketing budget in the USA. However, a research on 65 product categories showed that 84 per cent of trade promotions were unprofitable (Abraham and Lodish 1990, p.51).

During the past decade, the research priorities set by the Marketing Science Institute (MSI) progressively included different topics focused on marketing performance. In 2008–2010, accountability and return on investment (ROI) of the marketing expenditures emerged as the first item on the list of 16 top research priorities of the MSI (Marketing Science Institute 2008). In 2010, research was required to help firms evaluate and compare the long-term value of alternative marketing strategies. The identification of effective strategies of allocating resources to marketing activities became the seventh research priority (Marketing Science Institute 2010). The quantitative research on price promotion reflected this shift in marketing science priorities.

Measuring the impact of the marketing actions should not be limited to the assessment of the financial impact under the form of ROI. The reason is twofold. On one side, the calculation of the short-term ROI disregards the long-term impact of marketing expenditures. On the other side, laying the accent on ROI neglects effectiveness and may lead to diminished profits in the long term. The financial impact is only one facet of the marketing actions. Researchers suggest a productivity chain approach (Rust et al. 2004). According to this chain, the impact of marketing strategies and tactics is multifold. In essence, marketing strategies and tactics have customer impact (on customer awareness, associations, attitudes, attachment and experience), market impact (on market share, sales, competitive market position, etc.), financial impact (ROI, economic value-added, etc.) and impact on firm value (market value-added, stock market performance).

Researchers investigated the short-, medium- and long-term effects of price promotions. Until the end of the 1980s, most studies focused on the immediate effects registered in the week or weeks in which the promotion occurs, as well as on the intermediate effects which become manifest during the weeks or months subsequent to a promotion.

Emergence of a dynamic approach in modelling the long-term effects of price promotions

Almost two decades ago, marketing scientists and practitioners were looking for answers relative to the marketing effectiveness in the long term. The major question 'Are marketing efforts able to affect long-term trends in sales or other performance measures?' (Dekimpe and Hanssens 1995a, p.1) required a precise answer to support businesses in their endeavour to devise strategies able to generate and sustain competitive advantage.

Many questions were raised about the long-term effects of price promotions. The detrimental long-term effects of price promotions were considered 'the most debated issue in the promotional literature' and 'one for which the jury is still out' (Blattberg et al. 1995, p.G127). At the beginning of the 2000s, no conclusive findings were available relative to the long-run effectiveness of promotions (Nijs et al. 2001, p.3).

Since then, an increasing number of researchers approached the long-term effects of price promotions. Promotion was the variable that attracted much more interest than other components of the marketing mix such as distribution, product and even advertising. Only recently, integrated modelling approaches of the long-term impact of several marketing-mix instruments evolved.

The research approaches evolved progressively from modelling stable/stationary environments to modelling dynamic/non-stationary markets. According to the traditional market-response models which assume a stable environment, the impact of the marketing strategies on the brand's performance consists in temporary deviations from a predetermined level. However, such models do not provide insights into the causes of long-term fluctuations in performance.

By the mid-1990s, researchers became aware that the concept of evolution had to be statistically defined to better understand the long-run marketing effectiveness. The analysis of a database of univariate time-series models published between 1975 and 1994 revealed that the incidence of evolution was 54 per cent. Out of these models, for the marketing performance models only, the incidence of evolution was 60 per cent (Dekimpe and Hanssens 1995b, p.G114). Evolution was identified as a dominant characteristic for sales and marketing-mix spending, while stationarity was identified as a dominant characteristic for market share (Dekimpe and Hanssens 1995b, p.G109).

The persistence modelling emerged in marketing science to discern the long-term impact of marketing strategies. According to Dekimpe and Hanssens (1995a, p.2), persistence is a measure of the extent to which changes in current conditions lead to permanent future changes. Persistence implies a carry-over of the short-term impact into the future performance.

In the late 1990s, the findings of an exploratory research on the use of UPC scanner data in the consumer packaged goods industry in the USA revealed several long-term needs in the field of academic research and marketing action (Bucklin and Gupta 1999, p.269). First, the orientation from tactics to strategy held the top of the list of long-term needs relative to the scanner data analysis. Second, another long-term need was the orientation from the study of the impact of marketing strategies on sales to the examination of the impact on short- and long-run profits. Third, the shift from descriptive models to prescriptive models was underlined in order to support managers in the decision-making process.

Since the end of the 1990s, times-series methods have served to quantify the long-term effects of marketing tools. Unit-root tests, co-integration tests, vector auto-regressive models with exogenous variables (VARX) and vector error-correction models (VEC) are several examples.

To evaluate the long-term impact of price promotions, researchers resorted to different models. Two dominant modelling approaches emerged, respectively the varying parameter models and the vector autoregressive models (Ataman et al. 2010, p.870).

Hereinafter, the use of such models for the investigation of the long-term effects of price promotion (usually in connection with one or more marketing mix variables) is presented.

Varying parameter models

Since the 1990s, varying parameter models have been developed to study the long-run impact of promotions on choice, incidence, quantity, market structure, brand sales and elasticity.

Impact on choice, incidence and quantity

In the long term, price promotions may lead to undesirable outcomes relative to consumers' sensitivity to price and price promotions. Mela et al. (1997) developed and empirically tested a distributed-lag (Koyck) response model in order to understand the long-term impact of promotion and advertising on the brand choice behaviour of consumers. The input for the model consisted in scanner data from 11 stores within a market, data from a panel of 1,590 households and demographic information. The long-term changes in consumer behaviour were analysed based on data for a period of eight-and-a-quarter years. The research focused on one frequently purchased non-food product in a mature category and considered price and non-price promotions.

The research of Mela et al. (1997) underlined that in the long term, price reductions increase the sensitivity to price of both loyal and non-loyal consumers. However, price promotions did not generate long-term effects on the brand market shares. The effects of price promotions on non-loyal consumers were four times higher than on loyal consumers. In the long term, a 1 per cent increase in price promotion led to changes of −0.61 per cent and −2.50 per cent respectively in the sensitivity to price of the loyal and non-loyal segments (the negative numbers reflect an increase in price sensitivity). In exchange, a 1 per cent increase in price promotion had an insignificant long-term impact on the sensitivity to price promotion of the loyal customers and increased by 0.11 per cent the sensitivity of the non-loyal customers. The changes in price sensitivity were greater than the changes in price promotion sensitivity.

Mela et al. (1998) examined the long-term impact of promotions on consumer stockpiling behaviour. They developed a varying-parameter model of purchase incidence (the likelihood of making purchases on subsequent shopping trips) and purchase quantity in which the household responsiveness to price and promotion was allowed to vary with changes in the exposure to promotion over long periods. The model was estimated and calibrated based on panel data relative to a frequently purchased, non-food, consumer-packaged good (such as a cleaning product) in one small city, during a period of eight-and-a-quarter years. The study revealed changes in consumer stockpiling behaviour over the analysed period. The long-term exposure to promotions led to a reduced likelihood of purchase incidence on a given shopping trip and to an increase in the quantity bought when the purchase was made. The findings indicate the strategy of households to wait for good promotions/deals and to stockpile when the promotion occurs. As stated by researchers, the study was the first to document the negative long-term effects of sales promotions on category profits. More precisely, promotion increases consumer price sensitivity, decreases promotion effectiveness, augments inventories and generates demand volatility.

The long-run impact of price promotions on brand choice and purchase quantity was approached by Jedidi et al. (1999) who referred to the management of advertising and promotion in order to achieve long-term profitability. They developed a heteroscedastic, varying-parameter joint probit choice and regression quantity model, a new approach in the marketing and econometric literature at the end of the 1990s. The study was based on household panel, store, demographic and trip data. The information referred to a non-food, mature product category, for a period of eight-and-a-quarter years. These researchers were among the first to study empirically the relationship between the depth and frequency of the price discounts, in a long-run frame. The findings showed that while depth elasticities are larger than frequency elasticities in the short run, they become smaller in the long run. Compared to previous studies of the long-term effects of promotions on brand choice, the research provided a perspective of the trade-offs between the short- and long-run impacts. More precisely, results showed that, on average, the long-term effects of promotions are negative and represent about two-fifths of the short-term effects which are positive. Compared to regular price elasticities, the price promotion elasticities are higher in the short term and respectively smaller in the long term. For the product studied, the total (long-term plus short-term) promotion elasticity (0.56) is 30 per cent lower than regular elasticities. Price promotions influence consumer's brand choice in the short term, but not in the long term. The findings show that in the long term, promotions have a negative impact on brand equity; they make consumers more price sensitive and less discount sensitive in their brand choice decision. Thus, companies have to apply ever-greater discounts to generate the same impact on consumer's choice. While in the short term, choice accounts for most of the promotion elasticity, when both short- and long-term effects are considered, quantity accounts for the majority of the promotion elasticity. In the long run, price promotion may have a larger effect on quantity than on brand choice. The simulations made to evaluate the profit impact of long-term changes in promotion policies led to the conclusion that price promotions are unprofitable in the long term.

Impact on brand sales and brand equity

The dynamic effects of price on brand sales were investigated by numerous researchers. Among them, Kopalle et al. (1999) studied the dynamic effects (over several periods) of price discounts on the sales of liquid dishwashing detergent. They developed a two-fold approach, respectively descriptive and normative. The descriptive approach consisted in estimating a varying-parameter sales response model that allowed variations in parameters (that reflect market response) with the discounting policy of the company. That model was predicated on the dynamic SCAN*PRO based model developed by Foekens et al. (1999). In addition, the normative approach aimed to identify the optimal prices for retailers and manufacturers over time. The descriptive model based on store data revealed that price promotions have negative future effects on baseline sales, even if the contemporaneous (immediate) effects are positive. The baseline sales are the value of retail sales that would be obtained in the absence of promotion. For optimal price promotion strategies and higher profitability, a trade-off is necessary between sales increase in the current period and the decline in baseline sales in future periods. However, the research findings revealed that brands with higher contemporaneous price effects also achieve larger dynamic price effects. In essence, Kopalle et al. identified a 'triple jeopardy' generated by the increased use of price discounts: i) decline in the brand baseline sales; ii) increase in customers' price sensitivity; and iii) diminished ability to use discounts to gain market share from competing brands.

Monitoring the dynamics of brand equity, Sriram et al. (2007) studied the impact of several marketing-mix variables (advertising, sales promotions and product innovation) on brand equity. They used a random coefficients logit demand model that was calibrated on store-level scanner data. Two consumer packaged goods categories (toothpaste and dishwashing detergent) were studied during 30 quarters in a retail chain. The sales promotion variable for a product variant was defined as the proportion of UPCs in the product variant that were available on sales promotion during a specific week. The findings in the second stage of the model revealed that sales promotions had a negative impact on brand equity. Nevertheless, the short- and long-term effects were not statistically significant. Consequently, researchers invited a reconsideration of the allocation of the communication budget between advertising and sales promotion. This was based on the empirical results that advertising has significant positive effects on brand equity in the short and long run, as well as on the result that advertising effects have a larger magnitude than sales promotion effects.

To identify the most effective marketing strategies for the introduction of new brands in the market, Ataman et al. (2008) developed a Bayesian dynamic linear model of repeat purchase diffusion. The researchers examined the introduction of 225 new brands within 22 repeat-purchase product categories. The model was calibrated on weekly sales scanner data obtained from a national sample of 560 stores operated by 21 different chains in France, during a period of five years. Marketing strategies were linked to both the growth and the market potential of a new brand. The research findings underlined the relative effect of each examined marketing strategy on the growth parameter and respectively on the market potential parameter (for each specific strategy, the effect being expressed in percentage terms, by dividing the absolute parameter estimate of that strategy by the sum of the absolute parameter estimates for all the marketing-mix strategies). The relative effects on the growth parameter were the following: distribution breadth 31 per cent, discounting 20 per cent, regular price 15 per cent, line length 12 per cent, feature/display 12 per cent, advertising 10 per cent and distribution depth 0.1 per cent. As regards the market potential, the relative effects were: distribution breadth 54 per cent, feature/display 20 per cent, distribution depth 9 per cent, line length 7 per cent, regular price 5 per cent, advertising 2 per cent and discounting 2 per cent. Price discounting ranges the second after distribution breadth in generating sales performance. In contrast, the impact of discounting on market potential lies far behind the effects of distribution breadth and depth and even behind the feature and display (sales promotion tools). In addition, the findings showed that except for discounting, all the other marketing strategies examined have a positive total effect on sales. Price discounts may be used to accelerate the diffusion of the new brands launched. However, in the long run, discounts have a negative impact on market potential.

Further research made by Ataman et al. (2010) examined the long-term impact of the integrated marketing-mix strategies not only on the base sales of a brand, but also on regular price elasticity. Base sales are defined as the sales of the brand when all marketing variables are at their means. They should not be confused with baseline sales which are the sales in the absence of promotion. The aim of the study was to identify the marketing-mix strategies that correlate most highly with brand sales growth and with the potential to command higher prices. The research was based on a Bayesian dynamic linear model (a multivariate dynamic linear transfer function model). The model was calibrated on five years of weekly stock-keeping-unit store-level scanner data for 70 national brands within 25 product categories sold in a national sample of 560 outlets from 21 retail chains in France. The researchers also used monthly brand-level advertising data for the analysed period. As regards price discounts, the results showed that in the short term, discounting is a tactical tool that generates strong sales bumps, but in the long term it is a strategic tool with negative effects on sales. The findings show that long-term elasticity of discounting (-0.02 per cent) lags far behind the long-term elasticities of product (1.29 per cent), distribution (0.61 per cent) and advertising (0.12 per cent). The results of this research show that the magnitude of the negative long-term effect of promotion is approximately one-third of the magnitude of the short-term effect. This result is in line with the findings of Jedidi et al. (1999). The total elasticity (short term plus long term) for each marketing tool and its share of the total elasticities are the following: 1.37 (60 per cent) for product; 0.74 (32 per cent) for distribution breadth; 0.13 (6 per cent) for advertising; 0.04 (2 per cent) for discounts.

Contrary to the previous research that showed the positive impact of price promotions on sales in the short run, the varying parameter models revealed the unfavourable impact of price promotions in the long term. Price promotions used as a strategic tool do not have positive effects.

Vector autoregressive models

The vector autoregressive (VAR) models represent another class of models developed to study the long-term effects of marketing-mix variables on aspects such as brand and category sales, market share, incidence, choice and quantity, margin, revenue and financial measures. From a VAR modelling perspective, a price promotion is 'an unexpected price shock relative to the expected price as predicted through the dynamic structure of the VAR model' (Srinivasan et al. 2004, p.619).

The long-run effectiveness of promotions is computed based on the impulse-response functions derived from the VAR models. An impulse-response function is based on a 'conceptual experiment' that examines the chain of events generated by a change to a marketing variable (Pauwels 2004, p.596). The net long-term effect of price promotion on sales is the overtime impact of the chain of events consisting in consumer reaction, competitor reaction and company decision rules such as inertia or supporting with other marketing actions.

Impact on brand sales and category demand

The long-term impact of price promotions on primary demand (industry sales) and secondary demand (brand sales) was analysed by Dekimpe et al. (1999). They applied long-term time-series techniques on scanner data relative to 13 brands within four consumer goods categories (ketchup, liquid detergent, soup and yogurt). Some of the empirical generalizations based on the unit-root econometric analyses are the following: a) in scanner markets, category sales, brand sales and brand prices generally follow a mean-stationary process; b) price promotions have a temporary impact on the future brand and market sales (long-term promotion effects with relatively low persistence were identified only in the highly concentrated soup market); c) price promotions applied by the market leaders tend to have the largest immediate effect, but limited and competitive cumulative effects; and d) promotions of the private brands can lead to market expansion and increase the performance of national brands.

The long-term impact of price promotions on category demand captured the attention of researchers to a lower extent than the impact on brand sales. However, the study achieved by Nijs et al. (2001) provided a thorough and broad perspective of the topic for 560 frequently purchased consumer product categories over a period of four years. The data referred to supermarkets in the Netherlands and reflected all the components of the marketing mix (price, promotion, advertising, distribution, new products). The long-run effects of promotion on category demand were examined based on multivariate time-series analysis.

The findings of the study made by Nijs et al. (2001) showed that category demand is predominantly stationary (around a fixed mean or a deterministic trend). In spite of their strong short-term effect, price promotions do not have a persistent impact on category demand (volume). Consumer price promotions do not generate market expansion in the long run. The effects last no more than ten weeks on average. In the long run, the effects of price promotions converge to zero for 98 per cent of the product categories. The oligopolistic product categories marked by the intense use of promotions are attractive to major competitors rather than to small ones or to new entrants due to the low profit margin. Thus, price promotions preserve the market status quo by keeping out the 'unwanted' competition.

Researchers also investigated the long-term impact of price promotions initiated in response to a competitor's promotion attack. A relevant example is the large-scale empirical study achieved by Steenkamp et al. (2005) that stands out from the market-response literature due to the wide array of frequently purchased consumer goods considered, respectively over 1,200 brands within 442 product categories. The weekly scanner data referred to the Dutch market over a period of four years. Data were also obtained from the Europanel household panel. Time-series modelling was applied to measure the short- and long-term differential impact of promotion and advertising attacks on competitive and sales response. The findings addressed the following questions: 'How do brands react to competitive attacks?', 'When are the competitive reactions more aggressive?' and 'Is the competitive reaction justified?' First, the results relative to the competitive reaction to promotion attacks revealed that passive reaction (no reaction) is the most common competitive reaction. However, companies respond more often to price promotion attacks than to advertising attacks. In the cases when price promotions are used to react to price promotion attacks, the approach is generally retaliatory. The impact of the competitive reaction manifests in the short term, without generating permanent changes in spending behaviour. Second, reactions consisting in price promotions are stronger in the following situations: the attacker is more powerful; the relative power structure favours the defender; the category is less concentrated; the inter-purchase time is higher. Price-promotion reactivity is stronger in impulse-buying categories. Third, the competitive impact of the promotion attacks is due to the consumer response, rather than to competitors' reaction.

The cumulative and permanent effects of price promotions were studied by Slotegraaf and Pauwels (2008) within a research on the impact of brand equity and innovation on the long-term effectiveness of promotions. The data were obtained from several sources: scanner panel data relative to the second largest supermarket chain in the Chicago area; the COMPUSTAT database and the company Web sites. A total of 100 brands within seven food and non-food product categories (bottled juice, toothpaste, laundry detergent, cheese, soft drinks, paper towel and toilet tissue) were investigated over a period of seven years and eight months. The data referred to the effects of price promotions besides display and feature advertising. Compared to previous empirical studies based on VAR models, the product categories included not only the top three or four brands, but also brands with medium, small and very small market shares. Due to the broad range of brands examined, the findings differed from previous empirical evidence which showed that promotion has positive cumulative effects on brand sales, but rare permanent effects. In contrast, the study of Slotegraaf and Pauwels (2008) underlined that permanent effects are common when 9–25 brands per category are analysed. Price promotion yielded a permanent elasticity of 0.06 per cent (lower that the average cumulative elasticity of 0.87 per cent).

Impact on market share

Researchers studied the impact of temporary and permanent price changes on market share. According to Srinivasan et al. (2000), a temporary price change may be a discount applied during a short period to a price that is quite stable along the year (e.g. 10 per cent off the price during a couple of weeks). After the discount period, the price reverts to the previous level. The permanent price changes can be either evolving or structural. Evolving price changes may correspond to a regular discount policy (e.g. 5 per cent off the price by the end of each month). A structural price change may consist in a one-time (substantial) price reduction (e.g. a 20 per cent price cut) and leads to a new price level.

The study made by Srinivasan et al. (2000) was based on a set of aggregate weekly store level scanner data on sales of beer brands and on a set of household scanner data on purchases of margarine brands. The methodology was based on two empirical frameworks: the VAR model and the vector error-correction (VEC) model. The time-series technique of co-integration analysis and impulse–response analysis were used to assess the impact of temporary and evolving changes in prices on market shares, and to calculate short- and long-run price elasticities. For the beer category, the findings showed that the long-run price elasticities response to evolving prices is lower than the short-run price elasticities response to temporary price changes. As regards competitors' reaction to price changes, the results revealed that a structural price change is preferable to frequent evolving price changes at least for two reasons. First, structural price changes lead to the desired market share sooner than the evolving price changes. Second, competitors react to a structural price change not immediately, but with a time lag of 12–13 weeks. Frequent promotions invite competitive reactions and have as a long-run effect the persistent price reduction for the entire category.

Impact on incidence, choice and quantity

The study by Pauwels et al. (2002) decomposed the long-term effects of price promotions on the following components of brand sales: category incidence (weekly number of consumers that made a purchase within the product category), brand choice share (fraction of the consumers who bought the brand out of the consumers that purchased within the category) and purchase quantity (average quantity per purchasing consumer). Unit-root tests, VAR models and impulse-response functions derived from the VAR models were applied.

The findings (Pauwels et al. 2002) showed that permanent promotion effects are virtually absent for each of the three components of brand sales (category incidence, brand choice and purchase quantity). The breakdown (on the three sales components) of the total effects (cumulative promotional impact reflected by the sum of the immediate effects and the effects during the adjustment period) of a price shock is 66 per cent/11 per cent/23 per cent for soup, respectively, and 58 per cent/39 per cent/3 per cent for yogurt. The breakdown of the immediate effect is 30 per cent/48 per cent/22 per cent for soup, respectively, and 14 per cent/73 per cent/13 per cent for yogurt. The importance of the effects on category incidence, brand choice and purchase quantity varies by product category and time horizon. In the long run, price promotions may be beneficial more to retailers (primary demand) than to manufacturers (selective demand). Brand choices are in equilibrium in a mature market and price promotions produce only temporary benefits for established brands. The study has two major managerial implications. First, 'playing the promotional game appears better than staying out of it' (Pauwels et al. 2002, p.437), due to the favourable immediate and adjustment effects of price promotion on the sales components. Second, price promotions are valuable to retailers, due to the positive impact on primary demand (category incidence and purchase quantity).

Impact on margin, revenue and financial measures

The long-term effects of price promotions on manufacturers and retailers have been less studied. In 2004, Srinivasan et al. stated that 'no empirical literature to date has systematically assessed these financial effects over time' (p.618).

The first large-scale econometric investigation to address the effects of price promotions on manufacturer revenues, retailer revenues and retailer margins (*total dollar margin or gross profit of the retailer for all the brands in the category*) was the study achieved by Srinivasan et al. (2004). To evaluate the cumulative effects of promotions, the researchers applied VAR modelling and impulse-response functions. The scanner database referred to a total of 63 brands within 21 product categories sold in a supermarket chain with 96 stores, during 265 weeks in a regional market in the USA. The findings show that price promotions do not have permanent revenue effects. Manufacturer revenue, retailer revenue and retailer margins are stationary (after a promotion shock, they revert to their mean or deterministic trend). Thus, the management of promotions has tactical rather than strategic character.

The long-term impact of promotion on financial metrics was also examined by Pauwels et al. (2004) within the framework of a study relative to new product introductions and promotional incentives as important performance drivers in the automobile industry. Multivariate time-series models were applied to investigate the impact on revenue (top-line performance), profits (bottom-line performance) and firm value (stock market performance). VAR models were used to measure the dynamic performance response and the interactions between performance and marketing variables. The data sources were JDPA (for weekly retail sales transactions for a sample of 1,100 California dealerships from October 1996 to December 2001), the Center for Research in Security Prices, COMPUSTAT and I/B/E/S for earnings forecasts. The findings show that in the long run, promotions have an intensified positive impact on the top-line performance only. The long-term effects of promotions are significantly negative on both the bottom-line performance and firm value. In the short term, managers are tempted to use sales promotions due to their positive impact on top-line and bottom-line performance, as well as on firm value. Rebates play an important part in the marketing strategy in the automobile market. However, managers should refrain from rebates because the stock market penalizes the companies that rely on sales promotions.

Impact on mind-set metrics

Recently, a new research track emerged in market-response modelling. This approach integrates two extant streams. The former consists in modelling the effects of the marketing-mix tools on brand and category sales, market share, financial metrics, etc. The latter evolved in connection with branding and advertising and focuses on the impact of mind-set metrics on sales.

One of the first examples of the new integrative perspective is the research of Srinivasan et al. (2010) which includes customer mind-set metrics in models that incorporate marketing-mix variables related to price, promotion, advertising and distribution. The main steps of the analysis were: application of unit root tests; specification of the VARX model; generalized forecast error variance decomposition (GFEVD); and examining the generalized impulse response functions (GIRF). The data referred to 60 brands from four food and non-food product categories (breakfast cereals, bottled water, fruit juice and shampoo) on the French market and covered a period of seven years and five months. The components of the marketing mix considered by researchers were: average price paid, value-weighted distribution coverage, promotion and total spending on advertising media. The mind-set metrics examined were advertising awareness, brand liking and inclusion in the consideration set. The effects of the marketing actions on the mind-set metrics range among the findings of the research. Distribution is the marketing-mix variable with the highest cumulative impact on the three mind metrics, compared to price, promotion (in-store communication, presence of in-store flyers, price promotions and bonus buys) and advertising. In response to a shock to distribution, the average cumulative elasticity is 0.887 for advertising awareness, 1.040 for consideration and 0.517 for liking. In contrast, in response to a shock to promotion, the average cumulative elasticity is 0.049 for advertising awareness, 0.032 for consideration and 0.149 for liking. A conclusion drawn from the study is that advertising has the highest cumulative impact on advertising awareness, while promotion has the highest cumulative impact on consideration and price has on liking.

The varying parameter model and the VAR model provided an in-depth perspective of the long-term effects of price promotions.

Overview of the impact of price promotions on performance

The use of the varying parameter model and the VAR model revealed several major long-term effects of price promotions. These effects are presented in Table 3.1.

A legitimate question requires an answer. Is there a long-term return on price promotions?

From a 'narrow' perspective focused on the financial essence of the word 'return', price promotions fail to generate a significant sales increase, diminish the baseline sales and may have a negative impact on profits. Price promotions could be considered by decision-makers a cost rather than an investment in the long run.

From a 'broad' perspective, the return may be an outcome that also refers to customers and markets. Such outcomes may be negative and undesirable from a practitioner's standpoint, among which range the increase in customers' sensitivity to price and price discounts, the erosion of the market price for an entire category and the deterioration of the brand equity.

Implications for the marketing practice

The price promotions have captured the attention of practitioners due to the immediate impact on sales. The widespread practice of price promotions generates legitimate questions on the long-term return on price promotions. Even if most decision-makers are enchanted by the potential favourable effects in the short term, experts state that 'the effects of discounts and of other components in the marketing mix – such as advertising, new products, and distribution – can be understood only over the long term' (Lodish and Mela 2007, p.108). Are practitioners aware of the long-term impact of price promotions? Do they evaluate the effects in the long run?

TABLE 3.1 Synopsis of the long-term impact of price promotions on performance based on varying parameter and VAR models

Models	Areas of impact	Long-term impact on performance
Varying parameter model	Impact on brand choice behaviour of consumers, incidence (stockpiling behaviour) and quantity	• increase in the sensitivity to price of both loyal and non-loyal customers • no significant long-term impact of a 1% increase in price promotions on the sensitivity to price promotions of the loyal customers • negative long-term effects that represent about 2/5 of the short-term effects which are positive • negative long-term effects on category profits due to stockpiling behaviour
	Impact on brand sales and brand equity	• negative future effects on baseline sales • limited ability to use discounts to get market share from competing brands • negative impact on brand equity • negative impact on market potential
VAR model	Impact on brand sales and category demand	• no persistent impact on category demand (volume) • no permanent changes in the consumer spending behaviour due to competitive reactions • rare permanent effects on brand sales (when 9–25 brands per category are analysed) • preservation of the status quo of competitors' market shares • no impact consisting in market expansion
	Impact on market share	• decline in category price due to competitive reactions to frequent promotions
	Impact on incidence, choice and quantity	• virtually absent effects in category incidence, brand choice and purchase quantity • positive impact on primary demand rather than on selective demand (more benefits for retailers than manufacturers)
	Impact on margin, revenues and financial measures	• no permanent revenue effects (price promotions are tactical rather than strategic tools) for consumer goods sold in supermarkets • in the automobile industry, positive impact on revenues only (negative impact on profits and firm value)
	Impact on mind-set metrics	• potential positive cumulative impact of promotions on the brand inclusion in the consideration set

Long-run strategic effects of price promotions

Before deciding to use price promotions, practitioners have to clarify if they are interested in attracting new buyers or in rewarding the existing/loyal customers. There are products/brands for which price promotions will more likely resonate with those that have already had a purchase experience. An example is represented by the leading brands of established packaged grocery goods. Evidence from a multi-country study made by Ehrenberg et al. (1994) showed that extra sales of a leading brand while promoted came to a large proportion from the brand's existing long-term customer base. The percentage of buyers during peak sales who had bought the brand two-and-a-half years before reached category averages of 95 per cent for brands of ground coffee in Germany, 93 per cent for brands of detergents in the USA and 91 per cent for brands of ketchup and yoghurt in the USA. Similarly, the category average percentage of buyers corresponding to purchases made two years before was 98 per cent for detergent brands in Germany, 91 per cent for carbonated soft drink brands in Germany, 91 per cent for soup brands in the USA, 90 per cent for instant coffee brands in the USA and 78 per cent for crackers brands in the USA. The overall average percentage of those who bought in the previous half-year was 67 per cent for the categories of leading packaged grocery brands included in the study. In essence, most buyers of brands promoted through price cuts are existing customers and the proportion of buyers purchasing a promoted brand for the first time is below a few percentages. For the leading brands of grocery packaged goods, consumers display a habitual buying behaviour. They have a portfolio of two to three familiar brands from which they choose and among which they switch over time depending on the availability of an offer. Buyers seem to consider that a price cut is not worth the risk/effort of switching to an unfamiliar brand. Under such circumstances, the practitioners should be aware that price promotions will not be capable of achieving ambitious objectives related to the attraction of completely new buyers that are unfamiliar with the brand.

Short-run tactical effects of price promotions

Practitioners have to use price promotions mostly as a tactical tool (to achieve short-term objectives) rather than a strategic one (for long-term objectives). The reason for this approach is the research evidence that reveals the nature of the long-term effects of price promotions that consist in: i) increase in the price sensitivity of loyal and non-loyal customers; ii) decrease in the discount sensitivity of consumers in their brand choice decision; iii) erosion of the price for an entire product category (due to the competitive reaction to frequent price promotions); iv) lack of effects on the market shares of major/established competing brands (no significant impact on market structure; a fact that leads to the preservation of the status quo for major brands and keeps out other 'unwanted' players); v) negative future effects on baseline sales (even if immediate effects are positive); vi) diminished ability to use discounts to gain market share from competing brands; vii) decline in the profits of the product and of the product category exposed to price promotion; viii) negative impact on brand equity; ix) negative impact on market potential or no expansion of the market; and x) benefits mostly for retailers (relative to the primary demand) than for manufacturers (related to the selective demand).

The impact of price promotions on channel partners

Another implication refers to the need to correlate the decisions related to price promotions within the marketing channels among participants that may have different individual objectives. The long-term impact of price promotions is limited. In practice, market players make use of price promotions for various reasons (Wierenga and Soethoudt 2010). Manufacturers may want to maintain the relationships with a preferred channel partner or to increase market share. Retailers aim to increase store traffic and generate profits based on sales of other products. One of the most frequent reasons is the fact that competitors apply price promotions. In such circumstances, an individual channel member faces a prisoner dilemma when trying to discontinue the discounting practice and will keep applying price promotions because all the other market players implement them. Channel coordination can be the solution for practitioners to avoid the double marginalization phenomenon according to which the decisions made individually by manufacturers and retailers generate a suboptimal profitability at channel level.

The above mentioned facts show that price promotions cannot be considered as a generator of long-term positive return. For companies, price promotions are a cost of doing business rather than an investment. The decision to use price promotions due to their effects in the short term must be substantiated properly in order to avoid or diminish the long-term negative impact on the company and the brand.

Implications for research

Price promotions represent a marketing-mix component which was intensively examined by researchers as regards the short- and long-term outcomes. Since the late 1990s, quantitative research focused on the long-term impact of price promotions in dynamic environments. Several implications revealed by this evolving body of knowledge are presented hereinafter.

First, researchers tend to apply a multifaceted approach to the measurement of the long-term effects of price promotions. Numerous empirical studies investigated the market response in terms of brand sales, category sales, market share, etc. Market impact and customer impact should be considered besides the financial impact on the organization that initiates price promotions.

Second, there is a visible trend towards the simultaneous investigation of several other variables of the marketing mix besides price promotions. Advertising, distribution and new product launches have to be integrated in models together with various forms of promotion (price promotion, display, feature advertising, etc.).

Third, the classical perspective resumed to the impact of price promotion on sales is challenged by new orientations. Fairly recently, several researchers analysed the impact of promotion and other marketing-mix components on mind-set metrics such as advertising awareness, brand liking and inclusion in the consideration set. The integration between two research streams comes to the foreground – the quantitative modelling of the impact of marketing actions on sales and the modelling of the impact of advertising and branding on mind-set metrics.

Fourth, most studies were based on data from the USA market. Evidence from other markets such as the Netherlands and France was available to some extent. In the future, studies centred on other markets may uncover differences in terms of the long-term impact of price promotions.

Finally, contradictory evidence resulted from the extant literature on the impact of price promotions. On one side, a substantial body of research underlined that price promotions have positive cumulative effects on brand sales, but rare permanent effects. On the other side, changes in the research approach consisting in selecting broader ranges of brands (9–25 brands with different magnitudes of the market shares/manufacturer brands and private labels) within each product category investigated pointed out that permanent effects are common. The analysis of the long-term impact of price promotions must consider both permanent and cumulative effects.

Future research and modelling of the long-term effects of price promotions have to clarify the managerial relevance of this marketing tool. Powerful insights are required not only relative to the short-term impact, but also related to the strategic/long-term aspects.

On one side, further research may extend to different product categories, wider ranges of brands from different tiers, markets in different stages of development and various customer segments, as well as to the blended evaluation of the market, customer and financial impact of price promotions.

On the other side, as regards the potential role of channel coordination in improving the profitability of price promotions further research may evaluate aspects such as: i) the sales and profit losses generated by the absence of coordination among channel members; ii) the impact of coordination in the case of price promotions for various product categories and brands from high-, medium- and low-tiers; iii) the relative gains or losses at the different levels (e.g. manufacturer, retailer) of the marketing channel when coordination could be achieved; and iv) strategic and tactical barriers that may hinder the support of the coordination by individual channel members, etc.

Further research may enhance the ability to quantify the long-term return of the price promotions and increase the capabilities of market players to balance the cumulative effects over the immediate effects of this widely applied tool.

References

Abraham, M. M. and Lodish, L. M. (1990) Getting the most out of advertising and promotion. *Harvard Business Review*, 68 (3), pp. 50–60.

Ataman, M. B., Mela, C. F. and Van Heerde, H. J. (2008) Building brands. *Marketing Science*, 27 (6), pp. 1036–1054.

Ataman, M. B., Van Heerde, H. J. and Mela, C. F. (2010) The long-term effect of marketing strategy on brand sales. *Journal of Marketing Research*, 47 (October), pp. 866–882.

Blattberg, R. C., Briesch, R. and Fox, E. J. (1995) How promotions work. *Marketing Science*, 14 (3), pp. G122–G132.

Bucklin, R. E. and Gupta S. (1999) Commercial use of UPC scanner data: Industry and academic perspectives. *Marketing Science*, 18 (3), pp. 247–273.

Dekimpe, M. G. and Hanssens, D. M. (1995a) The persistence of marketing effects on sales. *Marketing Science*, 14 (1), pp. 1–21.

Dekimpe, M. G. and Hanssens, D. M. (1995b) Empirical generalizations about market evolution and stationarity. *Marketing Science*, 14 (3), pp. G109–G121.

Dekimpe, M. G., Hanssens, D. M. and Silva-Risso J. M. (1999) Long-run effects of price promotions in scanner markets. *Journal of Econometrics*, 89 (March–April), pp. 269–291.

Ehrenberg, A. S. C., Hammond, K. and Goodhardt, G. J. (1994) The after-effects of price-related consumer promotions. *Journal of Advertising Research* (July–August), pp. 11–21.

Foekens, E. W., Leeflang, P. S. H. and Wittink, D. R. (1999) Varying parameter models to accommodate dynamic promotion effects. *Journal of Econometrics*, 89 (March–April), pp. 249–268.

Jedidi, K., Mela, C. F. and Gupta, S. (1999) Managing advertising and promotion for long-run profitability. *Marketing Science*, 18 (1), pp. 1–22.

Kopalle, P. K., Mela, C. F. and Marsh, L. (1999) The dynamic effect of discounting on sales: Empirical analysis and normative pricing implications. *Marketing Science*, 18 (3), pp. 317–332.

Lodish, L. M. and Mela, C. F. (2007) If brands are built over years, why are they managed over quarters? *Harvard Business Review* (July–August), pp. 104–112.

Marketing Science Institute (2008) *Research priorities: 2008–2010 guide to MSI research programs and procedures*. Retrieved 20 January 2013 from www.msi.org/pdf/MSI_RP08-10.pdf

Marketing Science Institute (2010) *2010–2012 Research priorities*. Retrieved 20 January 2013 from www.msi.org/pdf/MSI_RP10-12.pdf

Mela, C. F., Gupta, S. and Lehmann, D. R. (1997) The long-term impact of promotion and advertising on consumer brand choice. *Journal of Marketing Research*, 34 (2), pp. 248–261.

Mela, C. F., Jedidi, K. and Bowman, D. R. (1998) The long-term impact of promotions on consumer stockpiling behavior. *Journal of Marketing Research*, 35 (May), pp. 250–262.

Nijs, V. R., Deskimpe, M. G., Steenkamp, J.-B. E. M. and Hanssens D. M. (2001) The category-demand effects of price promotions. *Marketing Science*, 20 (1), pp. 1–22.

Pauwels, K. (2004) How dynamic consumer response, competitor response company support, and company inertia shape long-term marketing effectiveness. *Marketing Science*, 23 (4), pp. 596–610. doi: 10.1287/mksc.1040.0075

Pauwels, K., Hanssens, D. M. and Siddarth, S. (2002) The long-term effects of price promotions on category incidence, brand choice, and purchase quantity. *Journal of Marketing Research*, 39 (4), pp. 421–439.

Pauwels, K., Silva-Risso, J., Srinivasan, S. and Hanssens, D. M. (2004) New products, sales promotions, and firm value: The case of the automobile industry. *Journal of Marketing*, 68 (October), pp. 142–156.

Rust, R. T., Ambler, T., Carpenter, G. S., Kumar, V. and Srivastava, R. K. (2004) Measuring marketing productivity: Current knowledge and future directions. *Journal of Marketing*, 68, pp. 76–90.

Slotegraaf, R. and Pauwels, K. (2008) The impact of brand equity and innovation on the long-term effectiveness of promotions. *Journal of Marketing Research*, 45 (June), pp. 293–306.

Srinivasan, S., Popkowski Leszczyc, P. T. L. and Bass, F. M. (2000) Market share response and competitive interaction: The impact of temporary, evolving and structural changes in prices. *International Journal of Research in Marketing*, 17, pp. 281–305.

Srinivasan, S., Vanhuele M. and Pauwels, K. (2010) Mind-set metrics in market response models: An integrative approach. *Journal of Marketing Research*, 47 (August), pp. 672–684.

Srinivasan, S., Pauwels, K., Hanssens, D. M. and Dekimpe, M. G. (2004) Do promotions benefit manufacturers, retailers, or both? *Management Science*, 50 (May), pp. 617–629.

Sriram, S., Balachander, S. and Kalwani, M. U. (2007) Monitoring the dynamics of brand equity using store-level data. *Journal of Marketing*, 71 (April), pp. 61–78.

Steenkamp, J.-B. E. M., Nijs, V. R., Hanssens, D. M. and Dekimpe, M. G. (2005) Competitive reaction to advertising and promotion attacks. *Marketing Science*, 24 (1), pp. 35–54.

Wierenga, B. and Soethoudt, H. (2010) Sales promotions and channel coordination. *Journal of the Academy of Marketing Science*, 38, pp. 383–397.

4

PRICING MODELLING AS A STRATEGIC LEVERAGE FOR KNOWLEDGE-INTENSIVE START-UPS

An explorative case study in the luxury fashion industry

Stefano Denicolai and Federica Merli

1 Introduction: new paradigms for innovative companies

This chapter discusses theories and practices for measuring the impact of pricing strategies on firm performance. In particular, it focuses on knowledge-intensive start-ups. This is a hot topic for both academics and practitioners. Conditions underlying growth and success for high potential start-ups are vibrant arguments for the recent research in the strategic management field (Davila et al. 2010; Freeman and Engel 2007; Hart 2012; Neyens et al. 2010). Nevertheless, we know little regarding mechanisms for the definition of prices and ROI targets in the cases of new ventures and breakthrough markets (Hinterhuber and Liozu 2012; Peeters and Surry 2000). The argument is crucial especially for start-ups showing a diversified product portfolio: they simultaneously handle a number of variables and this reduces the effectiveness of intuitions, perceptions and informal feedbacks, which often are at the core of the decision-making process for novel entrepreneurs.

After a brief literature review, the chapter addresses an explorative case study, namely 'Moi Multiple' in the luxury fashion sector. The development of this start-up relies on an innovative business model which impacts on the pricing strategy. The methodology combines both qualitative and quantitative procedures (Di Pofi 2002; Kaplan and Duchon 1988). An overview of the industry is also considered. Finally, section 4 draws conclusions, managerial implications and sets the direction for future research.

2 Pricing models and start-ups: challenges and opportunities

This section defines the theoretical foundations for this study and proposes a literature overview regarding challenges and opportunities that creative start-ups face in their pricing decisions.

The argument always had a central role in the strategic management (Ghemawat and McGahan 1998; Kotler 2011). Price is an expression of a company's competitive positioning (Porter 1985) and its definition enables the organization to optimize investments and performance. Furthermore, the pricing activity may be itself an innovative element of the business/revenue model (Onetti et al. 2010) or a firm capability (Hinterhuber and Liozu 2012).

A large body of literature discusses the strategic relevance of pricing models within established firms (Cavusgil et al. 2003; Ghemawat and McGahan 1998; Kotler 2011). Price is a significant variable in order to influence organizational performance: financial, operational and strategic issues are intertwined to determine the success of the firm (Voss et al. 1998; Walters and Mackenzie 1988; Weng 1995).

However, the literature regarding pricing strategies implemented by creative and innovative start-ups is scarce if not absent (Hinterhuber and Liozu 2012). Nevertheless, the argument is crucial for such companies. Scholars demonstrated that pricing adaptation significantly affects innovation and international processes since the price should reflect the environmental characteristics of the new market (Mesak and Berg 1995; Sousa and Bradley 2008). We define a 'start-up' as a newly created company − initial phase in the firm life cycle − showing a scalable business model and high growth potential (Freeman and Engel 2007; Hart 2012).

Start-ups usually operate in complex environments: high turbulence, scarce information regarding the market features, demanding customers, unstable financial equilibrium, globally interconnected dynamics, and so on (Bruton and Rubanik 2002; Shan et al. 1994; Zucchella et al. 2007).

These conditions *per se* introduce challenging issues for the pricing definition. First, the gathering of data through market analysis and monitoring of the cost structure becomes expensive and time consuming, especially for small and micro enterprises (Cooper and Giuffrida 2000). Prior surveys showed that start-ups which find a solution to this dilemma − for instance through customer behaviour tracking on the web − experienced a higher growth (Lowe and Alpert 2010). Unfortunately, a limited number of start-ups spend money in these activities. Deficiencies in terms of capabilities − for example in the appraisal of the relation between pricing definition and ROI − are another motive in explaining the limited attention towards data management in the case of small and medium enterprises (Rivard et al. 2006).

Second, markets that do not exist cannot be analysed: breakthrough value propositions create new competitive arenas where mainstream pricing models may fail due to the lack of reliable data (Christensen 1997; Kim and Mauborgne 2004; Mesak and Berg 1995). In particular, the definition of the first price is challenging (Lin et al. 2011). It implies complex decision-making processes: reflect the cost structure – and related investment, usually relevant at the early stage – or pursue a strategic positioning goal, meaning an aggressive price to stimulate the innovation diffusion (Mesak and Berg 1995), or a premium price to foster the reputation as a first mover (Lieberman and Montgomery 1998). Lowe and Alpert (2010) showed that the start-ups, due to their prototypicality, have a significant influence on price perceptions of incumbents creating a systematic bias to both the definition and evolution of price in creative sectors.

Another critical issue for start-ups is the management of the relation between price and investments (Lowe and Alpert 2010). The declining prices of emerging technology products could lead companies to postpone investment and wait for lower costs (Eden and Ronen 1993; Watanabe et al. 2000). However, the entrepreneur may prefer to enter the market as soon as possible to exploit the first mover advantage (Lieberman and Montgomery 1998). The scarcity of resources to finance the start-up's investment is a further aspect which affects the price strategy (Gartner et al. 1999). In the case of novel entrepreneurs, it may lead to an underestimation of this relation (Tanrisever et al. 2012). They are often overly optimistic about how easy it will be to gain enough customers to justify investments. Anyhow, the influencing power of third parties – such as suppliers, banks, business angels and so on – on the pricing definition has to be taken into account since it is extremely relevant, even if it is an indirect effect (Wiltbank et al. 2009). Start-ups have to change this condition into an opportunity and leverage on the expertise of such actors to improve their pricing strategy.

Another critical issue is the role played by the supplier along the value chain (Gilbert and Cvsa 2003). Typically, it is in a firm's interest for its partners to invest in innovations: to the extent that innovations either reduce the partners' costs, they will tend to create benefits for the value chain as a whole. Nevertheless, opportunistic players may increase own prices in response to the innovations of partners. It could create a barrier for investment in innovation and a further demanding aspect to be considered in pricing strategy for start-ups. The engagement into diverse innovation ecosystems – and the implementation of diversified sale channels – is fundamental to mitigate these risks (Iyer 1998).

The start-up usually deals with such challenges through the concurrence of basic pricing functions and – above all – extensive adoption of intuitive processes (Clancy and Stone 2005). Surveys aimed at investigating if this mindset is efficient – or exploring other options – are limited. Carter et al. (1996) studied what entrepreneurs do in their day-to-day activities. The authors argued that informal practices for novel entrepreneurs who have successfully started a new venture are differentiated from the behaviour of entrepreneurs who failed. A new venture usually adopts aggressive behaviour in the early stage because they will quickly learn that business opportunities will reveal themselves either as a successful company or as a wrong direction that should be abandoned (Carter et al. 1996; Zahra and Covin 1995). The implication in terms of pricing strategy is remarkable. Entrepreneurs often use intuition to explain their actions, but the comprehension of the unexplained variance in entrepreneurial behaviour remains high (Mitchell et al. 2005). If and how much processes based on intuition or prior experience to define investment and price levels lead to a superior firm performance remains poorly investigated.

The above mentioned issues assume diverse nuances according to different pricing models, which usually reflect the entrepreneur's mindset as well as the special feature of the business. The mainstream literature distinguishes between cost-, competition- and customer value-based pricing models (Cavusgil et al. 2003; Ingenbleek et al. 2003). The 'cost-based pricing' (Pavia 1995) leverages on the cost structure to define the product price. Similarly, the markup method sets the product price in order to achieve a goal in terms of ROI (Narayanan et al. 2004). This approach is easy to implement as long as costs are known, whilst it poorly considers the effect of the target market's demand. They are major issues, especially if the firm operates in a highly competitive market. Moreover, the rigorous implementation of the cost pricing model in the case of a newly created company or innovative products runs the risk of being affected by investments and expenditures, which will decrease if the company grows.

The second class of methods explores competitors' prices as a source of information which drives pricing activity and feeds the competitive advantage of the firm (Blattberg and Wisniewski 1989; Kotler 2011; Porter 1985). This view embraces diverse methods. 'Below Competition Pricing' scans the market to keep prices lower than the competitors. New entrants may adopt this solution to boost sales and support the early growth of the company. At the opposite end, 'Above Competition Pricing' serves the purpose of fostering the brand image and being perceived as the market leader or a trend setter. It is a fruitful and risky strategy at the same time. The high potential start-up frequently adopts this solution to develop a reputation as a first mover and because of its attitude to taking risks. 'Parity Pricing' sets the initial price at the same level as competitors, in order to leverage on diverse strategic levers (such as quality).

The third approach focuses on the customer value, meaning the customer's maximum willingness to pay (Hinterhuber and Liozu 2012; Ingenbleek et al. 2003). Value is a function of the benefits that the buyer receives, delivered by the architecture of activities implemented by the firm's business model. Thus, both researchers and practitioners compare the value created with the costs incurred to obtain these benefits. According to these premises, a customer value-based pricing approach aims at defining prices and cost structure in order to maximize the firm's profit. In contrast with cost-based methods – which could lead to suboptimal profitability (Kortge and Okonkwo 1993) – scholars argued that the value-based approach increases firm performance, even though there are limited empirical studies confirming this assumption (Ingenbleek et al. 2003).

The customer value-based model represents the evolution of the market-price method since it reflects the change from a market orientation to a customer orientation. Instead of relying on market analysis or pure psychological logics – e.g. the higher the price, the higher the perceived quality – the customer-oriented view supports the development of breakthrough value propositions and thus the embeddedness into the price of the whole value created by the company: quality, customer experience, firm values, brand awareness, additional services and so on.

TABLE 4.1 Pricing strategies for innovative start-ups: challenges and opportunities

Key variables and challenges	Opportunities	Main references
Complex scenario: turbulence, scarce information, demanding customers, unstable financial equilibrium, globally interconnected dynamics	Establish innovative systems for data gathering, in order to support decision-making processes along the pricing strategy Combine different pricing models	Bruton and Rubanik 2002; Shan et al. 1994; Zucchella et al. 2007; Cooper and Giuffrida 2000; Lowe and Alpert 2010
Definition of the first price	Implement aggressive policies or develop a 'first-mover advantage' strategy	Lin et al. 2011; Mesak and Berg 1995; Lieberman and Montgomery 1998; Lowe and Alpert 2010
Uncertain dynamics of the innovation life cycle create unstable financial markets, whilst the declining prices of emerging technology lead companies to wait for lower costs	Figure out the right moment to enter the market, as a source of competitive advantage	Eden and Ronen 1993; Watanabe et al. 2000
Opportunistic behaviours of some suppliers	Engagement in diverse innovation eco-systems Implementation of diversified sales channels	Gilbert and Cvsa 2003
The need for funds may increase the influencing power of partners (e.g. suppliers, banks, business angels, etc.)	Leverage on partner's expertise to improve the pricing strategy efficiency	Gartner et al. 1999; Tanrisever et al. 2012; Wiltbank et al. 2009; Iyer, 1998

Scholars showed that companies tend to combine different methods (Maglaras and Meissner 2006; Monteiro and Page 1996; Noble and Gruca 1999; Pavia 1995). Nevertheless, as previously mentioned, little is known about the solutions implemented by high potential start-ups and the impact of such decisions on their economic performance.

Table 4.1 sums up key variables and issues that start-ups have to take into consideration in their pricing strategy.

3 An explorative study: the case of 'Moi Multiple'

This section develops an explorative study aimed at outlining empirical evidences regarding the reliability of the above arguments in the case of high potential start-ups. The survey develops a single case study based on theory building orientation

(Eisenhardt 1989). Features of this contribution call for qualitative analysis embracing many variables as well as some quantitative investigations regarding the pricing function. It allows a fine grained analysis of the mechanisms underlying efficient pricing policies. Literature accepts this practice: other surveys in the strategic management field have used a similar solution through the simultaneous adoption of both qualitative and quantitative procedures in the same research model (e.g. Burger et al. 2001; Di Pofi 2002; Kaplan and Duchon 1988; Magnier-Watanabe and Senoo 2010).

A selection process led us to choose 'Moi Multiple' (MM). Many motives suggested this company. Primarily because of the phase in the life cycle: start-up at the early stage. Second, it operates in a complex and high velocity sector – the luxury fashion industry – where innovation and creativity are crucial. According to a press review, MM is a high potential start-up. And finally, thanks to the availability of the company to provide accurate information.

The case study analysis relies on the following structure. Section 3.1 describes the competitive scenario in which MM operates, namely the luxury fashion industry. Then, section 3.2 introduces MM, while sections 3.2.1 and 3.2.2 deepen the pricing strategy of the company. In particular, the former section (3.2.1) is a qualitative analysis concerning the interplay between the innovative business model of MM and the pricing activity. The latter (3.2.2) develops a quantitative study aimed at outlining the causal relations between pricing strategy and sales performance in the mainstream distribution channels.

3.1 The luxury fashion industry: features, trends and factors of success

The luxury fashion industry has peculiar features. It is one of the few sectors showing a growing trend even in the middle of the global crisis. The forecast of the Altagamma Foundation points out positive performance for many firms in the field, not only for market leaders. The luxury sector experienced the enormous growth of 40 per cent in 2011 with an overall turnover of € 191 billion. The apparel segment data are also more than favourable: +10.9 per cent in the same period. Recently this sector has changed. For a long time only a few people, a sort of 'élite', bought luxury products. The diversified portfolio of luxury products – coupled with the new consumer behaviour in contemporary society – has significantly expanded this market.

Big, aged companies largely dominated the luxury industry. However, this arena is more and more attractive for innovative start-ups. Consider, for instance, 'Super Flou': born as a small company, it produces expensive electronic products – such as TVs – that are at the same time masterpieces of design. Another compelling case is Reebonz: this Singapore start-up offers members-only private sales of branded fashion goods and has received millions in venture funding from Intel Capital in 2012.

Fashion is one of the most influential segments of the luxury industry. It embraces sectors such as apparel (50 per cent of the whole industry), textile, leather, shoes and jewellery (Boselli 2009). The fashion industry is changing. It is becoming similar to other sectors such as electronics. The competitive advantage moves to breakthrough value propositions, design and innovation along the whole value chain. Fashion is less 'status symbol' and more 'style symbol': value delivered to the customer counts more than astonishing marketing campaigns. The 'fast fashion' is stealing more and more market share to the 'seasonal fashion'. This created significant challenges, especially for small and medium-sized enterprises. The customer is ever more demanding and also looks for better quality, higher levels of customization and novel sources of value. Until 20–25 years ago, multinational companies based on vertically integrated value chains dominated the apparel sector. In the last decades, the industry structure as a whole radically changed. Market leaders increasingly focused on a slice of their value chain. Emerging countries create 85 per cent of the garments through a low labour cost production. These dynamics dramatically affect the cost structure of a firm and open up the market to new entrants and innovative start-ups.

Luxury is a fruitful domain to deepen the relation between cost structure, customer value, prices and firm performance: it is a multi-product business, investments are high, creativity and innovation are vital sources to create premium prices and pricing policy varies along the firm life cycle. The development of a business model rooted on a premium price strategy is fundamental (Beverland 2005; Wilcox et al. 2009; Wong and Ahuvia 1998). Products embed intangible elements such as uniqueness, style and experiential significance. The exclusivity of a luxury product fosters the prestige of the brand. It is not just a price issue: it stems from the coherency that brand maintains all along the phases of the value chain. Companies pursue the continuous innovation coupled with a flawless experience. The market for luxury is growing, but is unstable. It is a constant competition towards excellence. Investments in brand, design and innovation are crucial. Extending the price range, developing a multi-product strategy and (re)positioning the brand – aiming at profit maximization – are options to reduce the influence of significant investments on the pricing policy. A ten-fold difference between the lowest and the highest product price may occur.

The luxury pricing lies in quantifying the value-to-customer regardless of competitors or market prices. Luxury goods prices are less linked to any costs and the identification of customer willingness to pay is crucial. Luxury goods have a strong emotional component, which make them difficult to compare to any other competitor's product. Companies usually adopt the same price all over the world and avoid discount policies to increase customer loyalty and trust.

According to these features, pricing policy has to target simultaneously sales growth, high production volumes, innovation, premium prices and a clear-cut strategic positioning. The simultaneous maximization of these variables, by taking into account the effect of the price definition, becomes a key consideration.

3.2 Moi Multiple: strategy, business model and pricing activity

MM is an Italian start-up in the fashion industry – women apparel, Prêt-à-Porter – mainly focused on the luxury segment and headquartered in Milan. Anna Francesca Ceccon founded this brand in 2008 after a rapid career as Head of Design for the well-known brand '*La Perla*' (lingerie sector). Opinion leaders and magazines immediately recognized the high potential of this new venture. For instance, Vogue's 'Who's on Next', a famous competition for emerging designers, awarded MM in 2009. The product concept aims at combining elegance with innovation into a unique value proposition. The strategy relies on the following cornerstones:

- Core competences in terms of design and pattern-making;
- Exclusivity and creativity along the whole value chain;
- Materials and methods by MM: the company explores continuously new pattern techniques and it looks for unusual materials to create distinctive garments;
- Lean structure. MM outsourced many activities, whilst the core competencies – R&D (research and development), design and pattern-making – remain internalized;
- Innovative business model: it increases the flexibility of the cost structure, feeds the exclusivity of the brand and supports the pricing strategy (see section 3.2.1).

Cost structure and pricing policy are essential to implement such a strategy and to deliver value to the customer. The value chain of MM is sliced up into several activities developed by independent domestic suppliers, to safeguard the well-known Italian quality of textile production. The 'Moi-Atelier' supports an innovative view to manage the seasonal trait of the fashion industry, which creates problems in terms of cash flow dynamics and production planning. The pricing activity usually occurs at the end of the design process – when products enter the production phase and just before commercialization – through a relatively informal approach largely based on the entrepreneur's perceptions and commercial feedback. A template sheet allows the collection of data regarding costs and price definition for each garment (see Figure 4.1).

An in-depth analysis of the two main sales channels of MM is fundamental to investigate the pricing strategy of this company. Indeed, an innovative business model is intertwined with the mainstream channel (showroom and intermediaries). The former serves the purposes to implement a breakthrough value proposition, reduce uncertainty in the production process, develop the brand and foster the pricing activity. Section 3.2.1 explores this argument. Section 3.2.2 completes the empirical investigation through a quantitative analysis aimed at providing a better understanding of the relation between pricing decisions and firm performance in the case of MM.

	TOTAL	€133,83
Stock	**100%**	
	TOTAL	€133,83
Markup	**200%**	
	TOTAL	€267,67
Royalty	**100%**	
	TOTAL	€267,67
Markup showroom	**115%**	
	TOTAL	€307,82
Gross profit		€173,99
Fix components		€6,03
TOTAL €313,85		
Retail price €314,00		

FIGURE 4.1 Template for pricing definition in Moi Multiple (example)

3.2.1 Moi-Atelier: an innovative business model fosters the pricing capability

Moi-Atelier is an initiative of MM aimed at replicating on the large scale the fascinating experience of Atelier Dior during the 1950s and through a contemporary formula. It increases the flexibility of the cost structure through the simultaneous achievement of both high customization and the advantages of Prêt-à-Porter, feeds the exclusivity of the brand and delivers an original way to support the pricing definition. Notably, Moi-Atelier also shows an intriguing application of the value-based pricing approach.

In addition to mainstream channels – showroom and wholesales – this project develops a parallel sales system based on an original solution. Moi-Atelier is a truly exclusive fashion and design laboratory where the customer may purchase both new garments (before they enter traditional shops) and last season clothes. Here, the Head Designer – Anna Ceccon – and a 'premiere' – i.e. an experienced pattern-maker – directly proposes the MM creations and discusses with customers regarding their wants and fitting problems. A high-value consultancy service and the presence of the MM's top designer enrich the purchasing process which becomes a rewarding experience in itself. Second, during these special events some adaptations of the garments are available, introducing significant degrees of customization in the Prêt-à-Porter paradigm.

It is a 'travelling' Atelier. Every time the location is different and chosen in order to highlight the exclusivity of such meetings: Milan, Paris, London, Dubai, Singapore and so on. Moreover, they are invitation-only events: only those who are invited by someone who is 'in the club' may attend a Moi-Atelier. After that, becoming a member of this élite assigns the right to introduce other people and participate in all following events. These aspects create a comfortable environment (high value) where the MM fans feel free to express their wants, suggest creative ideas and provide sincere feedback regarding style, quality and prices. The presence of designers and managers of the company at the Moi-Atelier event also increases the customer proximity, as such increasing the value of these interactions.

Moi-Atelier develops a pricing capability (Hinterhuber and Liozu 2012) which fosters the competitive advantage of the firm by adopting a value-based view. First, according to the above mentioned features, it is a critical source of high-quality feedback. The company gathers strategic information regarding the consistency between product price and willingness to pay of the customer, as well as concerning elements of MM's value proposition which are more appreciated. Moreover, it creates an agile system to respond quickly to market changes as well as comparison with quality and prices of competitors as perceived by the Moi-Atelier's attendees. It replicates the 'shop' environment with many additional advantages. The participants of these events show all characteristics of the so-called 'pioneer' clients. Prior scholars showed how crucial is the creation of direct relationships with such actors (Nooteboom 1994). Second, the series of Moi-Atelier events creates the conditions to develop pilot tests on small groups of clients in order to check the effectiveness of the price definition by using dynamic functions. Feedback from diverse groups of clients subjected to diverse prices for the same product – before it enters the market – permit a fine-grained adjustment of prices, combining both intuition and rational arguments. According to some scholars, the value-based pricing is costly (Hinterhuber and Liozu 2012): the above described organizational structure mitigates this circumstance through a strategic leverage of just a few key customers (pioneers/fans/brand advocates) and informal processes. Moi-Atelier supports the competitive advantage of MM by increasing the flexibility of the cost structure – through the simultaneous achievement of both advantages of Prêt-à-Porter and high customization – and by mitigating the seasonal effect which generates an unfavourable cash flow. Moreover, Moi-Atelier feeds brand awareness by stimulating a strong sense of identity in customers themselves, who become brand advocates.

3.2.2 Quantitative analysis: pricing function and the performance of Moi Multiple

A quantitative analysis deepens the pricing activity of MM in the mainstream channels. The aim is to figure out key factors influencing cost structure, customer value and the firm performance. This part of the survey does not consider the sales achieved through Moi-Atelier. The analysis relies on a database of 198 product items – jackets, coats, dresses, shirts, trousers and skirts – regarding four collections over a period of two years. Figure 4.2 and Table 4.2 describe the variables of the research model and the criteria for operationalization. In particular, 'best seller' is a dummy variable: all garments belonging to the first quartile of the best performers in terms of sales (number

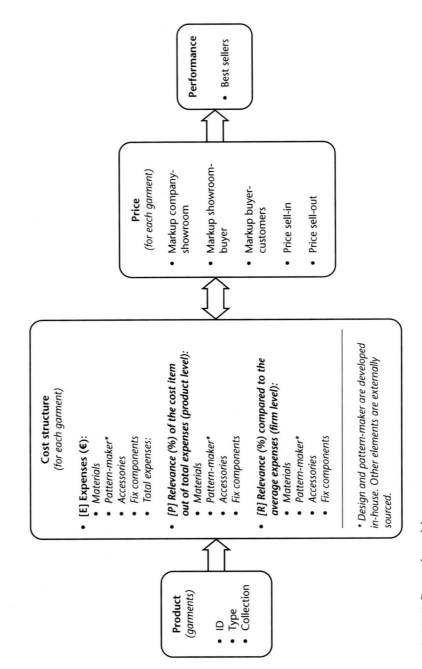

Product
(garments)

- ID
- Type
- Collection

Cost structure
(for each garment)

- **[E] Expenses (€):**
  - Materials
  - Pattern-maker*
  - Accessories
  - Fix components
  - Total expenses:

- **[P] Relevance (%) of the cost item out of total expenses (product level):**
  - Materials
  - Pattern-maker*
  - Accessories
  - Fix components

- **[R] Relevance (%) compared to the average expenses (firm level):**
  - Materials
  - Pattern-maker*
  - Accessories
  - Fix components

Design and pattern-maker are developed in-house. Other elements are externally sourced.

Price
(for each garment)

- Markup company-showroom
- Markup showroom-buyer
- Markup buyer-customers
- Price sell-in
- Price sell-out

Performance

- Best sellers

FIGURE 4.2 Research model

TABLE 4.2 Variables of the research model

Variable	Description	Type
ID code	Code and name of the garment	Scale
Type	Type of garment: jacket, coat, dress, shirt, trousers and skirt	Nominal (dummies)
Collection	Number of collection of the garment (decreasing order: coll.4 is the most recent collection)	Ordinal
Best seller	'1' = best sold garments; '0' = others	Dummy
E_Materials	Total value (€) of materials (tissues, leather, etc.) used for the garment production	Scale
E_Pattern-maker	Value (€) of the garment pattern-maker	Scale
E_Accessories	Value (€) of accessories used for the garment production	Scale
E_Fix components	Value (€) of fix components used for the garment production	Scale
E_Total	Total production cost of the garment	Scale
P_Materials	Percentage relevance of materials (e.g. textiles) out of total expenses for the garment production	Scale – percentage
P_Pattern-maker	Percentage relevance of pattern-maker out of total expenses for the garment production	Scale – percentage
P_Accessories	Percentage relevance of accessories out of total expenses for the garment production	Scale – percentage
P_Fix components	Percentage relevance of fix components out of total expenses for the garment production	Scale – percentage
R_Materials	Percentage relevance of materials along the production compared to the average cost structure of the firm = (P_Materials $_{\text{garment 'i'}}$) − (Mean 'P_Materials' all garments)	Scale – percentage
R_Pattern-maker	Percentage relevance of pattern-maker along the production compared to the average cost structure of the firm = (P_Pattern-maker $_{\text{garment 'i'}}$) − (Mean 'P_Pattern-maker' all garments)	Scale – percentage
R_Accessories	Percentage relevance of accessories along the production compared to the average cost structure of the firm = (P_Accessories $_{\text{garment 'i'}}$) − (Mean 'P_Accessories all garments)	Scale – percentage
R_Fix components	Percentage relevance of fix components along the production compared to the average cost structure of the firm = (P_Fix components $_{\text{garment 'i'}}$) − (Mean 'P_Fix components' all garments)	Scale – percentage

TABLE 4.2 Continued

Variable	Description	Type
Markup company-showroom	Markup applied by the firm to the showroom	Scale – percentage
Markup showroom-buyer	Markup applied by the showroom to the retailer	Scale – percentage
Markup buyer-customers	Markup applied by retailers to the final customers	Scale – percentage
Log_Sell-in	LOG (Sell-in pricing)★; price (€) at which MM sells the garment to the intermediary agent (showroom/wholesalers)	Scale
Log_Sell-out	LOG (Sell-out pricing)★; price (€) at which intermediaries sell the garment to the final customer	Scale

★ The log function increases the reliability of the regression model since it linearizes the function and supports a better interpretation of findings.

of products sold) have a value equal to '1'. Differences among prices/markup levels applied at the different stages of the value chain – 'from MM to intermediaries' and 'from intermediaries to final customers' – are taken into account.

Figures 4.3 and 4.4 and Table 4.3 show descriptive statistics (some data are not reported due to privacy reasons). Dresses and shirts count for 64 per cent of the total production. This is the main business for MM. Nevertheless, some of the most expensive garments are trousers or jackets: these products are not at the core of the company's production – because of quality and creative design – but they significantly support the differentiation strategy of MM as well as the brand image. The price range for MM products is extremely broad and significantly varies according to the type of garment: from € 140 to € 2,885.

In terms of cost structure – see Figure 4.4 – the pattern-making activity absorbs more than half of total expenses and, above all, the large majority of investments in MM. This activity concerns the design of garments and it drives the whole production process, thus the final quality. Raw materials are another significant cost item.

A logistic regression model serves the purpose of investigating which elements affect the firm performance in terms of sales. This is a widespread method for predicting the outcome of a categorical dependent variable 'best seller', on the basis of several predictor variables, by converting the dependent variable to probability scores. The aim is to provide a better understanding regarding the relations among best-seller garments, pricing activity and dynamics of the cost structure. Table 4.4 reports the outcomes of the regression analysis.

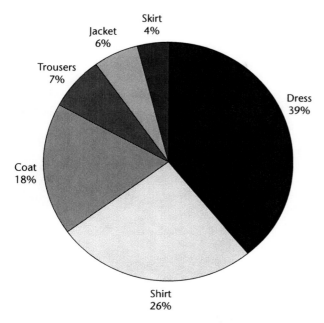

FIGURE 4.3 The production of Moi Multiple: types of garments

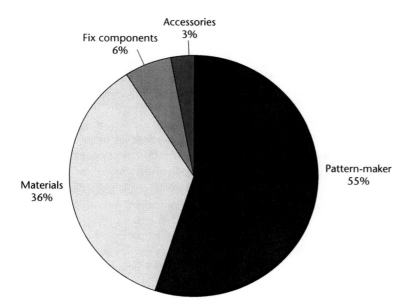

FIGURE 4.4 Percentage relevance of cost items in the production process within Moi Multiple (average values)

TABLE 4.3 Descriptive statistics

	Minimum	Maximum	Mean	Std. deviation
Best seller	0	1	0.247	0.432638801
T_Jacket	0	1	0.056	0.229642062
T_Coat	0	1	0.192	0.394808125
T_Dress	0	1	0.389	0.48873376
T_Shirt	0	1	0.247	0.432638801
T_Trousers	0	1	0.076	0.265280585
T_Skirt	0	1	0.040	0.197404062
P_Materials	6.3%	67.0%	35.7%	0.121027949
P_Pattern-maker	27.1%	88.7%	55.5%	0.118519773
P_Accessories	0.0%	41.6%	3.0%	0.052572211
P_FixComp	1.5%	21.6%	5.8%	0.031501315
R_Materials	−81.1%	99.6%	0.0%	0.332145432
R_Pattern-maker	−50.8%	52.0%	0.0%	0.202617644
R_Accessories	−100.0%	1067.7%	0.0%	1.52752732
R_FixComp	−68.0%	194.7%	0.0%	0.402330627
Sell-out_price	€ 140.00	€ 2,885.00	€ 675.87	351.6167859

Model 'A' is a preliminary study based on control variables, namely the type of garments. None of these elements is significant. Despite the strategy of MM leveraging on a wide range of dresses and shirts, this has not created a specialization in that sense. This model shows that best-seller products vary across different garments, also including coats, trousers or skirts.

Model 'B' studies the role of the cost structure. Outcomes of the regression analysis show that the production total expenditure does not affect the performance of the garments. Similarly, the composition among diverse variable-cost items – in terms of percentage relevance – is not significant. This evidence suggests that other aspects support the commercial success, such as fix costs, long-run investments or market-specific drivers.

Model 'C' investigates which cost item – materials, pattern-maker, accessories, fix components – is more, or less, relevant in percentage terms for each garment compared to the corresponding average value calculated by considering all similar products of the same collection. The following example clarifies the procedure: if the 'materials' (see Table 4.2) cost for the dress 'X' is € 120, whilst the average 'materials' cost considering all dresses of MM is € 100, then the relative relevance of dress 'X' is +20 per cent. Findings outline a significant coefficient in the case of 'pattern-maker' activity: if the value embedded in this phase is particularly significant for garment 'X' compared to other ones, then sales of the same garment 'X' tend to be higher. This is an intriguing outcome, especially when considering the nature of the pattern-maker activity and the principles of the value-based pricing view.

In general, pattern-making is a crucial activity in the apparel sector (Donohue 2012). It emerged when the industrial process entered the textile sector. This activity develops a production pattern without knowing who the final client is and by adopting standard measurements to produce a garment to any size. The pattern-maker converts the sketch created by the designer – Anna Ceccon in the case of MM – into a paper template. It is a critical upstream activity which generates high value, fosters the quality of production and supports the brand through ensuring that patterns reflect the image of the company. Pattern-making activity implies significant investments in terms of personnel expenses, technologies, facilities, initiatives for training and continuous learning. Notably, design and pattern-making are two intertwined activities within MM: the staffs of both functions collaborate in a complex iterative process.

In a nutshell, the performance of MM's product is high if the garment embeds a high value in terms of pattern-making and design, namely activities which imply significant investments, especially for a start-up such as MM.

Finally, Model 'D' deepens the customer-based views. Findings suggest that the pricing activity of the upstream company in the value chain – MM – may directly affect its performance, which is poorly dependent – under this view – on the intermediary's decisions downstream. According to Model 'D', a high markup level applied by MM to wholesale boosts the sales ('Markup_ws'), whilst findings do not report a similar conclusion regarding the markup established by intermediary agents (e.g. retailers) towards the final customers. The price level settled by the company – sell-in price ('Log_Sell-in') – affects the performance of the product, but through a negative relation. This result cannot be explained by a tension towards a low-cost strategy: in the investigated case, price variations affect the consumer behaviour (see 'Log_Sell-out' in Model 'D') while the reduction of production costs has no motives in explaining a better performance (see Model 'B' as a whole).

In a nutshell, in the case of MM the most efficient pricing strategy relies on a high markup to achieve top-class positioning in the market – and support investments – coupled with a 'below the average' positioning within the luxury segment in terms of price level; just a little below established brands (negative relation is significant, but the coefficient of 'Log_Sell-in' is little). It makes the entrant as a suitable alternative option compared to incumbents, in terms of both innovativeness and price. The Pseudo R2 of the whole Model 'D' is quite acceptable (0.1535) while the statistical significance (Prob > chi2) is reliable. Coefficients tend to remain stable across the four models, thus reinforcing the above mentioned considerations.

TABLE 4.4 Pricing activity, cost structure and performance in MM: logistic regression models

	Model 'A'	Model 'B'	Model 'C'	Model 'D'
_cons	−1.0986 (0.8164)	−4.8151 (9.7169)	−2.8497 (3.6807)	−5.8509 (16.2721)
T_Jacket	−0.4054 (1.1303)	−0.2604 (1.1564)	−0.4187 (1.1697)	−0.2892 (1.2166)
T_Coat	−0.7884 (0.947)	−0.4619 (1.0028)	−0.42 (1.0462)	−0.1196 (1.2009)
T_Dress	−0.6931 (0.879)	−0.3548 (0.9166)	−0.4926 (0.9449)	−0.569 (0.9675)
T_Shirt	0.976 (0.8652)	1.0864 (0.9265)	0.9919 (1.015)	−0.0724 (1.7374)
T_Trousers	0.6931 (0.9718)	0.9004 (1.0349)	0.4313 (1.1162)	−0.5197 (1.5418)
E_Materials		−0.3142 (0.6118)	−0.3391 (0.6223)	−1.1809 (1.1358)
E_Pattern-maker		−0.36 (0.6071)	−0.3857 (0.6186)	−1.2364 (1.1336)
E_Accessories		−0.3035 (0.6122)	−0.2542 (0.6182)	−1.0681 (1.1224)
E_Total		0.3371 (0.6077)	0.3592 (0.618)	1.3372 (1.1223)
P_Materials		−1.0959 (9.9162)		
P_Pattern-maker		4.4658 (10.1812)		
P_Accessories		−5.6196 (14.488)		
R_Materials			4.1497 (3.6251)	5.618 (4.1277)
R_Pattern-maker			**9.8382 (5.7802)★**	**12.5709 (6.4684)★**
R_Accessories			−0.1678 (0.3527)	−0.1914 (0.3958)
R_FixComp			0.5085 (1.0822)	−0.8945 (2.3012)
Log_Sell-in				**−0.0638 (0.0384)★**

TABLE 4.4 Continued

	Model 'A'	Model 'B'	Model 'C'	Model 'D'
Log_Sell-out				−5.6427 (8.1991)
Markup_ws				**9.2018 (5.17)★**
Markup_ret				−1.9522 (4.0879)
Number of obs	198	198	198	198
LR chi2(5)	21.47	25.3	29.02	34.01
Prob > chi2	0.0007	0.0135	0.0065	0.0008
Pseudo R2	0.0969	0.1142	0.1310	0.1535

★ significant values at 5%

4 Conclusion: not rational or emotional, but skilled

Despite the huge amount of theories on the pricing issue, there are few models addressed to innovative new firms and in particular to new ventures. This chapter explores theories and practices of measuring the impact of pricing policies on the performance of knowledge-intensive start-ups. Furthermore, it provides evidence suggesting that the value-based pricing could be a driver for higher profitability. It is a relevant issue for both academics and practitioners. Especially in the case of new ventures, traditional methods for price setting may lead to unsatisfactory performance and to underestimating the impact of strategic investments. Industry-specific habits or beliefs may lead a start-up to an ambiguous strategic positioning which slows down the firm growth in the early stages.

This study contributes to the debate through an explorative case study concerning an innovative start-up – 'Moi Multiple' – engaged in a complex sector such as the luxury fashion industry. Findings show both confirmations and unexpected outcomes. First, the company shows an intriguing way to implement a dynamic pricing function, based on both intuition and structured procedures, and to deal with challenges faced by start-ups. The key learning is that start-ups need both informal processes and entrepreneurial intuition to evolve, moving from improvisation to exploitation of this potential through novel solutions. Such as in the Moi-Atelier project, the goal is to gather data through original solutions, increase customer proximity and merge diverse pricing models: both cost- and market-based methods – through the maximization of profit in a value-based view. A better understanding of the value perceived and, above all, desired by the customer drives this process. In such a framework, a pricing capability is crucial. Second, in line with the prior surveys, the case study confirms that the implementation of diversified sale channels is a critical factor of success for emerging start-ups.

The quantitative analysis adds further elements. Products embedding a high value stemming from organizational capabilities and high customization – which require significant investments such as R&D, brand development and organization of special events – return the higher performance, even in the medium-short run. It highlights the relevance of 'pricing ROI' for innovative start-ups as well as the need for innovative practices in the appraisal of both firm capabilities and customer needs to support the firm growth. Moreover, market and, above all, value-based pricing methods emerged as more efficient than cost-based approaches. Evidences from both qualitative (Moi-Atelier) and quantitative (regression model) analyses converge to this finding. The stronger pricing strategy implemented by MM relies on a medium-high markup – to reflect the breakthrough value proposition – coupled with slightly lower prices compared to what incumbents propose in the wholesale market.

The good news is that pricing strategy developed by the innovative company matters: it directly affects its performance. The fundamental precondition, however, is the implementation of innovative solutions in order to gather data and then evaluate the price acceptance through pilot tests on small groups of customers.

Decisions made by intermediaries may play a minor role if the start-up leverages on pricing activity as a strategic element of the business model. The explorative regression analysis suggests that pricing activity has a significant impact even at the beginning of the value chain, namely in the relation between creative company and wholesale agents. The confirmation of this claim needs further research. Nevertheless, it sheds a new light on the assumption by which start-ups engaged in extended value chains are largely dependent on commercial decisions taken by downstream agents (e.g. distribution, resellers).

On the other hand, if the final price for customers stays high – due to the value embedded in the product and incurred by the start-up's investments – but the creative company maintains low prices at the wholesale level in order to foster its growth, then intermediaries retain the large part of value added. This study does not deepen this circumstance. However, evidences from the analysis of the Moi-Atelier experience point out the need for reducing customer proximity in order to manage such an issue and implementing customer value-based pricing models (Hinterhuber and Liozu 2012).

Not rational or emotional: mainstream pricing methods fail in the case of MM. A start-up is responsible for its destiny and may influence the economic performance through alternative pricing policies and investments for innovation, especially at the business model level. However, the above discussion evidences that entrepreneurial and managerial skills are fundamental to achieve that goal. Intuition is crucial, but it has to be integrated with an in-depth comprehension of cost structure and sources of value added within the firm to establish a pricing capability. Investments influence the pricing function and firm performance, but a new market – blue ocean – implies defining the strategic positioning while taking into account the perceptions and vision of the entrepreneur. Leadership is needed to play a relevant role in the supply chain, but customer proximity is the goal in the long-run horizon.

This survey has some limitations. The nature of the single case study method and the limited size of the sample do not permit us to generalize findings. Statistical validation implies further investigations. Second, available data do not allow us to implement a ROI analysis in its strictest sense. However, the discussion of empirical evidences draws promising insights to reshape the research proposition, highlight a literature gap and redirect future research agenda in the field. If, into at least one case, the consolidated assumptions fail, then the argument calls for further investigation, setting innovation in pricing activity – especially in the case of a start-up – as a promising area of research for the future.

Acknowledgements

The authors gratefully acknowledge Anna Francesca Ceccon, CEO of Moi Multiple, for her fundamental support in collecting data and revising the study and Valentina Marchese for the support in the case study analysis. Stefano Denicolai gratefully acknowledges financial support from Cariplo Foundation International Recruitment Call: The internationalization of Italian firms: the role of intangibles, managerial resources, and corporate governance.

References

Beverland, M. B. (2005) Crafting brand authenticity: The case of luxury wines. *Journal of Management Studies*, 42 (5), pp. 1003–1029.

Blattberg, R. C. and Wisniewski, K. J. (1989) Price-induced patterns of competition. *Marketing Science*, 8 (4), pp. 291–309.

Boselli, M. (2009) *Camera della Moda Italiana*. Assemblea Annuale: Camera della Moda Milano.

Bruton, G. D. and Rubanik, Y. (2002) Resources of the firm, Russian high-technology startups, and firm growth. *Journal of Business Venturing*, 17 (6), pp. 553–576.

Burger, C., Dohnal, M., Kathrada, M. and Law, R. (2001) A practitioners guide to time-series methods for tourism demand forecasting – A case study of Durban, South Africa. *Tourism Management*, 22 (4), pp. 403–409.

Carter, N. M., Gartner, W. B. and Reynolds, P. D. (1996) Exploring start-up event sequences. *Journal of Business Venturing*, 11 (3), pp. 151–166.

Cavusgil, S. T., Chan, K. and Zhang, C. (2003) Strategic orientations in export pricing: A clustering approach to create firm taxonomies. *Journal of International Marketing*, 11 (1), pp. 47–72.

Christensen, C. (1997) *The innovator's dilemma: When new technologies cause great firms to fail.* Boston, MA: Harvard Business School Press.

Clancy, K. J. and Stone, R. L. (2005) Don't blame the metrics. *Harvard Business Review*, 83 (6), pp. 26–28.

Cooper, L. G. and Giuffrida, G. (2000) Turning datamining into a management science tool: New algorithms and empirical results. *Management Science*, 46 (2), pp. 249–264.

Davila, A., Foster, G. and Jia, N. (2010) Building sustainable high-growth startup companies: Management systems as an accelerator. *California Management Review*, 52 (3), pp. 79–105.

Di Pofi, J. A. (2002) Organizational diagnostics: Integrating qualitative and quantitative methodology. *Journal of Organizational Change Management*, 15 (2), pp. 156–168.

Donohue, N. (2012) The pattern making primer: All you need to know about designing, adapting, and customizing sewing patterns. *Library Journal*, 137 (19), p. 85.

Eden, Y. and Ronen, B. (1993) The declining-price paradox of new technologies. *Omega-International Journal of Management Science*, 21 (3), pp. 345–351.

Eisenhardt, K. M. (1989) Building theories from case-study research. *Academy of Management Review*, 14 (4), pp. 532–550.

Freeman, J. and Engel, J. S. (2007) Models of innovation: Startups and mature corporations. *California Management Review*, 50 (1), pp. 94–119.

Gartner, W. B., Starr, J. A. and Bhat, S. (1999) Predicting new venture survival: An analysis of 'Anatomy of a Start-up.' Cases from Inc. magazine. *Journal of Business Venturing*, 14 (2), pp. 215–232.

Ghemawat, P. and McGahan, A. M. (1998) Order backlogs and strategic pricing: The case of the US large turbine generator industry. *Strategic Management Journal*, 19 (3), pp. 255–268.

Gilbert, S. M. and Cvsa, V. (2003) Strategic commitment to price to stimulate downstream innovation in a supply chain. *European Journal of Operational Research*, 150 (3), pp. 617–639.

Hart, M. A. (2012) The lean startup: How today's entrepreneurs use continuous innovation to create radically successful businesses. *Journal of Product Innovation Management*, 29 (3), pp. 508–509.

Hinterhuber, A. and Liozu, S. (2012) *Innovation in pricing: Contemporary theories and best practices*. New York, NY: Routledge.

Ingenbleek, P., Debruyne, M., Frambach, R. T. and Verhallen, T. M. M. (2003) Successful new product pricing practices: A contingency approach. *Marketing Letters*, 14 (4), pp. 289–305.

Iyer, G. (1998) Coordinating channels under price and nonprice competition. *Marketing Science*, 17 (4), pp. 338–355.

Kaplan, B. and Duchon, D. (1988) Combining qualitative and quantitative methods in information-systems research – A case-study. *MIS Quarterly*, 12 (4), pp. 571–586.

Kim, W. C. and Mauborgne, R. (2004) Blue ocean strategy. *Harvard Business Review*, 82 (10), p. 76.

Kortge, G. D. and Okonkwo, P. A. (1993) Perceived value approach to pricing. *Industrial Marketing Management*, 22 (2), pp. 133–140.

Kotler, P. (2011) Reinventing marketing to manage the environmental imperative. *Journal of Marketing*, 75 (4), pp. 132–135.

Lieberman, M. B. and Montgomery, D. B. (1998) First-mover (dis)advantages: Retrospective and link with the resource-based view. *Strategic Management Journal*, 19 (12), pp. 1111–1125.

Lin, M., Li, S. J. and Whinston, A. B. (2011) Innovation and price competition in a two-sided market. *Journal of Management Information Systems*, 28 (2), pp. 171–202.

Lowe, B. and Alpert, F. (2010). Pricing strategy and the formation and evolution of reference price perceptions in new product categories. *Psychology & Marketing*, 27 (9), pp. 846–873.

Maglaras, C. and Meissner, J. (2006) Dynamic pricing strategies for multiproduct revenue management problems. *M&Som-Manufacturing & Service Operations Management*, 8 (2), pp. 136–148.

Magnier-Watanabe, R. and Senoo, D. (2010) Shaping knowledge management: Organization and national culture. *Journal of Knowledge Management*, 14 (2), pp. 214–227.

Mesak, H. I. and Berg, W. D. (1995) Incorporating price and replacement purchases in new product diffusion models for consumer durables. *Decision Sciences*, 26 (4), pp. 425–449.

Mitchell, J. R., Friga, P. N. and Mitchell, R. K. (2005) Untangling the intuition mess: Intuition as a construct in entrepreneurship research. *Entrepreneurship Theory and Practice*, 29 (6), pp. 653–679.

Monteiro, P. K. and Page, F. H. (1996) Non-linear pricing with a general cost function. *Economics Letters*, 52 (3), pp. 287–291.

Narayanan, S., Desiraju, R. and Chintagunta, P. K. (2004) Return on investment implications for pharmaceutical promotional expenditures: The role of marketing-mix interactions. *Journal of Marketing*, 68 (4), pp. 90–105.

Neyens, I., Faems, D. and Sels, L. (2010) The impact of continuous and discontinuous alliance strategies on startup innovation performance. *International Journal of Technology Management*, 52 (3–4), pp. 392–410.

Noble, P. M. and Gruca, T. S. (1999) Industrial pricing: Theory and managerial practice. *Marketing Science*, 18 (3), pp. 435–454.

Nooteboom, B. (1994) Innovation and diffusion in small firms – Theory and evidence. *Small Business Economics*, 6 (5), pp. 327–347.

Onetti, A., Zucchella, A., Jones, M. V. and McDougall-Covin, P. (2010) Internationalization, innovation and entrepreneurship: Business models for new technology-based firms. *Journal of Management and Governance*, Special Issue on 'Entrepreneurship and Strategic Management in Life Sciences. Business Models for High-Tech Companies'.

Pavia, T. M. (1995) Profit maximizing cost allocation for firms using cost-based pricing. *Management Science*, 41 (6), pp. 1060–1072.

Peeters, L. and Surry, Y. (2000) Incorporating price-induced innovation in a symmetric generalised McFadden cost function with several outputs. *Journal of Productivity Analysis*, 14 (1), pp. 53–70.

Porter, M. E. (1985) *Competitive advantage*. New York, NY: The Free Press.

Rivard, S., Raymond, L. and Verreault, D. (2006) Resource-based view and competitive strategy: An integrated model of the contribution of information technology to firm performance. *Journal of Strategic Information Systems*, 15 (1), pp. 29–50.

Shan, W. J., Walker, G. and Kogut, B. (1994) Interfirm cooperation and startup innovation in the biotechnology industry. *Strategic Management Journal*, 15 (5), pp. 387–394.

Sousa, C. M. P. and Bradley, F. (2008) Antecedents of international pricing adaptation and export performance. *Journal of World Business*, 43 (3), pp. 307–320.

Tanrisever, F., Erzurumlu, S. S. and Joglekar, N. (2012) Production, process investment, and the survival of debt-financed startup firms. *Production and Operations Management*, 21 (4), pp. 637–652.

Voss, G. B., Parasuraman, A. and Grewal, D. (1998) The roles of price, performance, and expectations in determining satisfaction in service exchanges. *Journal of Marketing*, 62 (4), pp. 46–61.

Walters, R. G. and Mackenzie, S. B. (1988) A structural equations analysis of the impact of price promotions on store performance. *Journal of Marketing Research*, 25 (1), pp. 51–63.

Watanabe, C., Wakabayashi, K. and Miyazawa, T. (2000) Industrial dynamism and the creation of a 'virtuous cycle' between R&D, market growth and price reduction – The case of photovoltaic power generation (PV) development in Japan. *Technovation*, 20 (6), pp. 299–312.

Weng, Z. K. (1995) Modeling quantity discounts under general price-sensitive demand-functions – Optimal policies and relationships. *European Journal of Operational Research*, 86 (2), pp. 300–314.

Wilcox, K., Kim, H. M. and Sen, S. (2009) Why do consumers buy counterfeit luxury brands? *Journal of Marketing Research*, 46 (2), pp. 247–259.

Wiltbank, R., Read, S., Dew, N. and Sarasvathy, S. D. (2009) Prediction and control under uncertainty: Outcomes in angel investing. *Journal of Business Venturing*, 24 (2), pp. 116–133.

Wong, N. Y. and Ahuvia, A. C. (1998) Personal taste and family face: Luxury consumption in Confucian and western societies. *Psychology & Marketing*, 15 (5), pp. 423–441.

Zahra, S. A. and Covin, J. G. (1995) Contextual influences on the corporate entrepreneurship performance relationship – A longitudinal analysis. *Journal of Business Venturing*, 10 (1), pp. 43–58.

Zucchella, A., Palamara, G. and Denicolai, S. (2007) The drivers of the early internationalization of the firm. *Journal of World Business*, 42 (3), pp. 268–280.

5

MAKING THE BUSINESS CASE FOR VALUE-BASED PRICING INVESTMENTS

Stephan M. Liozu

Introduction

Of the three main approaches to pricing in industrial markets—cost-based, competition-based, and value-based—the last is considered superior by most marketing scholars (Anderson et al. 2010; Hinterhuber 2004; Ingenbleek et al. 2010) and pricing practitioners (Cressman Jr 2010; Forbis and Mehta 2000). Paradoxically, few firms have adopted it. A meta-analysis of pricing approach surveys between 1983 and 2006 reveals an average adoption rate of just 17 percent (Hinterhuber 2008b). Cost-based and competition-based approaches still play a dominant role in industrial pricing practice.

There are many published reasons for the low adoption of value-based pricing. Scholars focus on the difficulty of defining value and the lack of market orientation (Anderson et al. 1993). Practitioners often mention issues with value assessment, internal communication breakdowns between marketing and sales teams, and the lack of incentive alignment (Cressman Jr. 2009; Hinterhuber 2008a). One of the least-mentioned barriers to the increased adoption of value-based pricing is the difficulty of measuring and selling the required investment and the ROI internally. While the role of champions at the top is a key to successful implementation (Liozu et al. 2011), it remains very difficult to justify the investment for value-based pricing and pricing in general to top management in the C-suite. What, then, are the roadblocks to justification?

Difficulties in making the business case for value-based pricing

Difficulty in scope definition

The first possible difficulty lies in defining the scope of the value-based pricing concept. What are the relevant programs, activities, and costs? Our recent academic paper published in January 2012 in the *Journal of Revenue and Pricing Management* reveals the difficulty in conceptualizing value-based pricing (Liozu et al. 2012). Practitioners create their own social construction of the method and include what is needed based on their current context. This contextual framing is dynamic. Thus the scope of value-based pricing will also vary based on progress along the journey, changes in the market dynamics, and new developments in pricing theories.

Long transformational journey

Our study of the adoption and deployment of value-based pricing reveals that it is a long journey, lasting anywhere from three to seven years. This journey requires an organizational mobilization that is the equivalent of a deep organizational transformation, as shown in Figure 5.1.

It can be difficult to analyze and project the exact duration of this journey. Some firms will spend more time in the experimentation phase to create a sufficient number of successful case studies to maximize buy-in (Anderson et al. 2007; Liozu et al. 2011). But, generally speaking, firms never reach the terminal status of successful implementation. Implementing value-based pricing requires constant investment in pricing, continuous pricing innovation, and significant investment in training as the organization integrates new businesses and personnel. Knowing when to stop the investment "meter" is a real challenge. This also complicates the process of defining the scope of value-based pricing implementation.

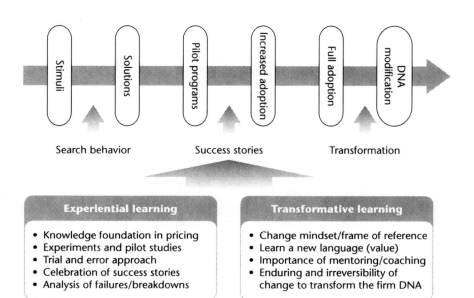

FIGURE 5.1 The transformational journey

Benchmarks and case studies are not enough and may be misleading

Firms internalizing value-based pricing move at various speeds and with various intensities. The nature of their programs is also adapted to their environmental context and to their existing internal capabilities. External benchmarks typically consist of qualitative case studies available through the Professional Pricing Society, other practitioner organizations, or consulting firms. Conducting benchmarks of successful transformation can help, but it does not provide the necessary rationale and scientific support. Benchmarks encourage imitations (Pfeffer and Sutton 2006) and copy/paste behaviors (DiMaggio and Powell 1983) that can be detrimental to the accuracy of the project cost evaluation.

Lack of documented success of value-based pricing performance

Most pricing practitioners agree that the lack of scientific and systematic ROI calculations for pricing strategies constrains the visibility of pricing in the corporate executive suite and restrains firm adoption of modern pricing approaches. In addition, the marketing and pricing literatures are silent both about the effect of firm pricing orientations on overall company performance and, more specifically, about how modern pricing practices might lead to superior firm performance (Hinterhuber 2008b; Liozu et al. 2011). This silence impedes the ability to quantitatively and statistically demonstrate that firms using value-based pricing deliver superior sales, pricing, and profit performance. The lack of academic research on this direct link makes it virtually impossible to convince CEOs and other C-suite executives who are bombarded with economic and financial analysis. The case for value-based pricing is typically based on qualitative case studies and incomplete data, leading to reduced credibility.

The pains and gains in value-based pricing

A recent survey conducted with 557 CEOs and business owners around the world showed that they pay little attention to pricing. When asked how they would allocate 100 points of attention between cost-cutting, growth programs, and pricing initiatives, they awarded pricing an average of just 16 points. Most (54 percent) of their time is spent on fixed- and variable-cost control (see Figure 5.2).

Clearly, and even though they realize the power of strategic pricing, top executives do not pay enough attention to it. What is behind this lack of interest and attention? I conjecture that it stems primarily from the fact that the pricing function does not excel at identifying, measuring, and communicating the business pains of poor or no pricing management. The pricing function also has difficulty measuring the gains generated by pricing activities as well as calculating the ROI of pricing activities, including the payback for investments in value-based pricing programs.

So here are some tips for getting started and making progress with this difficult exercise.

CEOs' perceptions towards pricing (1 = strongly disagree to 7 = strongly agree)	Total (n=557)
Strategic pricing can increase profitability	6.29
My employees actively engage in the pricing process	5.36
I have seen what other companies can achieve with pricing	5.08

CEOs declare understanding the importance of pricing ...
but they barely pay attention to it!

Allocation of 100 points of attention	Total (n=557)
Variables and fixed cost reduction programs	54%
Growth initiatives	30%
Price management programs	16%
	100%

FIGURE 5.2 CEOs' attention to pricing

Show the pains

Pricing professionals should spend more time up front identifying and articulating the pains relating to pricing. This can be done by conducting a pricing capability assessment and performing the fundamental pricing analysis: cost-to-serve, waterfall, pricing cloud, segmentation gaps, and so forth. These pains must then be "packaged" in a dramatic fashion with one or two critical numbers that might turn into a story "hook." These numbers must then be communicated inside the marketing and pricing organization in a mindful manner without created tensions or fear of rejection.

Articulate the gains

Once the financial and efficiency pains are identified, measured, and articulated, the next step is to evaluate the potential gains of investing in value-based pricing. This remains a difficult exercise. A focus on short-term gains may be necessary to attract some initial attention. As with the Lean Six Sigma methodologies, quick wins are greatly appreciated by top executives, as they tend to focus on short-term impact. That gives you an opportunity to get a foot in the door, to tell your story, and to come back for more "face time" later.

Create a story

Once pains and gains are identified and somehow measured, the next step is to create a story. That story must be adapted to the business context, the dynamics of the external environment, the culture of the organization, and the management style of the top leaders. The story must begin with a strong hook, which in this case is the pains: "Every year, our organization loses $1 million in profit due to poor pricing." The hook grabs attention and creates the opportunity to give your one-minute nontechnical elevator speech. The message is to convince top executives of what you can deliver for them in gains to help reduce the pains. That story should be repeated in business meetings and in pricing discussions, and might be translated into goals and objectives for the pricing team. The story has to be crisp, credible, well-articulated, and somewhat dramatic.

Be ready to compete internally

In an organization, you compete for attention. You also compete for human and financial resources. This competition is internal and consists of functions that are in the mainstream and are able to calculate their ROI very well, such as R&D (research and development), operations, innovation, technology, and IT. For these functions, calculating ROI and demonstrating payback is expected and second nature. The pricing function must be able to do the same.

Keep It Simple, Stupid (KISS principle)

Top executives are busy people with very short attention spans. Therefore, you might have to talk to them like a two-year old child suffering from ADD. It is recommended to keep the message simple, well-articulated, and business-like. If you manage to get 30 minutes of top executive attention, do not bore them with long analytical explanations, super-technical pricing methods, or 30 pages of PowerPoint presentation. Work on a very simple storyline using plain terms. It might sound like this:

> We are currently leaving $2.5 million on the table by not managing our profit leakages and not fully capturing pricing opportunities through value-based pricing. With an investment of $300,000, we could get some quick wins, get our company on the path to pricing excellence, while getting a payback and three points of ROS for it within two years.

Practical recommendations for making the business case

Bottom line: justifying investments with top executives in value-based pricing is not easy. It requires a thorough understanding of what the transformation requires and a clear delineation of the value-based pricing scope. There is no silver bullet or template that I can recommend. I propose that you consider the following ideas to strengthen your case and to win attention from top leaders.

Include costs associated with all organizational and behavioral programs

Based on the transformational nature of the implementation, I recommend breaking the value-based pricing story down into several modules or sub-projects. These modules might be based on the 5-C model I recently presented at the last Professional Pricing Society annual conference and shown below (champions, capabilities, center-led management, change, and confidence). Then, for each of the "organizational Cs," you can list five strategic initiatives with related critical investments. It might be virtually impossible to list all programs, but you can adopt the 80/20 rule (see Figure 5.3).

They should include change-management programs and confidence-building initiatives, which are essential to increasing organizational commitment and organizational self-esteem. Value-based pricing is a real transformation of the firm DNA from cost or competition to value (Forbis and Mehta 1981; Liozu et al. 2011). Besides typical costs of building capabilities (models, software, tools, pricing training, market research, etc.), firms will have to think holistically and include all relevant costs.

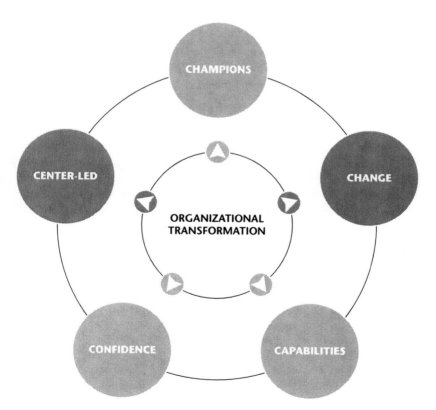

FIGURE 5.3 The 5-C model of transformation

Create a formal pilot program and make the case for increased scope

Another very good option is to voluntarily reduce the scope of the value-based pricing project and to focus first on one or two pilot projects in a region, a business unit, or a product line. Narrowing the scope of the case in the short term will reduce the uncertainty associated with an entire organizational transformation. The relevant costs will be easier to calculate. Choosing a "friendly" region or business unit led by a champion who is aware of the potential positive impact of value-based pricing will open the door for more collaboration and support to create a powerful financial case to be presented to upper management. Having the regional or business unit leader on board from the get-go will help justify the project.

Define specific value-based pricing KPIs in the business case

A critical element of the business case is the definition of clear, relevant, and quantitative KPIs (key performance indicators) for tracking success. These need to be specific to the value-based pricing implementation. Top executives need to be reassured that progress will be measured and that success will be reached. Including the value-based pricing cockpit in the business case presentation would help answer some of the following questions: "how do we win?"; "how do we know when we are done?"; or "what defines success?" These KPIs might include number of trained people, pricing realization index, incremental pricing with new products, to name just a few.

Diagnose where you stand in the pricing maturity model

The most important question to be asked before preparing the business case for significant investments in value-based pricing is "what is the existing level of pricing maturity?" Understanding where the organization stands in the pricing maturity model is important to defining the scope of the project and the intensity of the needed investments. Some organizations may require significant initial training programs to bring everyone in the organization to the same level. Others may require upfront investments in systems and tools. Therefore, conducting a diagnostic of the current pricing capabilities is primordial and must be included in the overall business case. Before one knows where to go and what is needed, one needs to know where one stands!

Bring the outside in to showcase successful transformations

Inviting thought leaders who have no commercial interests can bring a candid and transparent understanding of the required investments and necessary steps to get started. During one- to two-hour sessions with executive committees, I was able to explain the 5-C model of that transformation and the need to understand "short-term pains for long-term gains." Investments in value-based pricing do not pay off quickly. Payback periods for these transformational investments are longer than those for traditional investments. Bringing the outside in generates more pragmatism and realism in the value-based pricing story, which can sometimes be subjective, vague, and difficult to grasp.

Start with innovative products

One way to start on the road to value-based pricing is to integrate the methodology in the strategic innovation process. Keep all existing products under the current pricing strategy or orientation and integrate value-based pricing into your new-product development process. By doing this, you can compare and contrast and focus on initial quick wins that should open some eyes and gain some attention from the C-suite.

Implications for the measurement of pricing ROI

Additional academic research in the area of value-based pricing and pricing excellence is greatly needed. It is imperative to demonstrate academically and statistically that the adoption and internalization of value-based pricing leads to superior firm performance. Until this body of knowledge is formally brought to the worlds of practice and academia, pricing professionals must do a better job of measuring the impact of value-based pricing investments. There is no silver bullet solution; value-based pricing is a complex methodology that requires change and organizational attention. In this chapter, I offered some tips and recommendations to practitioners. To be able to compete for funds and attention, they will have to adopt a better approach to making the case and show some tangible results. The use of quick wins, pilot projects, and innovation success stories is certainly one step in the right direction. Pricing practitioners must also learn to create stories and make a strong case using the elevator speech concept. They must first grab attention; once they have it, they must then deliver an impactful business case that will trigger additional discussions. If you have your 15 minutes of fame in the C-suite, build a strong storyline, tell this story with conviction and confidence, and deliver a strong punch line.

Be bold—join the value-based pricing revolution!

References

Anderson, J. C., Jain, D. C. and Chintagunta, P. K. (1993) Customer value assessment in business markets: A state-of-practice study. *Journal of Business-to-Business Marketing*, 1 (1), p. 3.

Anderson, J. C., Kumar, N. and Narus, J. A. (2007) *Value merchants: Demonstrating and documenting superior value in business markets*. Boston, MA: Harvard Business School Press.

Anderson, J. C., Wouters, M. and van Rossum, W. (2010) Why the highest price isn't the best price. *MIT Sloan Management Review*, 51 (2), pp. 69–76.

Cressman Jr, G. (2009) Why pricing strategies fail. *The Journal of Professional Pricing* (Second Quarter 2009), pp. 18–22.

Cressman Jr., G. (2010) Selling value-based pricing strategies: Making pricing strategy work. *The Journal of Professional Pricing* (First Quarter 2010), pp. 16–19.

DiMaggio, P. and Powell, W. (1983) The iron cage revisited: Institutional isomorphism and collective rationality in organizational fields. *American Sociological Review*, 48 (2), pp. 147–160.

Forbis, J. and Mehta, N. (1981) Value-based strategies for industrial products. *Business Horizons*, 24 (3), pp. 32–42.

Forbis, J. and Mehta, N. (2000) Economic value to the customer. *The McKinsey Quarterly*, 4, pp. 49–52.

Hinterhuber, A. (2004) Towards value-based pricing—An integrative framework for decision making. *Industrial Marketing Management*, 33 (8), pp. 765–778.

Hinterhuber, A. (2008a) Customer value-based pricing strategies: Why companies resist. *Journal of Business Strategy*, 29 (4), pp. 41–50.

Hinterhuber, A. (2008b) Value delivery and value-based pricing in industrial markets. *Advances in Business Marketing and Purchasing*, 14, pp. 381–448.

Ingenbleek, P., Frambach, R. T. and Verhallen, T. M. M. (2010) The role of value informed pricing in market oriented product innovation management. *Journal of Product Innovation Management*, 27 (7), pp. 1032–1046.

Liozu, S., Boland, R. J. J., Hinterhuber, A. and Perelli, S. (June 2011) *Industrial pricing orientation: The organizational transformation to value-based pricing.* Paper presented at the International Conference on Engaged Management Scholarship, Case Western Reserve University, Cleveland, Ohio.

Liozu, S. M., Hinterhuber, A., Boland, R. and Perelli, S. (2012) The conceptualization of value-based pricing in industrial firms. *Journal of Revenue & Pricing Management*, 11 (1), pp. 12–34.

Pfeffer, J. and Sutton, R. (2006) Evidence-based management. *Harvard Business Review*, 84, pp. 1–12.

6

EVALUATING THE IMPACT OF PRICING ACTIONS TO DRIVE FURTHER ACTIONS

Antonio Ruggiero and Jered Haedt

Introduction

Pricing actions are performed in everyday operations. We present how to evaluate ongoing pricing actions to determine their effectiveness and, more importantly, drive further actions. The use of analytical methods, statistical metrics, and useful reports and dashboards is presented. We discuss how to evaluate ongoing pricing actions in terms of hard ROI and soft ROI, using business intelligence reporting and business analytics methods.

Although pricing functions have begun to take centre stage at corporations, not all aspects of pricing are implemented. The road to adoption is slow. For example, many corporations devote serious manpower and effort to creating their price lists or their price books. These price lists may be published in catalogues; exposed on corporate websites; and/or shared externally with customers. Interestingly, these price lists are not revisited very often during their life cycle. In our experience, new price lists are created annually with minor adjustments occurring throughout the year. What is most intriguing is that very few corporations devote resources and effort to monitoring and reporting on the market responses to pricing actions once implemented.

Pricing actions are not only limited to mature/everyday pricing issues, like producing price lists. For example, many pricing actions originate in marketing campaigns that may include short-term promotional pricing, long-term rebate pricing, new product skimming campaigns, mark down strategies and even liquidation strategies. In essence, pricing actions are all actions that corporations undertake that address all components of the product and service life cycle curve. This will include strategic, operational, and tactical decisions as defined by the military definition of tactics. Executives will set policy and drive both short-term focus and long-term strategic growth plans. Senior management in the operational level will decide the best methods to implement the strategies into their respective operational units. Lastly, junior management will effect day-to-day operations to realize strategic goals. Because of the different goals driving each level, the types of reporting and analytics are going to be different.

However, it has been our experience in pricing seminars that has revealed very few corporations employ any set standards for evaluating new price actions in their market place. At one such event, two questions were offered to a group of approximately 250 attendees regarding price lists. The first question pertaining to how many of the attendees put considerable effort and analytics into preparing price lists or a book of prices saw approximately 80 per cent of the attendees respond favourably. However, the second question of how many of the attendees perform any sort of pricing evaluation or price testing after the new price list is published received considerably less of a response: only a single attendee performed this type of analysis. To be fair, this type of analysis can be difficult and is confounded by the fact that data may not be readily available for analysis. For these reasons, it is typically difficult to determine the ROI from a pricing action.

Both hard ROI and soft ROI can be considered to evaluate a pricing action. Hard ROI is a statistical evaluation of a pricing action accounting for possible external factors during the test periods. Whereas, soft ROI are ancillary benefits gained by a pricing action. An example of soft ROI was a customer that implemented a cost-to-serve methodology to address contribution margin versus gross margin on sales. Although there was a successful hard ROI evaluation, a soft ROI emerged that pertained to the elevated education level of the sales representatives. While at first, the sales force neither cared for nor understood the concept of contribution margin, in time and with training, the sales force eventually understood how to suggest and alter orders to offset high cost drivers. In fact, the executives deemed the soft ROI of more importance than the hard ROI in this case, since they saw the sales force expertise as more important to continued sales and profit growth in the future.

A bird's eye view of how to evaluate a pricing action, with regards to hard ROI, is presented in Figure 6.1. To reiterate, hard ROI involves setting an evaluation scenario, and using available data to statistically evaluate the pricing action or actions.

Every pricing action is really the result of solving a business issue. Hence the first stage is adequately defining the business issue. The second stage involves collecting the people and data to perform the analysis. From a perspective of people resource, typically IT resources are required to understand the data and where the data are located. However, IT does not drive business processes and Subject Matter Experts (SMEs) are necessary to help focus the request for data. But this only addresses internally available data such as transaction data. Externally available data such as USA government financial data, indexes, and industry published data can be extremely powerful in analysis. Obtaining and updating this external data set requires the aid of both SMEs and IT.

Once we have the available data, the process of setting up and evaluating the modelling begins. This is typically an iterative process where different data variables and methods may be tested. Once the models are defined, testing the pricing action

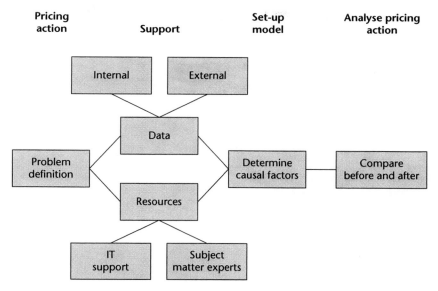

FIGURE 6.1 Bird's eye view of price action evaluation

will occur. Typically this involves defining a base set of data (the prior period), and a new set of data (the post period) to which is compared the base set of data. Our goal is twofold. First, we wish to introduce executives, senior management, pricing analysts, business analysts, and data analysts to several concepts of pricing action evaluations. Second, we wish to present a solution that is built on non-complex and established methods.

We begin with addressing the typical type of data required for this analysis. The next section describes the types of business intelligence and reporting that should be part of any monitoring process. We then follow with business analytics that can be used to analyse and report on pricing performance. A case study will be presented to try to cement some of the methods presented. Lastly, we will present some concluding remarks.

Data for monitoring ongoing pricing actions

Once a pricing action has been implemented, it is typically forgotten until it is time to implement a new action. Before we can address business intelligence and reporting or business analytics, we must address data. Without a doubt, the single task that is most troublesome is collecting the proper data. This is compounded by the fact that every IT system can have multiple functions and they overlap across software systems. Figure 6.2 highlights some of the sources that may be included in your reporting.

Your Enterprise Resource Planning (ERP) implementation likely processes quotes, orders, and invoicing. This transaction-level detail drives most of the

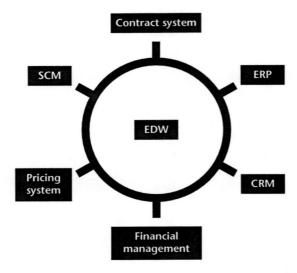

FIGURE 6.2 Possible sources of data for business intelligence and business analytics

reporting, metrics, and analytics. Your ERP may also be your source for marketing plans and campaigns, financial reporting systems, supply chain, and research and development. In many cases, price lists will be created outside the ERP but the ERP will manage discounts. If you employ a pricing system, then it may contain old price lists, contract information, special pricing agreements, discount structures, and rebate structures. Your Customer Relationship Management (CRM) system contains customer information for sales processes. In some cases, customer specific pricing and contracts may be stored in your CRM systems, including discount structures and rebate structures. Your CRM systems may also contain marketing information and campaigns. If you use a separate Contract Management system then it will likely contain all contract and customer specific pricing, terms and conditions, discount and rebate structures, and contract start and end dates. Your financial management systems will contain account receivables, refund information, terms and conditions, customer delinquency, financial costing (both variable and fixed), and rebate payments to name a few. The Supply Chain Management (SCM) system will contain inventory information and costing information. In some cases, new product research and development is initiated in the SCM and then moved into the other systems.

All these sources contribute data elements that drive different aspects of different reports and intelligence gathering. Furthermore they are the underpinning to any analytics you wish to perform. The old adage comes to mind: GIGO, garbage in garbage out. However, there is saving grace. For many corporations, the data revolution has spurred IT departments to invest in Enterprise Data Warehouses (EDWs) or Central Data Warehouses (CDWs). If an EDW exists then collecting the correct data may be somewhat simpler. We say 'may' because the EDW may not house all the data that you would like in your reports or analytics. If your corporation does not employ an EDW, then the data will likely have to be pulled from many source systems each with their unique idiosyncrasies. There will be extraction, transformation, and loading (ETL) issues with which to contend. Furthermore, there will surely be some data cleansing exercises. These may include, but are not limited to, outlier identification, special market considerations (e.g. the financial crisis), and/or master data hierarchical consistency. Without the necessary processes in place, analysts typically have to wait long periods and jump through IT resource hoops before the necessary data are collected.

The following list is an abridged version of the fields necessary for business intelligence and business analytics:

- Quote, order, and invoice information – both header and line item values
- Customer identifier – both sold-to and ship-to information
- Shipping/freight information
- Product name and identifier
- Order quantity, ship quantity, invoiced quantity
- Unit of measure information – selling versus stocking
- Pricing information: list price, contract price, distributor price, Original Equipment Manufacturer price, volume discount, contract discount, marketing discount, manual override price
- Distribution centre/sourcing information
- Customer terms and conditions
- Accounts receivable
- Customer delinquency status
- Inventory – either end of day, end of week, or end of month levels.

Typically there are master data which define the dimensions by which data are recorded. Some fields for master data include:

- Product dimension and hierarchical levels
- Customer dimension and hierarchical levels
- Geographic regions dimension – both local and global
- Business unit/industry dimension
- Date dimension – for comparison purposes e.g. quarter over quarter.

This list is by no means exhaustive but effectively highlights the fields of data required to properly evaluate pricing actions.

Business intelligence

Business intelligence is the ability to *slice and dice* data. Typically it may focus on historical reporting. There are many types of reports and methods to publish the results to ensure the right report is getting to the right person, at the right time, in the right format. Reports can be presented in dashboards, pre-defined standardized reports, embedded in specialized reporting systems, or embedded in one of the sources identified in Figure 6.2. Furthermore, what will drive actions are the metrics and associated workflow. Hard ROI is related to testing that produces a statistically confident analysis of return on a pricing action. Soft ROI is related to soft benefits associated with a pricing action. For example, a reduction in customer complaints because you aligned new product sales more closely with supply chain production plans such that customers received their orders in a more timely manner would qualify as a soft ROI.

Dashboards are often a very effective and quick methodology utilized to measure the ROI of any given pricing action. Identifying proper trend analysis for determining levels of ROI or pricing actions generally takes a trained eye for analysis. However, with proper Key Performance Indicators (KPIs) and thoughtful use of the formulations behind these metrics, even a novice user base can expand the group pricing function to a greater portion of the business and therefore help achieve the overarching goal of pricing becoming a part of the corporate DNA.

As with any tool or analysis, dashboards should be one of many tools in your corporation's pricing tool kit. Due to the expanded audience user group that will interact with and without the pricing group's guidance, it is paramount to create an audit trail, identify information levels and barriers to reduce abuse of the dashboard tool, and create ongoing training to reaffirm key learning points. In this section, we analyse most common time selections for reporting; common and advanced metrics; use cases to determine hard ROI and soft ROI; and strategies for determining new pricing actions. This section examines common and advanced metrics, their definitions, and describes a use case for each indicator to create a framework that can be expanded upon to create determinations for soft and hard ROI. Furthermore, actionable pricing decisions will arise that will be explored at the end of this section. Please note this is not an exhaustive list of potential variables, and depending on your particular industry, variables will change accordingly. The variables identified in this section are generalized and pertinent to any pricing corporation.

For each variable we identify a generalized definition to relate across the organization as a common ground of communication; a formula-based definition where this formula is important in analysing your pricing actions; and finally an example of an analysis that would impact this arena. Note that basic metrics, like sales, gross margin, discount off of list, customer count, etc., while important, will not be discussed.

First, *price* as a metric is not price in the formal sense. For this metric we are identifying the change in price from one period to the next based on the time component discussed earlier. The component of understanding how price is being affected on an acute level allows for actionable results to be driven. Furthermore, this is a significant launch point in the determination of an ROI analysis.

- Price: The portion of sales growth dollars attributable to a change in price, this is only measured on repeat sales where the same account (group, region, segment, etc.) bought the same product in both (current and prior) periods.
- Formula:

$$\text{Price change} = (\text{ASP}_{current} - \text{ASP}_{prior}) \times \text{Qty}_{current}$$

where
ASP = Average Selling Price
Qty = Quantity

Where is this important? When you have a price change (regardless of quantity) and truly want to know how price has been affected. This is valuable in understanding if the customer is price testing you; how well the salesperson/sales channel is upholding price; and finding strategic areas of pricing improvement. By isolating price and volume implications, policy changes become a clear decision point.

Pricing decisions that the price metric can identify and also be an expression of hard ROI are: willingness to pay and pass-through. Whereas, price metric for soft ROI is: (short-term) mean time reaction and (long-term) price adoption. Note in the price adoption technique an internal metric can be analysed for price realization based on the salesperson. By looking for this effect, it can lead to valuable insights on how to align training.

Second, *volume* as a metric goes hand-in-hand with the price metric, in that it is a derivative of the previous formulation. However, volume in this case does not factor any change in price. Therefore, most analytics driven from this will be the softer side of pricing within the scope of a volumetric industry. There is a significant downfall to this variable; significant velocity must be achieved, for the action in question, coupled with relevance to the grouping. Therefore, this analysis is generally not recommended for investigation of outliers, cycle volatility, and new product introduction (unless analysing cannibalization).

- Volume: The portion of sales growth dollars attributable to a change in volume. This is only measured on repeat sales where the same account (etc.) bought the same product in both (current and prior) periods.
- Formula:

$$\text{Volume change} = (\text{Qty}_{current} - \text{Qty}_{prior}) \times \text{ASP}_{prior}$$

where
ASP = Average Selling Price
Qty = Quantity

Where is this important? Volume as a metric is critically important in determining if an account is willing to sustainably increase its volume commitments period over period and it is very important for long-run analysis. Furthermore, by isolating volume, the muddiness of reactionary price loss (opposite of the pass-through) volumetric gains is a clear differentiator when creating ROI analytics. Thus, a consideration of volume considerations would utilize continual product pricing breaks by segment and then analyse the floor movement in the next time period.

Pricing decisions that the metric price can identify and be an expression of hard ROI are: net price optimization (in particular pricing floors) and acquisition analysis in M&A (mergers and acquisitions); for soft ROI practices: customer decile analysis as a function of purely volumetric change to identify at-risk behaviours and channel stuffing as an internally focused study.

Third, *churn* is a powerful metric. This metric shows the number of dollars an account (measuring component) has gained or lost on items purchased in one period but not in the other. While churn is usually shown as one metric, a more in-depth and telling version is splitting the metric into a positive and negative churn.

- Churn: The portion of sales growth (or loss) dollars attributable to the net change in non-repeat sales; this is all of the sales where price and volume were not able to be measured due to non-repeat sales.
- Formula: (Products in Current Period − Products in Prior Period): On both sides of the equation, products in the current period that were not in the prior period is considered a positive, products in the prior period that were not in the current period is considered a negative.

$$\text{Churn change} = PC - NC$$
$$PC = (PB_{current} \neq PB_{prior})$$
$$NC = (PB_{prior} \neq PB_{current})$$

where
PC = Positive Churn
NC = Negative Churn
PB = Product Bundle

This is particularly useful for sustainable, consistent accounts that buy period over period, and as an analysis we are creating a pricing action based upon product expansion/penetration of the account. Alternatively, one can use churn as a deterministic variable of the effectiveness in upselling/down-selling (with down-selling being deterministic of better margin performance thus yielding more marginal dollars for the account). Other uses of the metric include: analysing critical accounts on product shifting to determine the likelihood the account is seeking an alternative; another determining analysis, 'cherry picking' or short ordering items to use your corporation as a backfill.

Pricing decisions that the metric price can identify and be an expression of hard ROI: churn can be used in several different methodologies such as product penetration reporting, share of wallet, and identifying adoption rates of new products. In regard to soft ROI, churn is very good at identifying new product bundling opportunities, secondary cannibalization rates, and internally understanding the expansion (or limitations) of sales groups in expanding portfolio of products.

Fourth, *Win/Loss Gross Margin Dollars* (W/L GM$): this metric encapsulates the economic value to the unit being measured. This unit can be of any of the previous levels we have discussed thus far from a product or product group, to the measurement of people, business unit, or the entire corporation. This provides visibility into whether the margin dollars on the volume gained were worth the price dollars given up to gain the volume. This metric brings the entire dashboard together; when the sales channel is pointing to an account rejoicing on a (volume, price, contract, product expansion, etc.) increase you can turn to this metric and simply say: was the action worth it?

In short, this metric provides the quickest look into whether an 'action' was worthwhile to the corporation. Further metrics can be used to dissect more deeply, but this can be considered a marquee 'scorecard' item and should be the key point in your training exercises when expanding the user base.

- W/L GM$: An economic measure showing if a pricing action had net positive or negative effect on the unit (sku, product, product group, people, business unit, etc.)
- Formula:

$$\text{Win/Loss GM\$} = (\text{Sales}_{current} - \text{Sales}_{prior}) \times \text{GM\$}_{current}$$
$$+ (\text{GM\$}_{current} - \text{GM\$}_{prior}) \times \text{Sales}_{prior}$$

where
GM$ = Gross Margin Dollars

Figure 6.3 is an example of a price management dashboard using the afore-mentioned metrics. Notice that the overall feel of the dashboard has been broken into three sections: current period, previous period, and the metrics we have discussed in this section. Please note Figure 6.3 has been split into two sections to enable readability.

Business analytics

Business analytics uses the available data and any externally available data to drive strategic plans, and determine operational and tactical actions. Business analytics includes typical mathematical modelling techniques such as segmentation, fore-casting, and price-setting processes. Our focus is to present analytics to monitor an existing pricing action. In summary, after a pricing action is implemented, we wish to monitor its effectiveness and be alerted as soon as possible, in effect minimizing the risk that the pricing action goes awry. Armed with this type of information, effective decisions are made that limit the downside risk.

This section shows how business analytics can be used to model and track ROI associated with a pricing action. This section will define the business issue; define some terminology; describe how to select important drivers; describe a regression based signal decomposition method; and lastly we will touch on more advanced techniques of analysis of covariance and regime shift analysis.

Drill downs	Current period						vs. Prior period				
Sales decile	Customer count (parent level)	Sales	Sales per order	C/D	Discount off list	Potential C/D lost	Δ Customer count	Δ Sales	Δ Sales per order	Δ C/D	Win/ Loss C/D $
1	6	$4,288,516	$1,432	15.41%	71.6%	94.2%	20.00%	34.1%	25.9%	−0.77%	$143,446
2	14	$4,712,251	$1,348	21.15%	71.7%	92.3%	0.00%	42.1%	38.9%	−2.69%	$206,275
3	19	$4,612,629	$1,005	20.16%	65.0%	90.2%	0.00%	13.8%	−2.7%	2.54%	$215,908
4	28	$4,708,374	$1,110	23.36%	62.4%	87.7%	3.70%	16.8%	16.0%	0.97%	$197,548
5	42	$4,566,947	$927	23.52%	63.4%	88.1%	2.44%	9.7%	8.1%	0.24%	$105,333
6	67	$4,598,606	$1,035	25.79%	64.7%	87.7%	3.08%	17.5%	−1.0%	2.57%	$277,089
7	109	$4,619,962	$710	25.14%	61.3%	86.3%	3.81%	−3.1%	−5.2%	1.41%	$30,279
8	181	$4,585,962	$719	27.04%	65.6%	87.6%	9.04%	12.9%	6.2%	1.14%	$188,251
9	373	$4,599,598	$608	29.78%	62.0%	84.6%	8.43%	−24.2%	−21.3%	5.04%	−$131,702
10	3,365	$4,573,864	$290	35.97%	60.4%	80.9%	−1.64%	−52.5%	−46.1%	4.79%	−$1,358,785
Grand total	4,204	$45,866,709	$9,184	24.77%	65.2%	88.3%	−0.07%	−2.8%	−2.5%	0.43%	−$126,358

Price	Volume	Churn	Price %	Volume %	Churn %	PVC overall	Growth drivers P / V / C
$ (36,106)	$2,679,363	$ (1,552,475)	-1.3%	83.8%	-48.7%	14.73%	
$ (78,406)	$2,867,071	$ (1,391,426)	-2.7%	86.5%	-42.5%	16.09%	
$ (184,185)	$2,429,227	$ (2,053,442)	7.3%	59.9%	-52.0%	11.21%	
$ (271,557)	$2,709,359	$ (1,759,759)	-9.8%	67.2%	-44.7%	6.33%	
$ (313,332)	$2,092,018	$ (1,372,980)	-14.7%	50.2%	-33.3%	1.05%	
$ (198,336)	$1,819,896	$ (936,605)	-10.3%	46.3%	-24.6%	3.83%	
$ (122,522)	$1,905,785	$ (1,929,395)	-6.2%	39.8%	-41.0%	0.64%	
$ (275,018)	$1,696,467	$ (896,529)	-15.9%	41.8%	-22.3%	0.14%	
$ (64,412)	$1,322,524	$ (2,726,982)	-4.8%	21.7%	-45.1%	-4.89%	
$ (286,008)	$982,419	$ (5,757,330)	-28.3%	10.2%	-59.9%	-23.07%	
$ (1,829,882)	$20,504,129	$ (20,376,923)	-7.0%	43.4%	-43.7%	0.80%	

Price / Volume / Churn

FIGURE 6.3 Example dashboard layouts built around pricing analytics

Note: Numbers are for illustration only.

The fundamental premise is that there are two periods that are being compared: the prior or base period, and the new or post period. In order to be able to statistically model and create an ongoing metric, the time period component must be discretized. That is, do not compare, for example, the revenues of a single quarter to another quarter. Instead compare the average weekly revenue between the two periods. We can then create measures to monitor the process and determine if the new period's revenues are different from the old period's revenues.

Without loss of generality and to facilitate discussion, let us assume that the price action is a product, or a family of products, that is sold at a fixed price during each period under test. That is, the price does not change frequently. The time dimension can be rescaled in the case of commodity-like products that change price frequently. The business issue is: *Given I have implemented a pricing action, tell me how is it performing? Specifically, are we losing, gaining or is there no change.*

Figure 6.4 graphically describes the problem. The business issue is to determine if the corporation is performing better, worse, or statistically the same as before the pricing action. Without additional information, we can solely analyse the quantity between the two periods. However, it becomes more interesting and more informative (and more difficult) if we have additional information that we can leverage to explain the variability in the data. If we can account 'control' for the variability then we can achieve a better evaluation of performance.

Figure 6.1 introduced a bird's eye view of how to monitor an ongoing pricing action. The solution is to decompose the data somewhat similar to signal analysis. If we think of the price action effect as a signal then we are trying to isolate it from the background noise. In the simplest sense, one estimates the noise first and then removes it from the signal. Then what is left is due solely to the signal. Hence the exercise is to find both internal data and external data that can be used to statistically isolate the pricing action, and then analyse the remainder to determine how successful the pricing action is.

FIGURE 6.4 Graphical view of a price action over time

Unfortunately, there are many over-used and, as such, confusing terms and terminology in statistics. To facilitate discussion, we must define a few variable terms. Most people are familiar with the two main variable types used in regression: the dependent variable and the independent variable. The dependent variable is the presumed effect in an experimental study – the output. The values of the dependent variable depend upon, or are functions of, another variable, the independent variable. The independent variable is the presumed cause in an experimental study – the input.

For the purposes of our analysis, we must describe covariate variables. A covariate variable is typically a continuous scale variable. It is an extraneous variable that an investigator does not wish to examine in an experiment. Thus the investigator wants to control this variable, or reduce its effect. Hence it is also known as a control variable. In this context, the covariate is always continuous, always a control variable, and always observed (i.e. observations weren't randomly assigned their values – you just measured what was there).

A simple example to explain a covariate variable's effect is to consider a study looking at the effect of a training programme on maths ability. Let the independent variable be the training condition, that is, whether participants received the maths training or some irrelevant training. The dependent variable is defined to be their maths score after receiving the training. But the problem is that within each training group, there will be a lot of variation in people's maths ability, that is, their maths ability starting point. Hence, if we do not 'control' or account for the difference in starting maths ability, then it is just unexplained variation. This unexplained variation leads to noise and if we have a lot of unexplained variation then it is difficult to see the actual effect of the training. The signal gets lost in all the noise. So the solution is to use a pretest maths score as a covariate, then we can control for the starting maths ability of each person. This results in a clearer picture of whether people do well on the final test due to the training or due to the maths ability they had coming in.

While internal data were extensively discussed in the *Data for monitoring ongoing pricing actions* section, here we discuss external data that will prove useful as covariates to explain variation in the data. There are certainly data that are collected internally that at first thought would not appear useful for analysing financial time series. This type of data is outside the frame of the issue but they may have contributed to reasons as to why the sales were what they were. For example, we may be interested in store traffic, aisle traffic, attendance levels, occupancy rates, and even out-of-stock inventory indicators to help explain variation in sales, revenues, and profits. For example, sales would certainly be impacted if there was a shortage of supply for a short time period. Either these data are identified as outliers and excluded from any study, or covariate data are used to reduce their sphere of influence on the analysis.

There are many powerful methods that perform variable selection for OLS (Ordinary Least Squares) regression modelling. We will focus on two of these many methods: the Leaps and Bounds (LAB) method (Furnival and Miller 1974; Miller 2002), and the Least Angle Regression (LARS) method (Efron and Hastie 2003; Efron et al. 2004). The LAB function provides a way to select a few promising regressions (sets of explanatory variables) for further study. The end result is the collection of explanatory variables that best explain the variability in the underlying data set. The best-known criterion for regression is the coefficient of determination (R^2), or goodness-of-fit. This has definite limitations in the context of LAB method since the largest R^2 is the full set of explanatory variables, or over-fitting the data. Hence it is necessary to balance the power (or goodness of fit) of the model with the complexity of the model.

To take account of the number of parameters being fit, an adjusted R^2 can be used. Another more powerful method is to use an information criterion, like Bayesian Information Criterion (BIC), with a penalizing function that limits or balances adding additional variables to increase the R^2 value with the increased complexity of the model (Raftery 1995). For example,

$$BIC = n\log(1 - R^2) + k \log(n)$$

where
k is the number parameters fitted in the model
n is number of observations
R^2 is proportion of variance explained by the model

This approach has the advantage of relative simplicity and, consequently, ease of computation. Fundamentally, LAB performs stepwise regressions. If we consider forward stepwise regression then LAB selects the best covariate that describes the data. Then LAB selects another covariate to create a best fit in combination with the first selected covariate. This process is repeated *ad infinitum*. The end result is the best collection of covariates that explain the variation in the data. LARS is fundamentally an algorithmic generalization of many methods like LAB and better methods.

Signal Decomposition (SD) attempts to remove all known effects except for price. Then the remainder is analysed for any structure, and this is attributed to the price action change. Everything but the pricing effect is considered noise, and the pricing action effect is the signal we wish to isolate and analyse. That is, we wish to 'normalize' the data for all explanatory covariate variables for which we can account, and the remainder will contain the pricing action effect. The methodology first fits a generalized linear model to the data. That is,

$$\text{Signal} = f_0(t) + f_1(t)g_1(t, x_1) + f_2(t)g_2(t, x_2) + \ldots + f_n(t)g_n(t, x_n)$$

By signal we mean either quantity or volume, sales revenue, or profit. This formula is generic in that there are $x_1, \ldots, x_n$ covariates in m time periods. The demand is a function of general functions f and g of the covariates. However, in the Ordinary Least Squares (OLS) space, this simplifies to:

$$y = \beta_0 + \beta_1 x_1 + \beta_2 x_2 + \ldots + \beta_n x_n$$
$$\beta = (X'X)^{-1}X'y$$

These are the typical equations for linear regression. Using OLS, the normalized data are calculated as the mean of the series plus the residuals or, for m time periods, and n covariates then,

Normalized Signal$_t$ = Series Mean + Residuals

$$= \frac{1}{m} \sum_{t=1}^{m} f_i(t)g(t,x_i) + \left(\text{Signal}_t - \sum_{i=1}^{n} f_i(t)g(t,x_i) \right)$$

Note, the normalized signal will still contain any unexplained variation in the data.

Once we obtain the normalized signal, then we can perform a two-sample student t-test to evaluate the mean of the prior period against the mean of the post period. We have reduced our complex problem to a readily available test in Microsoft Excel. The normalized signal variable is then used to evaluate a price action. Variable refers to quantity, sales, or profit. A test period before, the prior period, and after the price action change (the post period) would be tested for statistically significant change of the corresponding means of the post and prior periods. The following equation demonstrates how to setup the statistical test. Using this test, either there is a significant change implying that the price change had some effect, or there is no significant change. It is typically simpler to report the p-value from the two sample t-test. In order to draw a conclusion from a p-value, a significance level α is required.

For prior period i
For post period j
$H_0 : \mu_f - \mu_i = 0$

where

$$\mu_i = \frac{\displaystyle\sum_{t=j-k}^{t=j} \text{Normalized Signal}_t}{k}$$ represents the mean before the price action

$$\mu_f = \frac{\displaystyle\sum_{t=j+1}^{t=j+k} \text{Normalized Signal}_t}{k}$$ represents the mean after the price action

j represents the time point where the price action occurs
k represents the time period duration for the test

The method we demonstrated is part of a family of methods called Generalized Linear Models. The method we demonstrated simply used OLS regression to fit the data. There are more advanced techniques like Analysis of Variance (ANOVA) and Analysis of Covariance (ANCOVA) that can be used. While both methods are used to test a treatment effect or the pricing action, ANCOVA (Cochran 1957; Neter et al. 1990) is an extension of the SD method. Regime Shift or Change Point Analysis is an additional method that has proven useful to identify shifts in underlying time series data. ANCOVA combines features of both ANOVA and regression. It augments the ANOVA model with one or more additional quantitative variables, called covariates, which are related to the response variable. The covariates are included to reduce the variance in the error terms and provide more precise measurement of the treatment effects, in this case pricing actions, and ultimately gain power. The ANCOVA method is well-documented in the literature.

Regime Shift or Change Point Analysis is a method to identify thresholds in the relationship between two variables (Easterling and Peterson 1995; Lanzante 1996; Rodionov 2005). In the typical pricing action case, we have a time series of quantity, revenue, or profit. More specifically, it attempts to identify a critical point along a distribution of values where the characteristics of the value before and after the critical point are different. It has long been studied and employed in ecology, oceanography, and climatic studies. A number of methods have been developed to detect regime shifts or change points in time series data at the National Oceanic and Atmospheric Administration (NOAA) (Rodionov 2005; Rodionov and Overland 2005). Specifically, a researcher developed a sequential algorithm for early detection of a regime shift called Sequential T-test Analysis of Regime Shifts (STARS) (Rodionov 2004). The notion is quite basic and easily implemented. Consider any time series where new data arrive regularly. When a new data point arrives, it is tested to see if it is different to the mean value of the current regime or prior state. If it is different then it is marked as a possible change point that identifies a new regime, the post state. Successive new data points will either reinforce the hypothesis that it is a true change point or reject it. A student t-test is employed to compare the mean of the current regime to the mean of the new proposed regime. Regime shifting algorithms are also available in the open source statistical software, R.

At the heart of SD is linear regression. Hence it is susceptible to all that ails linear regressions. First, we have assumed that the relationship between the dependent variable and all the covariates is linear within the range of data. Second, OLS is greatly influenced by outliers. This is a general issue with regression of all degrees, including linear. Since we consider other covariate data, then it is possible to have 'multivariate' outliers that we do not identify; for example, if we are using age and salary as covariates. While an age of 16 years is not an outlier, and while a salary of $75,000 is not an outlier, the combination is a likely outlier. That is, there are very few 16 year olds who earn $75,000. Third, the linear regression will suffer if any of the covariates are strongly correlated. The question is what we should define as 'strongly'. Fourth, the data may not be as independent as we assume, especially since we are dealing with time series data.

ANCOVA is really an extension of ANOVA, and as such contains all assumptions applicable to ANOVA. The basis of ANCOVA is to reduce variability by statistical process, rather than employing other data collection or experimental processes. Second, ANCOVA is built on the linear regression and is susceptible to all limitations with linear regression. Third, ANCOVA assumes that the covariates are measured exactly and without error.

STARS is limited by the fact that some experimentation is required to choose the probability cut-off, the cut-off length, and also the outlier parameters. Furthermore, it does not explicitly account for any autocorrelation in the time series.

A case study

In this section, we apply the SD methodology to analyse a pricing action to determine if statistically we are better off. Without loss of generality we will consider a pricing change on a product family. Let us assume that we are charged with analysing the performance of a family of a product in an amusement park. The product family is fairly mature, and an everyday pricing increase was applied to the product family. We are charged with evaluating the pricing action. We examine the relevant metrics to determine how the quantity of sales was affected, how the sales revenue was affected, and how the net profit was affected. We are driven by profitability but a secondary constraint is that we do not wish to affect our reputation too adversely. That is, we do not wish to appear as price gouging and ruining the experience of the amusement park visitor.

In the case of our pricing adjustment example, the solution is a straight-forward application of the regression methodology. First, we define the measures to test. Quantity will examine weekly sum of volume sold before the pricing action and compare to weekly sum of volume during the pricing action. Gross revenue compares weekly sum of revenue which is simply the quantity price. Lastly, gross profit examines weekly sum of profit, which is quantity (price-cost). That is, for each measure we sum the daily measure to a weekly value. Second, we define the prior period to be 12 weeks and the post period to be 12 weeks.

We present information about the raw quantity, pricing, and covariate data. Figure 6.5 shows the pricing and quantity information. In the case of our pricing adjustment for our amusement park, we considered many possible covariates (see Table 6.1). These covariates were tested for their ability to explain variation in the data not attributed to the pricing action. The methodology used was LARS with BIC. R-statistical packages, glars, bicreg, and BMA were used for this analysis. (Marsden 1995). The results set were the following covariates. That is, the following covariate variables were selected as powerful explanatory variables of the variance in the data (Table 6.2).

Table 6.3 presents the correlation matrix for the reduced set of covariate data. The matrix shows that, at most, some variables are moderately correlated.

The charts in Figure 6.6 display the time series plots of the covariate information over the same time period. Using the covariates, a linear regression is performed.

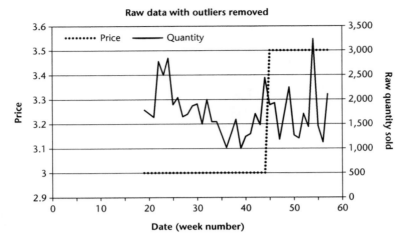

FIGURE 6.5 The raw pricing and quantity sold data for the price action evaluation

TABLE 6.1 Case study: possible covariates

Covariate name	Description
In park	Customer staying in park
Out park	Customer staying out of park
Local resident	Local resident to city of amusement park
Tourists	Foreign or outside local city of amusement park
Travel group non family	Adults only in group
Travel group w LT 13	Family with kids younger than 13
Tourist ticket	Tickets bought for visit
Annual ticket	Annual ticket holders
Salary LT 59K	Annual salary less than $59,000
Salary GT 59K	Annual salary greater than $59,000
First time	Is this their first trip to the amusement park?
Revisit	Revisiting the amusement park
Ethnicity	Caucasian, vs non-caucasian
Rain	Rain level on each day park is open
Temperature	Maximum temperature on each day park is open
Attendance	Daily attendance of amusement park on the whole

TABLE 6.2 Case study: selected covariates

Covariate name	Description
Attendance	Daily attendance of amusement park on the whole
Travel group non family	Adults only in group
First time	Is this their first trip to the amusment park?
Ethnicity	Caucasian
In park	Customer staying in park

TABLE 6.3 Case study: correlation of covariates

Correlation matrix	In park	Travel group non family	Ethnicity	First time	Attendance
In park	1.00				
Travel group non family	0.57	1.00			
Ethnicity	0.64	0.71	1.00		
First time	−0.53	−0.55	−0.68	1.00	
Attendance	−0.45	−0.73	−0.28	0.12	1.00

Excel can be used to evaluate the model (Figure 6.7). Using the regression method available in the Excel addin *Data Analysis ToolPak*, we see the setup window Figure 6.7. We select the quantity as the 'Input Y Range', select all the covariate variables for the 'Input X Range', accept the default confidence level, and, lastly, select 'Residuals'. Excel will provide the regression fit parameters and corresponding P-values; the residuals and the predicted values. Next, we calculate the average of the 'Predicted Quantity' (coincidentally, the average of the quantity will equal the average of the Predicted Quantity). Lastly, calculate the sum of the average of the Predicted Quantity and the residual values. This is the Normalized Signal or Normalized Quantity. This forms the bases of the two-sample t-test of unequal variances.

The Data Analysis ToolPak also provides the 'Two Sample Assuming Unequal Variances t-test', as shown in the setup window Figure 6.8.

The 'Variable 1 Range' is the 12 data points in the prior period. The 'Variable 2 Range' corresponds to the 12 data points in the post period. The 'Hypothesized Mean Difference' is set to 0. That is, we are testing for equal means. Lastly, 'Alpha' is set to 0.10.

Table 6.4 presents the test of whether the mean weekly quantity in the prior period is equal to the mean weekly quantity in the post period. The results indicate that the normalized means of weekly quantity are NOT significantly different at $\alpha = 0.10$. Recall, the test is,

if $p > \alpha$ accept H_0 ($\mu_1 = \mu_2$)
if $p \leq \alpha$ accept H_A ($\mu_1 \neq \mu_2$)

For quantity, the P-value is 0.38 which is greater than 0.10. Therefore we accept the hypothesis that the means are equal. This means that the price caused neither an increase nor a decrease in average weekly sales over the prior and post periods. The identical analysis for sales revenue and profit showed that both are significantly different. The results seem to reinforce the premise that the pricing action is successful thus far. We expect an increase in revenue and possibly profit since there was no change, statistically, in average weekly quantity sold.

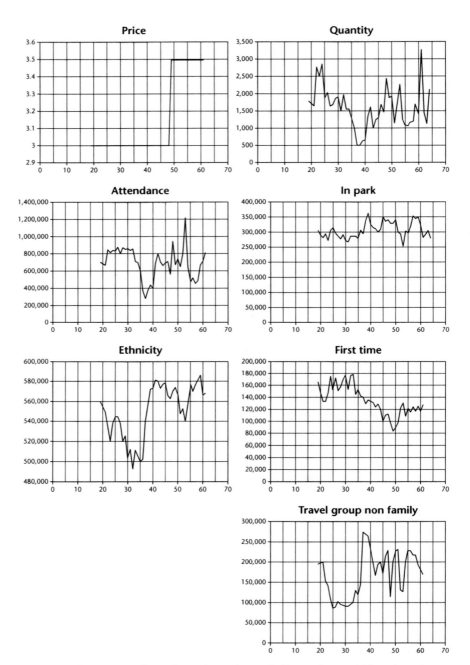

FIGURE 6.6 Time series plots of quantity, price, and all covariate variables selected

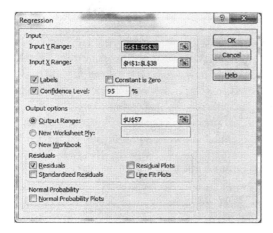

FIGURE 6.7 Excel setup window for regression in the data analysis package

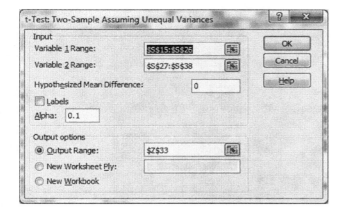

FIGURE 6.8 Excel setup of t-test in analysis ToolPak

TABLE 6.4 Test result: before and after mean weekly quantity

Metric	Before price action		After price action		t-test P-values
	Mean	Variance	Mean	Variance	
Quantity	1,616	63,905	1,767	272,149	0.38
Sales revenue	4,871	772,933	5,884	3,057,210	0.09
Profit	4,047	570,663	4,982	2,203,614	0.07

Contributions to the measurement of pricing ROI

While we are driven to plan and implement new actions, we do not assign resources, or pay much attention, to monitoring how well our current pricing actions are progressing. We typically take a reactive approach instead of a proactive approach. In this chapter we presented how business intelligence and business analytics, coupled with reporting, can provide the necessary tools to evaluate ongoing pricing actions, report on the progress of pricing actions, and take corrective actions if needed to reach incremental benefits. These are the tools that help keep us relevant and help the pricing profession justify its existence. Pricing is by nature a scientific and analytic function. Our goal was to demonstrate that our analytical strengths can be used to better justify the measuring and tracking of pricing actions. We therefore encourage pricing experts to experiment with these tools and to pay more attention to the statistical impact of pricing tactics. The discipline of measurement is key to pricing execution. Using the most sophisticated statistical analysis can also prove very powerful to present rational and documented ROI to top management.

References

Cochran, W. G. (1957) Analysis of covariance: Its nature and uses. *Biometrics*, 13 (3), pp. 261–281.

Easterling, D. R. and Peterson, T. C. (1995) A new method for detecting undocumented discontinuities in climatological time series. *International Journal of Climatology*, 15 (4), pp. 369–377.

Efron, B. and Hastie, T. (2003) Lars software for R and S-Plus. Retrieved April 2013 from http://www-stat.stanford.edu/_hastie/papers/lars

Efron, B., Hastie, T., Johnstone, I. and Tibshirani, R. (2004) Least angle regression. *The Annals of Statistics*, 32 (2), pp. 407–499.

Furnival, G. M. and Miller, A. J. (1974) Regressions by leaps and bounds. *Technometrics*, 16 (4), pp. 499–511.

Lanzante, J. R. (1996) Resistant, robust and non-parametric techniques for the analysis of climate data: Theory and examples, including applications to historical radiosonde station data. *International Journal of Climatology*, 16 (11), pp. 1197–1226.

Marsden, P. V. (1995) *Sociological methodology*. Oxford: Blackwell.

Miller, A. J. (2002) *Subset selection in regression* (Vol. 95). New York, NY: Chapman & Hall.

Neter, J., Wasserman, W. and Kutner, M. H. (1990) *Applied statistical models* (3rd ed.). Homewood, IL: Irwin.

Raftery, A. E. (1995) Bayesian model selection in social research. *Sociological Methodology*, 25, pp. 111–164.

Rodionov, S. (2004) A sequential algorithm for testing climate regime shifts. *Geophysical Research Letters*, 31: L09204. Regime_detection.zip, retrieved April 2013 from http://www.beringclimate.noaa.gov/regimes/index.html

Rodionov, S. N. (2005, June) *A brief overview of the regime shift detection methods. In large-scale disturbances (regime shifts) and recovery in aquatic ecosystems: Challenges for management toward sustainability.* Unesco-Roste/Bas Workshop on Regime Shifts, Varna, Bulgaria (pp. 17–24).

Rodionov, S. N. and Overland, J. E. (2005) Application of a sequential regime shift detection method to the Bering sea ecosystem. *Ices Journal of Marine Science: Journal Du Conseil*, 62 (3), pp. 328–332.

7

USING VOC TO ENSURE PRODUCT LAUNCH SUCCESS

A case study showing how one firm prevented a launch misfire

Linda Trevenen

Introduction

Market launches represent a high investment cost for any firm. There is usually discovery research, feasibility research, development and validation work with the target customers in the market that would make up the minimum effort required before launch. However, why is it that some launches fail so miserably or don't meet their planned targets? Sometimes, leaders of product development teams miss the most basic of all market checks: is the solution providing the expected benefit for the customer? Unfortunately, some leaders focus so much on meeting the original specifications or hitting a launch date that they forget who is using their solution. One may argue that the specifications should be in tune with customer needs and would be differentiated; but, unless you are testing your solution often with customers throughout the process, you may not know if recent competitive entries have altered their expectations by the time you are ready to launch. Markets are dynamic and many factors are in play that impact expectations by the time you are ready to test.

Pricing is the output of how well the team has identified the value the solution they are developing is providing their customer. Value can be defined here as meeting the desired benefits of the customer who needs the solution to do a particular job for them. This job or jobs may have different levels of value, but an astute leader will do the proper voice of customer (VOC) work to determine these critical inputs. VOC is not something done only once, but rather good VOC is done throughout the design process of a new solution development. Either the solution will deliver upon its promise or it won't. To plan for success, a smart leader plans regular VOC checks into their product development process.

This chapter focuses on the strategic pricing decision a new product development team faced and the objective data required that influenced their launch decision.

Company A prevented a product launch misfire by conducting conjoint analysis to determine the best combination of features and likely adoption rate. The data were then used to determine launch readiness and whether the team should: a) do nothing; b) delay the solution launch to make a development change; or c) introduce the solution as is and mitigate what was learned from the research in the market.

Background

Pete, a Product Manager for Company A, was recently assigned to develop a new medical device that is worn by a patient while receiving therapy. Pete has been in this business a while and knows that certain key factors are important for a successful launch. One factor is designing for effective therapy delivery while providing a comfortable patient experience. Another factor is visual appeal, as the patient is usually shown several competitive devices and it is up to the patient to choose the one they prefer for their therapy.

Over the past few years, Company A had been losing position in this particular segment of the market and a competitor, Company B, grew to become dominant in the segment with market shares over 50 per cent. Pete knew that he would need a disruptive solution to get the attention of customers who had switched to his competitor. Pete's key market assumptions are shown in Figure 7.1.

- Aesthetics for this category are not important and were perceived as having little to no value, thereby not considered part of the selection criteria.
- Performance criteria were the central part of the selection criteria with patient comfort and effective therapy delivery as key decision factors (Efficacy).
- Competitor would counter new market entries in this segment with a concession on price to their key customers.
- This category would continue growing among the other categories, propelling it to the leading category in this market.
- Brand reputation of Company A with its new entry is solid and reputable. However, in this class of product, its reputation was a distant #2 to its main competitor.
- Company A had some past missteps in the market with quality and durability issues that resulted in a tarnished brand reputation, therefore new launches were suspect and went through more scrutiny by current customers.
- New product in development was benchmarked against Company B's existing product which was already in the market for several years.
- Company B launched a newer version that focused on the patient's impression and experience, putting more emphasis on improved aesthetics accompanying an already established performance expectation.
- Company B's strong design patents forced all firms in the market to find new ways of solving key design issues as they each had to have their own solution for functional designs.
- Patient compliance and comfort are more important than initial cost of solution.

FIGURE 7.1 Key market assumptions

Company A had reasons to be excited about their latest development. It represented some brand new design elements that would address known customer concerns related to current products. Company A's new design and solution offered:

- Improved performance results compared to existing marketed products.
- A less complex design compared to the existing competition. This could result in higher perceived ease of use.
- A real design improvement vs. its current marketed version.

The heart of the problem

The project was moving along and the team was ready to transfer their final prototype into development. The schedule was locked and any design change would potentially delay the launch date. When designs reach this stage, there is a higher commitment level to tooling, thus increasing the cost of failure if the device does not deliver upon its promise in the market. Therefore, the project team asked a key question: 'Are we absolutely certain that the design will indeed satisfy our target customer as per the business case?' To help them answer this question, they reviewed their internal user trials and external trials with current patients using a similar device for therapy. Pete was being told by his project team that the trial data passed some of its original criteria, but not all of them. Key trial requirements were NPS (Net Promoter Score) score/comments, trial retention rate, performance/attribute ratings and patient comments. Pete was concerned that his product would not meet its intended value proposition. Additionally, when Pete showed the prototype to prospective target customers, it was poorly received. Contrary to internal opinion about probable good customer acceptance, customers strongly disliked the design and voiced their concern for possible discomfort due to plastic components touching the skin. When he expressed his concerns to his superiors that the latest trial data did not meet all of its criteria and that customers' reactions were not acceptable, he advocated for a product redesign and launch delay. Management disagreed, stating the need to get a competitive product into the market immediately as Company B continued to take share and a launch delay would further solidify their leadership position.

Proposed approach – investments in VOC

When Pete realized he had to convince his superiors that putting the current design into the market was a poor strategic move, he chose to conduct a choice-based conjoint study to gather the right data points to justify a redesign. A choice-based conjoint study was chosen among other market studies because it compares attributes of one product with attributes of competing products to demonstrate which attributes resonate with the target customers. These attributes have varying levels, such as different price points, different brands and different attributes and types of materials (see Table 7.1). Conjoint methodology surfaces how buyers 'value' different product and service attributes. Beyond measuring perceived value, conjoint analysis can determine optimum mix of attributes, price elasticity and sensitivity, and can quantify the market share effect of subtracting or adding features. Conjoint analysis is effective in helping to prioritize offering elements for products and services, either in research, development or already on the market. In this case, the product design was finalized, so the conjoint data would have to be very strong for this team to even consider design changes prior to launch.

How a conjoint study is calculated:

- A respondent is presented with several bundles of attributes with each bundle representing a 'product' or 'service'. The respondent is asked to accept one bundle and reject the others or reject all bundles. As a respondent accepts one bundle and rejects the others, the respondent is then presented with several new and different bundles of attributes, each representing new products or services. As the respondent accepts bundles and rejects others, the conjoint software determines the respondent's utility value (i.e. relative importance) of each attribute.
- The conjoint software normalizes the utility value of the attributes to equal 100 per cent.
- If all six attributes were equally important, each attribute would have a utility value of 16.7 per cent (100 divided by 6).
- However, each attribute is not of equal importance; some attributes are above 16.7 per cent and some are below.
- The farther attribute levels are from each other within the same attribute, the more important the difference is to the respondents. (Meaning, it could signal that some customers value one attribute a lot more than another and it is then necessary to understand that attribute among the others.)

When conducting conjoint analysis, it is recommended to conduct the research blind and not identify the company sponsor. For this study, Pete surveyed three different customer groups in his value chain so he could understand if customer's perceptions differed across audiences.

The conjoint study's objectives were to project the new product's market share, project competitive market share once his new product was introduced and

TABLE 7.1 Attribute options

Attribute name	# of levels
Brand	3
Material used for device	4
Configuration of attribute #1	3
Configuration of attribute #2	3
Configuration of attribute #3	4
Price	5

TABLE 7.2 Key features ranked in order of importance

Attribute name	% of levels
Material used for device	28%
Configuration of attribute #1	22%
Price	19%
Configuration of attribute #2	11%
Brand	10%
Configuration of attribute #3	10%

determine how much market share impact there would be if the design changed. Conjoint analysis was used to compare the existing design to new designs in order to determine if design changes would generate the additional share needed to justify the launch delay. It is important to note that too often companies do not consider the short- and long-term costs and risks of degrading the brand if an inferior product is introduced. It is generally believed that brands are easier to grow once you are in a dominant position, but much harder if you are coming from behind and not in a leadership position, which essentially reflects Pete's position.

The conjoint study summarized the six key features ranked in order of importance (see Table 7.2).

When conducting this research, other qualitative data were gathered to provide context for why some features were chosen over others. It is this context that supplies the company with the intensity of the respondents' choices. When showing the design's current material to customers, it was disliked strongly and the alternative received higher preference ratings. The conjoint analysis projected expected market shares for the current design and the proposed design alternatives. The conjoint results showed a low preference and market share for the current design and a much higher preference and market share for the alternative design. This research allowed Pete to recommend and justify the redesign and launch delay in order to incorporate the new material into the product.

The power of VOC and pricing research

During the conjoint work, price sensitivity was also tested and showed that these designs were price sensitive only above a certain threshold price, driven by the customer's own profit models. Relative to pricing strategy, it was concluded that lowering price to enter an already dominant market by Company B would not result in new market share gain because the research showed product features outweighed lower cost. Therefore, when determining optimal price, the range just below the 'sensitive' point made sense. All stakeholder responses to price and product attributes were layered on a graph to understand if there were large variances between customer sets.

Pete held a meeting with the General Manager, the Director of Marketing and the Project Team to review the conjoint methodology and the results. The results were projected to show utility value for materials (Figure 7.2), prices (Figure 7.3) and four other important attributes (not shown).

Various product configurations were constructed and those configurations' utility values were converted to 'preference shares' (a proxy for market share) versus competition. Figure 7.4 shows one of the scenarios using a combination of attributes at various price points.

The conjoint analysis also projected shares for line extension feature sets contemplated within one to three years. The ability to translate feature sets into preference shares and, more importantly, dollars, was powerful.

The conjoint methodology was hailed as a new 'best practice' for this business unit. The scenario above, using the new configuration, shows that a market share impact of a $60 price point versus a $30 price point is minimal. All parties immediately saw the value of delaying the launch and modifying the design as soon

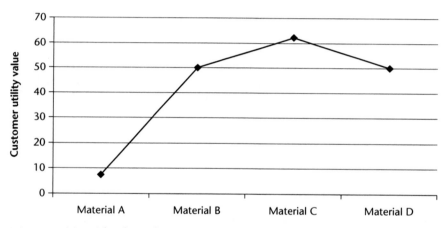

FIGURE 7.2 Material utility values across all stakeholders and all configurations

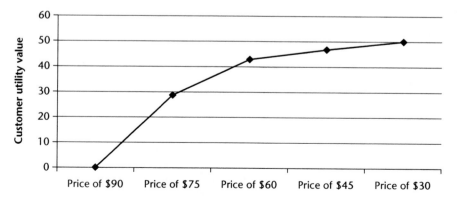

FIGURE 7.3 Price utility values across all stakeholders and all configurations

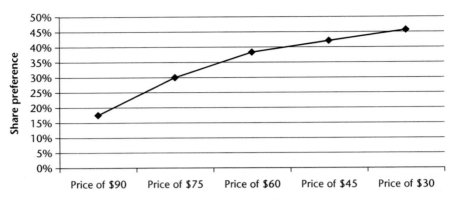

FIGURE 7.4 Share preference for a single product configuration at various prices

as the results were unveiled. There were no longer any objections. Calculating the dollars gained (or lost if the project continued) allowed the stakeholders to easily support and defend the decision to delay launch and invest in the changes. They made a 'data driven decision' rather than a 'date' driven decision. One of the key 'lessons learned' from this effort is to test out the product configurations earlier in the development process. Company A followed Pete's recommendation to redesign the product and delay the launch by six months. The business continues to embrace and deploy conjoint analysis for new projects, as needed.

Before Company A made their decision to delay the launch, Pete combined the conjoint analysis results with previous research findings that emphasized that launching the product without a redesign would create a 'mis-step' in the market affecting both brand and future customer willingness to try new products.

Contribution to the measurement of the impact of pricing

This short case study demonstrates the power of conducting VOC research and more particularly of running conjoint analysis. When done right, conjoint analysis can become a powerful tool to finalize the alternative designs of innovative solutions and to derive the ideal pricing level based on customers' preferences. Pete took the initiative to conduct VOC research versus the option of doing nothing and launching the product as it was originally designed with all the risks that it entailed: inferior design that was known not to be well accepted by customers; missed sales targets; damage in the customer relationship; and loss of trust. The reputation of Company A, relative to its ability to provide innovative solutions, would have been further eroded. Measuring the impact of the 'do-nothing' option is somewhat difficult to do. The best way to start is to calculate the value of the decision to delay and not to conduct additional research. The price of this new product would have been set below current market level due to Company A's market position and the internal beliefs that they should price 20 per cent below their main competitor. The conjoint analysis results that demonstrated the utility of price in the overall offering enabled Pete to set price 20 per cent higher than their original intentions. The additional research also provided a stronger value proposition story for the sales force to communicate at the time of launch. As a result, the impact of this exercise led to a 7 per cent point margin improvement for the new offering and a 20 per cent price improvement. The first six months' sales were estimated to be 60 per cent above where they would have been had the company not made the necessary changes to the design. In a market segment worth $500 million in revenues, the incremental investments of $30,000 in VOC research was money well spent for Company A.

This short case study illustrates a success story for conjoint research investments based on a real experiment. Because the product was ready for launch and all launch parameters were clearly defined, Pete was able to measure the real impact of the pricing research investment. This 'before and after' exercise served as a real life controlled experiment that demonstrated that $30,000 in additional research investment could lead to increased business results. Besides that, the confidence built with the innovation, the product marketing and the sales force was priceless.

8

THE POWER AND IMPACT OF QUICK WINS

Stephan M. Liozu and Mathias Chenal

Introduction

Making the case for large pricing investments and calculating the impact of these investments remain preoccupations of pricing leaders and pricing practitioners. Large-scale transformational pricing projects are difficult to scope and to operationalize over multiple years. While certain types of investments in pricing are easier to justify than others (pricing software, for example), investments in people, training programs, and pricing strategies are a real challenge to measure, to operationalize, and to control for payback.

In order to show the positive impact of pricing, and borrowing from the Six Sigma methodology, we conjecture that quick wins are a good tool for demonstrating the short-term impact of pricing initiatives and for gaining the interest of top executives in pricing projects. Quick wins may be used to promote success stories in the organization and to gain attention from top management for larger pricing programs.

In this chapter, we propose one way to calculate quick wins using a new pricing methodology based on a "before and after" experiment. Although all names, numbers, and information have been disguised for this case study, the foundation, storyline, and process are based on a real experiment as part of an organizational transformation toward value-based pricing.

An experiment to capture quick wins

The journey to pricing excellence is long and sometimes tenuous. It requires continuous change and the integration of pricing knowledge and pricing capabilities. This long journey may take up to ten years, based on some of the corporate presentations given at numerous Professional Pricing Society conferences. Our

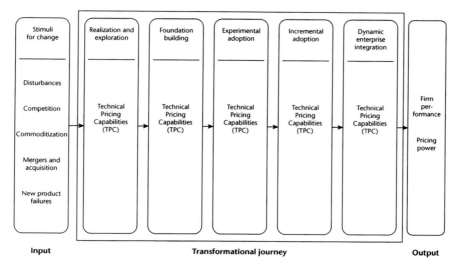

FIGURE 8.1 Stages of the pricing transformation

research shows that firms undergo several stages of transformation in order to build momentum, generate organizational confidence, and create the needed internal success stories, as shown in Figure 8.1. The change process begins with a period of exploration and realization of the internal difficulties related to pricing. During the first three stages of the transformation, quick wins can be used to demonstrate the power of pricing activities and to document pilot-project payback. This is particularly true in the phase of experimental adoption during which pilot programs are deployed.

During this particular phase, quick wins can be used as part of pricing experimentation and problem-solving searches. They can be used as an instrument to generate organizational confidence around successes and quick payback stories to be communicated, celebrated, and elevated to the C-suite. But the preparation, scoping, measurement, documentation, and promotion of these quick wins cannot be improvised. Leaders in charge of the pricing-transformation project must design them up front in order to be able to leverage them when the time comes to request large-scale investments in enterprise-wide pricing resources.

One way to prepare for quick wins is to design and operationalize a "before and after" experiment during the phase of exploration, experimentation, or when the team is ready for a pilot deployment. This type of experiment requires full attention from the pricing leader as well as the support of the business sponsor. It also requires the combining of the legacy price-setting method with the new method being implemented. In our case study, we compared a legacy cost-plus price-setting mechanism with a new value-based price-setting method being introduced to the business teams. In order to operationalize this experiment, we allowed the business teams to set the price for a new product without asking them to consider value-based pricing. Thus, the process was based on cost-based pricing and was pursued "as usual." Then, slowly, through continued discussions, the new methodology was introduced and the team was asked to go back and conduct additional analysis.

Here is a short description of the experiment:

1) Request by the CEO to discuss price setting for innovative product.
2) **First Meeting**: Legacy Pricing Method
   a) Presentation of price to CEO based on cost-based pricing.
   b) Discussion of the method used to set pricing.
   c) Negotiation between CEO and team based on cost-based pricing as well as documentation of main arguments and facts entering in the price-setting process.
   d) Rejection of price level.
   e) Request by CEO to consider value-based pricing and the dollarization process.
   f) Instruction by CEO to the pricing team to assist with this new request.
3) **Second Meeting**: Value-Based Pricing Consideration
   a) Presentation of price to CEO based on value-based pricing: discussion on value drivers, value pool, and value sharing; discussion on the method used to set pricing.
   b) Rejection by CEO of the first pricing level and request for further modelling and consideration of differentiation and value-sharing mechanism.
4) **Third Meeting**: Value-Based Pricing Refinement
   a) Discussion between CEO and team on the dollarization process, price-setting moderator, and revised pricing level.
   b) Rejection by CEO of second pricing level based on revised value models.
   c) Discussion on the need for behavior change in the price-setting process.
   d) Request by the CEO to the pricing team to engage the business team with creative thinking in pricing this innovation.
5) **Fourth Meeting**: Final Price Setting Based on Value-Based Pricing
   a) Team discussion about the revised value models and dollarization levels.
   b) Final price setting of the innovative process and consensus building.
   c) Discussion of the before and after price levels with mindful conclusions.
   d) Exploration of the behavioral and organizational blockages to set prices using the dollarization process.
   e) Request by the CEO to the pricing manager to include a tracker for legacy pricing versus value-based pricing in the pricing council cockpits to demonstrate the success of the customer-based price level.
6) **Pricing Council Meeting**: Debriefing and Discussions
   a) Review the monthly status of sales of new product and situation with price acceptance in the market.
   b) Discuss the "what we did not leave on the table" situation by looking at the tracker.
   c) Celebrate the incremental profits generated by the new product.
   d) Build a case study for the pricing of future innovative products.

This experiment is not a scientific one and is certainly not perfect. But it was planned in advance and allowed us to capture the necessary information to make a point: that there is a better way to price our innovations and that, as an organization, we need to capture the value of our innovation. By formally following the process without telling anyone except the pricing team, we were able to demonstrate the power of psychological and behavioral roadblocks. This allowed us to demonstrate the incremental profits created by the new methodology and to communicate heavily on the success. Finally, it was critical to have the tough discussion with business leaders to challenge them on their approach to pricing and on the need to fully capture value through progressive pricing. Because the CEO was involved in the process, the experiment was operationalized according to plan and delivered the intended outcome. The new product that was launched happened to be a true success for the firm, and the incremental margin delivered through the experiment was significant.

Case study: price setting for an innovative product technology

Product description

The product under consideration was a new and unique veneer plaster product to be applied to interior walls in construction sites. The product is applied once the plaster boards have been installed and the wall requires some finishing. The unique selling propositions of the legacy product and the new product to be introduced were overall coverage and quick drying time, as shown in Table 8.1.

The new product, Veneer Plaster 300 (VP300), clearly shows superior performance in terms of its coverage as well as some improvement in drying time once applied. However, the main innovation resides in the thin layer of application and the superior coverage that cannot be matched by competition. The question became how to price this superior product coverage versus the legacy technology called Veneer Plaster 150 (VP150).

TABLE 8.1 Product description

Products	Veneer plaster 150	Veneer plaster 300
Price	$15.34	To be determined
Proposed bag size (lb)	50	50
Type of plaster	Finishing	Finishing
Color/finish	White	White
Color tint available	No	No
Coverage/bag (sq. ft.)	150	300
Set time (minutes)	50	50

The legacy pricing approach and the rationale

The initial pricing discussion focused heavily on how to price VP300 based on the performance of and prices for VP150. The initial pricing proposal from the business team was to position the product at less than $20 per bag and at slightly over $2 per bag more than the price of VP150, as shown in Table 8.2. The price setting for VP300 represented a 14 percent increase in price and an increase of gross margin of 5 percentage points. This price level also reduced the price per installed square foot from $0.10 to $0.06, thus delivering some excellent savings for the applicators. However, based on an estimated sales projection of 50,000 bags, this pricing level delivered only $60,980 incremental dollars in gross margin.

This exercise clearly showed that the initial pricing decision for VP300 did not capture value in the market sufficient to reflect its superior product performance. The pricing decision was rejected, and further analysis on the basis of customer value was requested of the business team and the pricing experts. An important point is that the threshold of $20 per bag was considered to be a barrier one should not exceed in the plaster industry. The discussions on VP300 pricing also revealed the level of fear and stress in the minds of managers when dealing with the introduction of innovations. A general lack of confidence in the technology was noted and led to some level of irrationality in pricing decisions.

The tough discussion and reformulating process

The initial discussion on customer value and the dollarization exercise led to the identification of the value drivers to consider as well as the main performance criteria to highlight. The consensus led to a focus on superior coverage as a main unique

TABLE 8.2 Legacy and cost-based pricing method

Legacy pricing/cost-based pricing	Veneer plaster 150	Veneer plaster 300
Bag size (lb)	50	50
Coverage/bag (sq. ft.)	150	300
Increase in coverage	Ref.	100%
Cost of goods/bag	$12.27	$13.20
Cost of goods/lb	$0.25	$0.26
Cost increase		8%
Price/bag	$15.34	$17.49
Price/lb	$0.31	$0.35
Price increase/lb		14%
Price/sq. ft.	$0.10	$0.06
Margin	20%	25%
Annual estimated sales volume (bags)	50,000	50,000
Gross profit	$153,400	$214,380
Increase in gross profit	Ref.	$60,980

TABLE 8.3 Main value drivers to dollarize

Value drivers	Veneer plaster 150	Veneer plaster 300
Coverage/bag (sq. ft.)	150	300
Price/sq. ft.	$0.10	$0.06
Brand	Not dollarized	Not dollarized
Value/bag	Ref.	$15.34

selling proposition and on keeping the value story simple and impactful. Therefore, branding was considered "nice to have" and would not be dollarized, as shown in Table 8.3.

The tough discussion at this point consisted in convincing business managers to look at the real value of VP300 and to consider launching the product at a higher price based on real performance differentials between the two products. The issue might have been that these managers understood that the price of the new product could potentially be doubled because of the doubling of its application coverage. The resistance level was already strong at this point of the discussion, as the managers were anticipating a price of more than $30 per bag just by doing some basic math. These managers were considering the uncertainty of this pricing decision under these new considerations and expressed their concerns not only verbally but through their body language.

The outcome of the price-setting exercise: the before and after math

As discussed during the presentation of the experiment, the pricing interaction consisted of several meetings, with additional analysis being requested of the business and the pricing teams. Two iterations of pricing based on the dollarization exercise are presented in Table 8.4. The first iteration consisted of an increase of 45 percent in the price per bag with a bag remaining at 50 pounds. The pricing level of $22.17 per bag generated some additional tough discussion given that the psychological barrier of $20 would be breached.

However, at $22.17 per bag, the gross margin would increase to 40 percent, and incremental gross-margin gains would have been $294,915. The discussion at this point centered on the price per installed square foot and the $20 price-per-bag threshold. This price per bag acted as a strong moderator to price setting for VP300. These are important considerations to keep in mind when setting the price. The bottom line of the experiment is to train leadership and let them experiment with dollarization and value-based pricing. It is not time to play hardball and to get the highest price possible. Based on the $20 psychological ceiling, the group decided to reposition the bag size at 45 pounds, to maintain the price per installed square foot at $0.07, and to maintain incremental margin levels. The goal was achieved as a team, and we protected gross margin while delivering an additional $250,084 in incremental gross margin (see Figure 8.2).

TABLE 8.4 Cost-based versus value-based pricing methods

Products	Pricing options			
	Veneer plaster 150	*Veneer plaster 300*	*Veneer plaster 300*	*Veneer plaster 300*
Cost-based pricing versus value-based pricing	*Existing product*	*New product cost-based pricing*	*New product value-based pricing*	*New product value-based pricing and smaller bag*
Bag size (lb)	50	50	50	**45**
Coverage/bag (sq. ft.)	150	300	300	270
Increase in coverage/bag	Ref.	100%	100%	80%
Cost of goods/bag	$12.27	$13.20	$13.20	$11.88
Cost of goods/lb	$0.25	$0.26	$0.26	$0.26
Cost increase	Ref.	8%	8%	8%
Price/bag	$15.34	$17.49	$22.17	$19.95
Price/lb	$0.31	$0.35	$0.44	$0.44
Price increase/lb	Ref.	**14%**	**45%**	**45%**
Price/sq. ft.	*$0.10*	*$0.06*	*$0.07*	*$0.07*
Margin	20%	25%	40%	40%
Annual estimated sales volume (bags)	50,000	50,000	50,000	50,000
Gross profit	$153,400	$214,380	$448,315	$403,484
Increase in gross profit	Ref.	$60,980	$294,915	$250,084

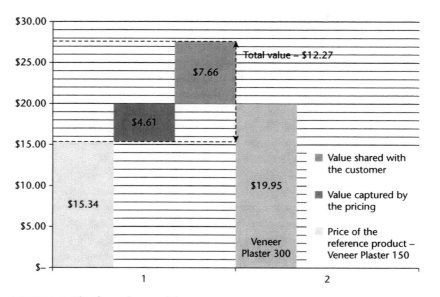

FIGURE 8.2 The first value model

The pricing team had prepared what would become our first value model based on the dollarization exercise we conducted as a team. This value model showed how much value we were capturing based on our pricing decisions and how much value was passed on to final installers. As a team, we felt comfortable with this decision given that the plaster industry is a fairly traditional industry characterized by few behavioral changes. We had to provide an incentive for professional installers to try the VP300 technology. One way to do this was to give them a greater share of the value pool.

Items to be discussed: cannibalization and volume elasticity

Two important elements were to be considered during the price-setting process. The first was a risk of cannibalization between VP150 and VP300 since both products were in the same market space and in the same category (see Table 8.5).

We anticipated little cannibalization based on the price differential and the targeted marketing strategies. The second element we considered was the estimation of volume elasticity based on the volume projections. We had to revisit our volume projections because the price was increased from $17.49 to $19.95 per bag. A quick estimation of volume and gross margin was conducted by the pricing team, as shown in Table 8.5, and we anticipated a minor drop in volume.

Communication of quick wins

The communication of quick wins is as important as their design and documentation. Communicating how the team delivered additional contribution to the bottom line is an excellent way to interest people in learning more about the new pricing method and to get on board with the overall pricing program. The best place to communicate and celebrate the wins is during the pricing council meetings where pricing ROI is formally tracked. Start by walking through the quick win with all relevant decision-makers and identify the main story. Next, document the specific quick win with an internal case study and focus on the positive elements of the win. It is important not to dwell on the way price setting was conducted before or on the psychological breakdowns of some business leaders. It is important to celebrate the new method, the impact of the win, and to communicate this across the organization. That includes discussion in the pricing council but also in the pricing reports, the project newsletter, and the innovation council. At the end, it is all about celebrating success!

TABLE 8.5 Volume elasticity estimations

Elasticity analysis	Veneer plaster 300—value-based pricing—$19.95			
Annual estimated sales volume (bags)	20,000	30,000	40,000	50,000
Gross margin	40%	40%	40%	40%
Gross profit	$161,393	$242,090	$322,787	$403,484

Implications for the measurement of pricing ROI

When designed and operationalized with purpose and with care, informal experiments can be a powerful tool for measuring and communicating the impact of pricing programs. In our case, we used a "before and after" experiment to show the power of the dollarization process in the price-setting process. We also showed a stark contrast between a price-setting process based on legacy and cost-based pricing and one based on customer value and the dollarization method. Our experiment was not perfect and was not rooted in science. It was designed to demonstrate to business leaders that they need to capture the value of their innovation by embracing the economic value estimation process and by dollarizing performance improvements.

This experiment showed the incremental gross margin generated by the same product priced using two different methodologies. The incremental gain of $60,980 for cost-based pricing versus $250,084 for value-based pricing demonstrates the power of customer value-based pricing as a methodology. The quick win of a $189,104 incremental gross margin for 50,000 bags on one product sold in the market can pay for considerable investments in pricing. One can only imagine the power of over 20 or 30 innovative products priced using value-based pricing and sold in the commercial building-materials market.

We make a strong contribution to the topic of pricing ROI by demonstrating the power of quick wins as a tool to:

1) Build organizational confidence among team players.
2) Promote the power of pricing and celebrate success stories.
3) Demonstrate the power of pricing to top executives and to organizational skeptics.
4) Change behavior in price setting and increase the adoption of value-based pricing.
5) Generate quick bottom-line dollars that can pay for a lot!

9

ILLUMINATING VALUE CAPTURE WITH RETURN ON PRICING INVESTMENT

Navdeep Sodhi

Introduction

Managers appreciate the importance of the pricing function within their companies when top leadership starts pressing for increasing profitability. As a result, they strive to enhance their value propositions and sharpen their pricing tactics for expanding products or services, bundling or unbundling features, or improving the customer experience in other ways. But how should companies choose from among many possible initiatives when resources are limited and shareholders demand high returns as well as transparency into strategic decisions?

Senior managers often find their hands full having to decide which of the initiatives should get serious consideration. Complicating choices is the fact that some of the initiatives may be 'strategic' focusing mainly on topline growth over several years – for example, setting up a new high cost plant in an emerging economy – without offering much certainty on benefits or payback. In such cases, sponsorship from the top leadership may allow poorly positioned projects to get started, but without visible results such initiatives could still fail to gather organizational support. Therefore, managers would benefit if proposed solutions were vetted at least on a first cut based on quantifiable outcomes.

Although in theory, every major pricing decision should be supported with analysis at the proposal stage followed by post-facto validation for success, in reality, business environments are rife with gut-feel decisions at the outset and no validation after the initiative. There are flawed practices, such as viewing profitability at the general-ledger level or pricing inadequately with maybe a single ASP (average selling price) for an entire product line or even entire product portfolios irrespective of transaction size, customer set or geography. An example is that some companies run price promotions so frequently that instead of attracting new customers they inadvertently offer deep discounts to existing customers thus eroding margins.

Therefore, it is important to measure the potential impact before and actual impact after completion of each pricing initiative. This should also be done cumulatively for multiple actions to gauge the effectiveness of the company's pricing overall. The basic goal of business is always related to the improvement of the return of improvement (Sloma 1980).

To help managers do that, I start by discussing various hurdles in measuring the return on investment (ROI). After having measured ROI for pricing actions at a major US-based airline, I found the need to adapt current calculation methodologies to meet the nuances of different business environments. I conclude by making a case for return on pricing investment (ROPI) as a standard pricing metric to bring critical focus to pricing and to secure much-needed support from senior management and other internal stakeholders.

Obstacles to accurate price measurement

Changes in regulation or economic conditions, inflation in raw material cost, rising competitive pressure, mergers or organizational reshuffles compel managers to measure and secure bottom-line performance. However, price measurement should not be any less important in normal circumstances when tracking progress of annual business plans or gauging traction of a pricing strategy in the market place. When companies tap the market place for price-related information, customers and channels are reluctant in sharing accurate data. Even internally, managers cannot assume reliable access of their own data given limited or inconsistent senior management support, divergent motivations inherent in organizational silos, scattered legacy systems as well as billing errors that may be out of control.

Senior management support for pricing

In the Wall Street culture, executives manage to quarterly cycles and near-term objectives even when business conditions are good. In pricing, there are various

Pricing level		Organizational level	Frequency of review/ decision-making
Strategic		Senior management	Annual (quarterly, sometimes)
Operational	Tactical planning	Middle management	Monthly/quarterly
	Execution	Managers and their teams	Daily (or continually)

FIGURE 9.1 Timelines associated with pricing activities

timelines for pricing decisions as shown in Figure 9.1. For longer-term initiatives, they require justification which, unfortunately, few pricing departments are able to provide without insightful data. Therefore, short-term focused pricing initiatives that are self-financing get attention over others.

Organizational barriers

There are multiple roles and functions involved in executing pricing strategy (see Figure 9.1). It is important to note that strategic actions invariably require operations support from individuals at different levels in the company (Sodhi and Sodhi 2007). The actual processes vary by industry and/or by company depending on the expertise of those involved and the complexity of the strategy. Whether market facing or internally focused, these processes require pricing people to work with their colleagues in marketing, sales, finance, customer service, IT, inventory management and legal. Since companies are typically organized by business unit, product line, geography, B2B or B2C, direct sales versus other channels and reinforced by separate profit and loss goals, organization silos emerge which not only inhibits collaboration but sometimes encourages unproductive and contradictory behaviour. In this backdrop, measuring pricing or value of a customer relationship across multiple silos becomes challenging.

Pricing process/stakeholder	Strategic (S) or Operational (O)?	Divisional Head	Brand Director	Finance Manager/Analyst	Director Marketing	Marketing Communications	Legal	Global Account Manager	Sales Rep	Customer Service Manager/Rep	Product Manager	Sales VP/Director	Country/Territory Manager	IT Manager/Analyst	Sales Manager	Pricing Director	National Pricing/Contracts Manager	Pricing/Contracts Analyst
Standard list price change	S & O	■		■	■	■			■	■	■	■	■	■	■	■	■	■
Price promotions	O				■	■			■	■	■	■	■		■	■	■	■
Price communication to customers	O				■	■	■	■	■	■	■		■		■	■	■	■
New product launch pricing	S & O	■			■						■	■			■	■	■	■
Multi-brand pricing	S & O		■		■						■	■	■	■	■	■	■	■
Market segment pricing	S & O				■			■			■	■	■	■	■	■	■	■
Custom product pricing	O				■				■	■	■	■			■	■	■	■
Volume incentive programmes and rebates	O		■					■	■	■		■	■		■	■	■	■
Multi-channel pricing	S & O		■					■			■	■	■	■	■	■	■	■
Global contracts	S & O	■						■	■		■	■	■		■	■	■	■
National or regional contracts	O							■	■		■		■		■	■	■	■
Competitive transactional pricing intelligence	O								■	■	■		■			■	■	■
Analysis, tracking and reporting	O			■										■	■	■	■	■
Product life cycle pricing	S & O										■	■		■		■	■	■
Discounts and concessions approval	O							■	■						■		■	■
Scorecards and price reviews	O			■												■	■	■

FIGURE 9.2 Typical roles in various pricing processes

Data governance

Companies amass copious amounts of data in scattered databases that are difficult to access let alone provide useful information. When newly adopted technologies or data systems do not integrate with the legacy systems, they have to be maintained separately thus exacerbating an existing problem (Mackris 2012). Global companies with tens of millions invested in enterprise software may still lack consistent data access across geographies. With rising regulatory requirements as those in the financial sector, companies face critical problems managing the demand for improved transparency and reporting. Even pricing software firms with expertise in converting disparate pricing data into fine-grain information find themselves constrained by geography and business unit architecture.

Skills and efficiency

Price measurement is fundamentally an analytical exercise. Many companies lack adequate analytical skills to convert data into business insight. A few years ago, the CIO of a multi-billion dollar firm was fired for being unable to deliver the various data elements required for a price water-fall analysis that was recommended by a major consultancy. At another company, pricing analysts routinely spend two to three days developing and circulating a semi-automated monthly report detailing price exceptions. Given the lack of clear process or accountability, few recipients review the report while others delete it right away to keep their email boxes under 100 megabytes! Such examples also underscore the need for establishing fit between the data shared with stakeholders and their needs and motivations.

Billing issues

Extensive price exceptions or 'custom' conditions also affect the quality of price-related data. When invoices are wrong due to system problems or human errors, upset customers demand revisions, return products or demand compensatory discounts. Aside from being bad for business, the resulting ASP becomes unsuitable for making sensitive business decisions. No wonder, companies with disciplined pricing and billing practices are also in a better position to communicate value to customers!

Box 9.1 Balanced scorecard

Measuring pricing ROI is not the end-game for companies looking for healthy topline or bottom-line growth. Senior managers would rather envision themselves as pilots in control of a dashboard full of indicators, including those for pricing, to develop strategies, direct decisions and oversee execution (see Figure 9.2). When seeking topline growth, companies may increase prices of products or services or decrease prices for highly profitable customers to gain share. Similarly, in the context of bottom-line growth, companies may eliminate large discounts for highly customized offering or increase prices for overly demanding customers. Viewing revenue or profits by product, service or at a customer level provides an opportunity for tracking the success or failure of past pricing strategies and re-pricing in future.

Pricing ROI measurement at an airline

A major US airline directed their yield and revenue management teams to regularly review bookings in order to minimize spoilage (planes flying with empty seats) in line with the carrier's revenue maximization strategy. If the bookings for a route, say, Minneapolis–London fell short, a price promotion could help reach planned loads.

However, the process for deciding on the appropriate discount level, length of promotion and getting various approvals could take so long that sometimes promising opportunities were missed. Some managers deliberately circumvented critical analysis trying to gain speed but ended up either discounting too deeply or not deeply enough. Given hundreds of such promotions worldwide, the airline decided to switch away from ad hoc decision processes and to carefully monitor which routes required promotions, how rich they should be and in which situations these promotions were most effective.

A senior executive took charge as the final authority for the entire process that included pre-analysis (responsibility of pricing), marketing copy (responsibility of passenger marketing), finalizing terms (also pricing), for legal check (legal) all of which were now completed within 48 hours. The Senior Vice-President personally reviewed assumptions and pre-analysis leading to expected ROI. He revisited the same analysis with actual results of the promotion in the monthly market review meetings.

To ensure consistent analysis and communication, the pricing team developed a single-page spreadsheet template containing five key sections:

1) *Offer Details*: Explained the purpose and description of offer, travel geography or specific routes, promotion period, applicable ticketing dates and travel dates.
2) *Restrictions or Terms*: An extensive menu of restrictions, such as including advance purchase, minimum and/or maximum stay, ability to get a refund, combination with an existing itinerary already purchased, transfer to another passenger or itinerary, eligiblity for frequent flier miles, etc., allowed choosing specific ones based on promotion objectives. Each of the restrictions was accounted for in financial terms, for example, there was a standard internal cost associated with frequent flier miles.

3) *Assumptions*: The assumptions were based on factual data and past experience. For instance, existing fare, average cost of carriage, production costs, number of base passengers in previous year and total forecasted passengers in current period as well as proposed promotional fare guided the estimation of total incremental passengers due to a promotion. Additional considerations to fine-tune the calculation of the true incremental passengers included:
   a)   Dilution (number of passengers who would have flown without the promotion)
   b)   Take-along (additional passengers who would join an already booked passenger to take advantage of a promotion)
   c)   Generation (number of passengers generated by the promotion).
4) *Calculations*: Once the assumptions were specified in the template, it calculated net incremental revenue, contribution per incremental passenger ($), net incremental cost or investment.
5)   ROI: The template calculated the expected ROI based on the formula:

ROI = Net Incremental Revenue/Investment

Net Incremental Revenue = Total Incremental Revenue − Investment
Investment = Total Incremental Cost associated with a pricing action

Figure 9.3 shows an example where 'Investment' includes dilution, credit card costs, carriage costs, production costs and other costs related to applicable. Regular discussions of ROI for pricing promotions during cross-functional market reviews provided consistency in the decision process thus enabling organizational learning to a degree never experienced before. Every business segment contributed in rolling up incremental revenue and incremental costs associated with promotions to develop a company-level view of ROI for all promotions.

ROI measurement at a manufacturing company

Declining price and margin of an industrial manufacturer for several quarters in a row brought critical attention to price leaks and underlying root causes. An important problem was the perpetual quarter-end promotions that were used to make sales plans. Product managers habitually forecasted slow sales by the second month of the quarter recommending quarter-end promotion in the last three weeks of the period. Price promotions always seemed to 'exceed' revenue expectations while no one mentioned the impact on margins. Whereas the objective for most promotions was to attract business from new customers, the lack of analysis or targeted communication, lower prices were offered inadvertently to the mass market.

A new pricing director hired by the company introduced breakeven analysis and ROI measurement for setting expectations for promotions and for measuring their true impact. The analytical rigour and standardized process to estimate revenue

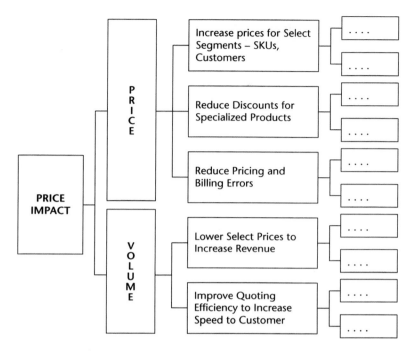

FIGURE 9.3 Balanced scorecard considerations
Source: Sodhi and Sodhi 2007

dilution as an interim step to calculating ROI revealed that the entire promotional strategy required rethinking. After all, happy customers were becoming dissatisfied and holding back on purchases, or buying forward when discounts were available. Senior management mandated an ROI review as part of the formal approval and validation process. In the following quarters, the product teams were able to rationalize the use to quarter-end deals to a bare minimum and with careful customer segmentation.

Case for ROPI (return on pricing investment)

The successful application of pricing ROI at the airline and subsequently at other companies encouraged renaming it ROPI (Return on Pricing Investment), primarily to bring attention to the importance of measuring price impact and to motivate mainstream adoption. To make ROPI an essential tool at any company requires initial preparation for understanding nuances associated with the business in order to define roles and responsibilities and required data elements and to develop a standardized process to gather and review this information. For instance, the data elements associated with net revenue and 'investment' would need to be defined and agreed upon by various stakeholders upfront. While adoption of ROPI may vary by organizational needs at different companies, the essential data elements are:

a) *Investment or total incremental cost*: Typical costs included in this calculation are related to discounts, rebates, giveaways, incentive payments, increased customer messaging with, say, production and distribution of promotional materials, consulting fees if an outside firm is hired and additional costs related to increased production time, overtime, etc. Typically, pricing related work is done by existing employees and does not count as an incremental cost with the exception of when a business unit may have to 'pay' for shared resources which can also be accounted for.

b) *Total and net incremental revenue*: Total incremental revenue is the net gain in sales because of customers buying more versus baseline sales (prior period or revenue forecasted without pricing programme) but accounts for cannibalization or dilution effects. Net incremental revenue is calculated by subtracting total incremental cost from total incremental revenue.

c) *Calculating and interpreting ROPI*: Although ROPI is derived easily from incremental costs and incremental revenues, the results need to be interpreted and discussed in the context of shared objectives and needs of the most important internal customers – the senior management. For instance, ROPI in the case of the airline example was a high positive number given relatively low cost and high dollar returns and therefore justified the action. In the case of the industrial manufacturer, high dilution to the effect of 60–70 per cent would deliver relatively low returns and thereby suggest targeted use pricing promotions (see Figure 9.4). Hence, ROPI is a useful indicator when prioritizing pricing actions, which can be presented more effectively along with the associated net incremental revenue.

I propose using ROPI for measuring not only discrete short-term activities but also medium- to longer-term initiatives (Brealy and Myers 1991) by calculating the

TOTAL INCREMENTAL REVENUE	$1,923,278
TOTAL DILUTION	($222,740)
TOTAL TAKEALONG	$15,652
TOTAL CREDIT CARD FEES	($44,428)
TOTAL CARRIAGE COSTS	($380,999)
TOTAL PRODUCTION COSTS	($25,000)
NET INCREMENTAL REVENUE	$1,265,763
CONTRIBUTION PER INCREMENTAL PASSENGER	$505.44
RETURN ON INVESTMENT	188.04%

FIGURE 9.4 Airline promotion showing high ROI

impact of all interim activities that are measurable. This way, a company can track success of major steps of price improvement initiative or accrue results in terms of building blocks of, for example, product, customer segment or geography.

A word of caution: ROPI is not useful unless companies ensure consistent process and measurement techniques across geographies, products and business units so pricing opportunities can be reviewed fairly. If used correctly and mandated as a discussion topic during business reviews, ROPI fosters accountability for pricing at all levels of the company.

Contribution to the measurement of pricing ROI

I advocate ROPI as a management tool for illuminating value capture through pricing. By adopting ROPI, companies can choose:

- *Organization for pricing*: Senior managers can ratify critical pricing decisions and follow-up based on analysis rather than gut feel or middle-management rhetoric. Pricing teams can enhance their standing in the broader organization by proving their value and, in turn, gain support from the top. Cross-functional collaboration required in compiling data elements and explaining assumptions and results improves organizational learning and agility in achieving shared goals.
- *Raising the bar*: While calculating ROPI, the process of assembling data elements, improving measurability followed by business reviews with engaged team members, leads the company on a path to continuous improvement.
- *From building blocks to balanced scorecard*: An incremental, building block approach comprised of existing and new analytical tools, increasing focus on processes standardization and burgeoning organizational capabilities, enables companies to measure and compare price effectiveness across multiple dimensions, such as by geography, product line, channel or customer segment. Improved visibility into analytically set shared goals helps lower organizational barriers. With greater trust in data analysis, companies can pursue the balanced scorecard in both spirit and practice.

References

Brealy, R. A. and Myers, S. A. (1991) *Principles of corporate finance* (4th ed.). Upper Saddle River, NJ: McGraw-Hill Education – Europe

Mackris, F. (2012) *Flying blind on the route to profits? Use strategic cost management to stay on course.* White Paper.

Sloma, R. S. (1980) *How to measure managerial performance*. London: Macmillan Publishing Co. Ltd.

Sodhi, M. S. and Sodhi, N. S. (2007) *Six sigma pricing: Improving pricing operations to increase profits*. Upper Saddle River, NJ: Financial Times Press.

10

CASE STUDY ON
BREAK-EVEN ANALYSIS

Kostis Indounas

Introduction

Empirical studies have indicated that cost-plus pricing is the most widely used pricing method in a number of different industries mainly due to the easiness related to its practical implementation. This method relies on adding a percentage to the unit cost of a product. However, the problem with this approach is that it does not take into account the market's conditions extensively since its fundamental aim is just to cover costs and have an adequate profit that permits the company to survive in its market. The objective of this short chapter is to highlight this problem and present the well-known pricing strategy of break-even analysis. Through describing the case of a Greek shipyard, the chapter illustrates the advantages of this method over the traditional cost-plus pricing method and the positive impact that it may have on the ROI of its use. More specifically, this method requires a scenario analysis on the basis of which the minimum level of sales that is required so as not to have losses but profits is estimated. Contrary to cost-plus pricing, this method does take into consideration market conditions in that a thorough examination of competitive prices and customers' responses to different price levels is needed in order to estimate this amount of sales.

The Greek shipyard industry

The Greek shipyard industry, like the wider European industry, is in crisis due to the broader economic crisis and competition from countries with low labour costs. The market's leading shipyards have traditionally been Skaramangas, Elefsina, Syros and Avlida. An important part has also been played, mainly with regard to repairs, by the Piraeus-Perama ship-repair zone, which operates on the basis of independent small and medium-sized enterprises. The activities of all these shipyards have at times represented more than 80 per cent of total repairs performed in Greece. The

Skaramangas shipyard is the biggest industrial shipbuilding unit, as far as turnover and number of workers are concerned. During the past 15 years, however, turnover in Greek shipyards has been steadily decreasing, as has the number of persons employed. Up to 1985, Greek shipyards employed about 15,000 primary workers, and around 20,000–30,000 peripheral workers in small industries in the Piraeus-Perama zone: at present, they employ no more than 4,500–5,000 workers. To this end, these shipyards have been forced to make a series of structural changes that are gradually creating the conditions for Greek shipyards to profitably re-enter international markets, where they can enjoy high profitability.

Shipyard A

Shipyard A is a small family owned business that started its operations in the mid 1970s and has traditionally operated in the vessel repair industry. Due to the inability in terms of infrastructure to compete with the large industry leaders, the company's management has decided to focus solely on repairing (not constructing) small yachts, thereby identifying a profitable niche for its activities. The shipyard has been traditionally developed to provide yacht owners with well-equipped facilities and a professional service. It has two dry docks, substantial quay space, fully equipped workshops, a comprehensive range of machinery and equipment and a total work-force of around 50 people. It covers a wide variety of repairing activities from typical machinery and painting repairs to more specialized projects such as re-decoration services.

Until recently, its main clients were Greek private vessels transferring passengers to various Greek islands in the form of boat cruises. However, the entrance of low-cost Asian competitors (especially Korean ones) has transformed the industry due to their low prices, which, in many cases may be 40 per cent lower than the average industry prices. Many traditional clients with relationships of more than ten years that were not quality oriented have preferred to turn to these competitors for lower prices. The saturation of the Greek shipyard industry forced the company to attempt to expand its activities abroad.

Recently, an export manager with considerable experience in exporting (in a fast-moving company) was hired and was appointed the person responsible for the company's export performance. He felt that private yacht owners were a much more lucrative segment than are cruise companies due to their lower price sensitivity and higher quality orientation. This segment would be less likely to be penetrated by low-cost Asian-based competitors. The European private yacht repairing market is estimated at approximately 200 million €. The main competitors are Dutch, Italian, French and German companies. The company would expand its international presence by targeting the most developed European countries where private yachting was popular, including the UK, Germany, France, Italy, the Benelux countries and the Scandinavian countries.

His main suggestions were to advertise the company in specialized shipping journals and various shipping exhibitions that are held all over Europe every year.

This promotional effort resulted in initial calls by prospective customers with similar project specifications, resulting in the expectation that five projects would emerge within 2012. Due to the uncertainties in the new venture, a decision was made to focus on projects facing similar repairing activities. Thus, the variable cost for undertaking these projects would be more or less the same.

The pricing problem in the new markets

Traditionally, for domestic customers, pricing decisions were mainly made through collaboration between the finance manager, the marketing manager and the CEO. However, this process was a rather informal one due to the long-lasting relationships with the majority of customers, which resulted in standard prices over recent years. However, the situation was completely different with foreign customers. All projects, except for some routine repair services, were characterized by specialized services, whose pricing required a completely different process. This fact forced the company to outsource many of these services to external partners (subcontractors).

Initially, the finance manager proposed a variation of the traditional cost-plus method. This method required the estimation of the cost per project as described below. The company's predicted fixed cost for 2012 is 700,000€ (Table 10.1).

The variable cost of each project has been estimated to be 800,000€ (with small variations in case a customer requires something specialized and customized) and is presented in Table 10.2.

Given that the repairing activities are exactly the same, the finance manager divided the fixed costs equally across the expected five projects, resulting in fixed costs per project equal to 140,000€. Thus, the predicted cost of each project would be 940,000€, and the costs of all projects would be 4,700,000€. To calculate the price of each project, the company could add a percentage of profit to this amount. A percentage of 15 per cent (used in the Greek market) was proposed, resulting in a final proposed price of 1,081,000€ per project and, thus, total sales of 5,405,000€ (1,081,000€ × 5) and total revenues of 705,000€.

TABLE 10.1 Shipyard A's fixed cost for 2012

Personnel wages	450,000€
Facilities and equipment maintenance	100,000€
Facilities insurance	30,000€
Electrical appliances	20,000€
Operating costs	50,000€
Depreciation	50,000€

TABLE 10.2 Shipyard A's variable cost of each project for 2012

Subcontractors	400,000€
Raw materials cost	300,000€
Extra personnel wages	100,000€

Although straightforward in its implementation, when discussing the afore-mentioned approach with the marketing manager and the CEO, the marketing manager raised some objections. He felt that market input was not apparent. How would competitors' prices be taken into account? How would customers' needs or the value that they attach to the service be taken into consideration? In a sense, he felt that these issues were considered solely on the basis of the percentage of profit added to the unit cost, constituting the ceiling that the final price can reach. Moreover, what if the scenarios for the five projects did not prove to be real? What would happen if only three or four projects appeared?

In light of the above objections, the CEO felt that a different, more market-oriented approach would be more appropriate. This approach could complement the current cost-plus method. To this end, he suggested that the company should ask the advice of an expert consultant with experience in the field of pricing.

The new pricing approach

When faced with this situation, the consultant suggested a new approach in a meeting with the CEO, the marketing manager and the finance manager. The underlying principle of this approach is that market conditions should be taken into account. Thus, he suggested the *break-even analysis* approach, which is based on the concept of a *contribution margin* given by the following formula:

$$\text{Contribution Margin} = \text{Price} - \text{Variable Cost}$$

The contribution margin (CM) represents the amount of cost that contributes to the firm's fixed costs and profitability. Divided by the price (P), it produces the contribution margin ratio, also called profit volume (PV) ratio, as follows:

$$\text{PV Ratio} = \frac{\text{CM}}{\text{P}}$$

The approach uses the above concepts and formulas to determine the amount of sales (in quantity or Euros) that is required to *break even* (BE), i.e., to cover total variable and total fixed costs (TFC). This is given by the following formula:

$$\text{BE} = \frac{\text{TFC}}{\text{CM}}$$

What is evident from the above, according to the consultant, is that the suggested approach is a value-based pricing method that endeavours to incorporate not only the cost but also competitors' and customers' inputs when levying prices into a single mathematical formula. More specifically, instead of pricing based on a service's cost, the cost contributes to estimating the amount of sales that need to be achieved. In contrast to marketers' perception that price should be based on what customers are willing to pay, price is a function of the value that customers attach to the product. Instead of the traditional approach in many companies where prices are set by only one department or the CEO, a wider, cross-functional co-operation is encouraged. Thus, the financial department could provide the necessary cost-related data, and the marketing department could provide market-related data, especially data related to customers' potential responses to different price levels. Finally, the company's top management could have the responsibility of approving this price.

Regarding market-related data in particular, both competitive potential reactions and customers' attitudes to different price levels must be considered. Thus, the company should understand the value that customers attach to their services. In addition to evaluating this value, the company also has much to gain by estimating the sensitivity of its customers (or, even better, the groups of customers that it targets in the market) to different price levels. As is evident, formal market research conducted either by the company's marketing department or through the aid of an external market research agency can assist a company in this direction. With reference to competitors' potential responses, formulating scenarios regarding how competitors are expected to react to different price levels was suggested as the only solution given the lack of familiarity of the company in the market. Investigating current prices through industry trade reports and industry experts' opinions would be another fruitful action.

To clarify his suggestions, the consultant presented scenarios referring to different proposed prices (Table 10.3). These scenarios reveal the break-even point (in the number of projects and sales) that must be achieved at every different suggested price. If the company desires a profit, it must find more projects than the suggested ones at each price level. To determine this, a thorough market analysis should be undertaken. In a growing market worth approximately 200 million € and consisting of thousands of private yacht owners, the consultant felt that all of the above break-even points (in Euros and number of projects) could be achieved. Although new to the specific market, the existence of long-term relationships within the broader Greek yacht market could result in positive word-of-mouth, and the intense promotional effort would also have results.

In addition, discussions with the editors of specialized shipping magazines were undertaken. These industry experts suggested that many of the vast number of private owners had established long-term relationships with local competitors (mainly Dutch, French, Italian and German ones) and were unwilling to switch to other shipyards. Additionally, yacht repair is a rather unpredictable job because a single yacht may not need any repairs for a considerable period. For a new company, five projects within a single year were an optimistic scenario. If they were in the consultant's shoes, they would not expect more than three projects.

If three projects appeared, each of them should be priced at not less than 1,033 million €. Was this price feasible? How would competitors react? How would customers find this price? The industry experts suggested that for the specific project requirements, an average market price would be approximately 1,000 to 1,020 million €. The strict customer specifications (in terms of raw material quality) limited the opportunity for differentiation. Thus, a higher price than the market average might not be justified and accepted.

The consultant felt that there were three solutions:

1) Lower the price by lowering the cost of the project. However, fixed costs were constant. Only variable costs could be reduced by, perhaps, finding alternative subcontractors.
2) Increase the break-even price by targeting quality-sensitive customers that emphasize criteria other than price when choosing among competing shipyards.
3) Choose a combination of the above solutions.

The third solution was proposed and accepted by the company's top management because its implementation would lead to higher profitability and, despite sacrificing volume, would permit targeting a niche market that would not be likely to switch to competitors in the future merely due to a lower price. To lower the cost, the consultant advised the company to follow the practice of competitive bidding, which would involve asking potential subcontractors to provide offers for particular goods or services. The subcontractor with the lowest bid would be selected, having ensured that the quality of the repair activities would not be sacrificed. The only way to find an adequate number would be through specialized magazines. The company could ask potential subcontractors to provide their offers within a pre-determined period of time. After three months, eight offers were made, which were more or less similar. The lowest bid (750,000€) was then selected.

Regarding the possibility of increasing the break-even price, 20 in-depth interviews were conducted with potential customers from the UK, the Netherlands, Germany, France, Italy and Sweden. The results were amazing. Ten of these customers indicated that they would be willing to accept a higher price if the time

TABLE 10.3 The alternative scenarios suggested by the pricing consultant

Fixed costs (in €)	Variable costs (in €)	Proposed price (in €)	Break-even point*	Break-even sales (in €)
700	800	940	5	4,700
700	800	950	4.67	4,433
700	800	975	4	3,900
700	800	1,000	3.5	3,500
700	800	1,033	3	3,099
700	800	1,081	2.49	2,693
700	800	1,100	2.33	2,567
700	800	1,200	1.75	2,100
700	800	1,500	1	1,500

* The amounts are in thousand €, and the break-even point refers to the number of projects.

of delivery was reduced (most of them suggested a period of not more than one month) and if the company offered the ability to pay the total amount gradually through instalments (two to four instalments were proposed within a time period of six months to one year). Five out of the ten even indicated that they would try the company despite their long-term relationships with competing shipyards. To identify competitive reactions, the technique of mystery shopping was adopted. An experienced marketing research agency's employee was appointed to pretend to be a customer and to conduct 30 interviews with selected competitors. The results were again amazing. Despite the existence of a loyal clientele basis for many of the competitors, most of them (19 in total) indicated that they would most likely examine the possibility of catering to a market segment that preferred to pay a higher price to receive its work on time.

The final solution

After the in-depth interviews, the consultant was satisfied. He suggested a final price of 1,050,000€. The CEO was also satisfied with this price. If more customers appeared, profits would be even higher. The CEO was persuaded that the premium image the company had selected to transfer through its skimming pricing strategy would pay off in the long term. A quality-sensitive market segment seems to exist that can prevent future useless price wars for the company. Thus, despite the willingness of some competitors to cater to this segment, avoiding the possibility of being affected by the increasing pervasiveness of Asian low-cost competitors would be worth the effort. Moreover, the CEO felt that this new pricing strategy would provide a guideline for the company's future pricing decisions, producing better financial results.

Contribution to the measurement of the impact of pricing

What emerges clearly from the above case is that, despite its easiness in use, the traditional cost-plus pricing method has the key disadvantage of not taking market conditions into account to a large extent. In particular, competitors' prices, customers' needs or the value that customers attach to the service are considered solely in an intuitive and informal way on the basis of the percentage of profit added to the unit cost, constituting the ceiling that the final price can reach.

The break-even analysis pricing strategy overcomes this problem. It is a value-based pricing method that endeavours to incorporate not only the cost but also competitors' and customers' inputs when levying prices into a single mathematical formula. Its premises rely on a) the concept of contribution margin, b) the determination of prices through a cross-functional collaboration and c) a scenario analysis on the basis of which the impact of different prices on finding that minimum level of sales that are required in order to have neither profits nor losses is evaluated. Instead of pricing based on a service's cost, the cost contributes to estimating the amount of sales that need to be achieved. In contrast to marketers' perception that price should be based on what customers are willing to pay, price is a function of the value that customers attach to the product. Instead of the traditional approach in many companies where prices are set by only one department or the CEO, a wider, cross-functional co-operation is encouraged where different departments provide different necessary data and top management makes the final pricing decisions.

The contribution of this pricing strategy on the measurement of its ROI relies on the fact that it ensures that the company will at least not have losses through its use if the minimum level of sales that is related to each different proposed price is achieved. Profits will be finally achieved if final sales exceed this level.

11

ALLOCATING PRICING RESOURCES WITH A MORE STRATEGIC ROI CALCULATION

David Dvorin and Vernon Lennon

Introduction

A dedicated pricing team can be an incredibly powerful driver of profitability and revenue improvement for a business. Since effective pricing execution requires alignment of activities, metrics, and behaviors across the entire organization, a central pricing function is uniquely positioned in a business to lead this alignment. A pricing function certainly needs smart talent, clearly defined organizational structure, and active executive support within the business to be successful (Baker et al. 2010). However, a pricing team that is shared across independent business units also requires an explicit and repeatable way to deploy itself across the enterprise.

Few other investments in performance improvement yield as outsized a return as explicit investments in pricing, and so the demand for a shared pricing team's services should quickly overtake the supply of the team's resources. A business with a shared pricing team must therefore have a method for allocating the limited team resources that tries both to minimize the investment required for implementing pricing improvement initiatives and to maximize the financial return achieved by the pricing actions. In short, a shared pricing resource needs a proficient approach to optimize return on investment (ROI).

The key to maximizing the ROI of a shared pricing resource is multi-step engagement sequencing. Rather than treating the investment of a shared pricing team's resources as a one-time event when determining where to deploy, the team must assess and anticipate the potential second- and third-order effects of implementing particular pricing initiatives with particular business units in order to allocate in the most beneficial way.

A brief note on terminology used in order to highlight the applicability of the suggestions contained in this chapter: the authors use the term "shared pricing resource" to specify a pricing team that simultaneously provides strategic, analytical, and tactical pricing services to multiple independent entities. The methodology outlined in this chapter applies equally to corporate pricing functions, internal consulting teams for holding companies, venture, or private equity investment firms, and even companies making a decision about using external pricing consultants. The suggested approaches will not be as directly applicable to single business unit pricing practitioners or teams.

A review of the traditional shared service resource allocation approach will highlight weaknesses with this approach when applied to a shared pricing team. This review will be followed by a discussion of an improved resource allocation approach and the implications of this refined approach on the calculation of ROI for a shared pricing resource.

Beyond traditional allocation

Traditional resource allocation methodologies present a single-step investment and financial return calculation (Bower 1986; Tomkins 1991). The established methodologies certainly include thoughtful approaches for incorporating different stakeholder and financial perspectives into the resource and investment allocation decisions, but they nevertheless fail to account for subsequent impacts across other business entities from a successful pricing initiative at one initial entity. They instead assess the immediate and direct pricing impact at an entity of the shared pricing resource allocation weighed against the investment of that resource allocation (Figure 11.1).

Traditional resource allocation approaches for a portfolio of individual businesses also do not provide a framework that can account for how investing in the pricing capabilities and performance of one business unit can later directly influence the pricing processes and execution of other business units. The well-known Boston Consulting Group's Growth Share or the GE-McKinsey Industry Attractiveness matrices provide strategic guidance on how to deploy resources and investments across a portfolio of businesses at a point in time, for example, but they do not in concept or practice involve second-order impacts or possible portfolio network effects (Coyne 2008; Henderson 1973).

Executing a strategic pricing transformation across an entire enterprise requires the deliberate sequencing of initiatives and entities to ensure uptake of improved pricing strategy and execution. Pricing improvement at its core is about changing commercial and financial decision-making behaviors. Ultimately this involves individual participants breaking away from habitual patterns through improved processes, tools, and training. Pricing improvement relies on the frontline resources in an organization—field sales, customer service agents, service engineers, product managers, and others—to act differently. To accomplish this change of behavior, a combination of top-down leadership together with bottom-up activities and dis-cipline is needed. The order in which initiatives are implemented and individual business pricing champions are created has a direct impact on how the frontline resources of different entities embrace pricing improvements of their own farther

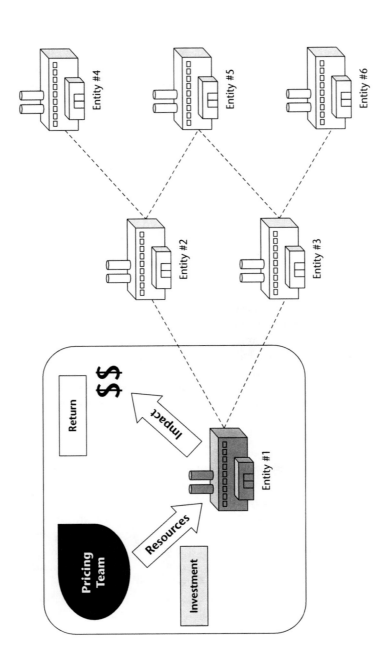

FIGURE 11.1 Impact assessment: one-step

down the line. A resource allocation approach that maximizes the return from a shared price function must therefore incorporate the possibility that a single business' pricing improvement can have immediate and direct domino or ripple effects on other businesses in the portfolio. Unfortunately, the traditional methodologies for allocating shared corporate resources do not overtly include this possibility.

The approach for allocating shared pricing resources outlined below overcomes the weakness of a single-step resource investment decision by explicitly acknowledging the expected impact of a single entity's pricing initiative on the improvement opportunities for other related entities. The suggested approach leverages the investment of resources at a particular entity into other entities by expecting one entity's pricing performance, leadership, people, and tools to directly influence pricing at other entities without requiring the full investment complement of the central pricing team.

Refined allocation approach

To improve on the traditional resource allocation approach, a shared pricing team should proceed through four distinct steps. The first step is the traditional outside-in assessment of potential pricing improvement opportunities at an individual entity. The second step is the estimation of the potential second- and third-order impacts of the individual entity's pricing improvement. The third step is the deployment of shared pricing resources based on the overall expected impact and costs. Finally, the fourth step is the tracking of actual investment costs and performance results post-engagement used to inform future resource deployment decisions.

Step 1: Conduct initial assessment

The Pricing Capabilities Assessment (PCA) process, as defined in "Pricing Due Diligence in the Mergers and Acquisition Process," provides a framework for rapidly analyzing an organization's current pricing performance and predicting its pricing improvement potential (Dvorin et al. 2013). The first step in the suggested allocation approach uses the PCA to complete an initial estimate of pricing improvement opportunity.

The PCA consists of a questionnaire on business pricing strategy and execution that is answered in a one- to two-hour interview with the financial and commercial leaders of a business. The PCA is designed to provide a quick evaluation of the pricing improvement opportunity for a business. The PCA questions are grouped into five categories (Figure 11.2):

1) Overall Strategic Clarity
2) Market Pricing Intelligence
3) Transactional Pricing Management
4) Price Performance Measurement
5) Pricing Organizational Alignment

FIGURE 11.2 PCA: five components

The Overall Strategic Clarity category determines whether a clear pricing strategy exists within the organization, is formally communicated vertically and horizontally in the organization, and is differentiated by markets, product groups, and customer type. The Market Pricing Intelligence category questions ascertain whether a formal knowledge capture process exists, if competitive and supply chain data are stored centrally and used for nominal price influence, and whether price tests are used for validation. The Transactional Pricing Management category questions revolve around the tools used for measuring price performance, the level of data granularity utilized, and whether this information is used to identify new potential selling opportunities. The Price Performance Measurement category evaluates the quality of reporting, dashboards, and scorecards disseminated throughout the organization, and whether pricing is a formal component of strategic plans and quarterly business reviews. Finally, the Pricing Organizational Alignment category determines whether pricing exists formally within the entity as a dedicated function, and if pricing roles and responsibilities are clearly defined.

When completed and compiled, the PCA interview process provides a quantitative estimate of the possible benefit for pricing improvement at an entity. The potential benefit is in the form of a percent improvement of the sales affected by the business. The percent improvement in the PCA ranges from 0 percent to 9 percent. In the original PCA scoring approach, used for adjusting the discounted-cash-flow valuation of an enterprise, negative changes are a possible outcome. When using the PCA for shared pricing team allocation, any negative changes will equal zero improvement opportunity for a business under consideration by a shared pricing team.

Once the PCA process has provided the possible benefit measure, the shared pricing team should then estimate the costs of improvement in order to determine a baseline expectation of return. Both hard costs and soft costs should be considered in this estimate. The hard costs are the salary and benefits for all of the full-time resources or equivalents (FTEs) required for completing the project by the shared pricing team and the business itself, software and hardware costs required, and other department costs if needed, like sales training or marketing collateral. Soft costs, while less intuitive, should also be considered when determining baseline return. Soft costs in this case are defined as leadership voids or change management hurdles that may dilute the potential impact of the project or may extend the time to completion. While soft costs are "gut feel" predictions of timeline extensions and organizational resistance, they may be inferred from the strength of responses to the Pricing Organizational Alignment category questions. The more center-led an organization appears to be from the PCA responses, the less are the soft costs. The soft costs should be quantified as a percent markup of the hard costs of the pricing improvement implementation and included as a contingency in the overall cost estimate of the business improvement.

At the end of this first step of the resource allocation approach, the shared pricing team will have an estimate of the first-order dollar impact for each entity assessed using the questionnaire of the PCA along with an estimate of the costs required to complete the improvement initiative at each entity.

Step 2: Estimate follow-on influence

The second step in the resource allocation approach is to estimate what influence pricing improvement by the entity or entities under consideration can have on other entities across the enterprise. The follow-on influence can take several different forms. There can be an influence on another entity that shares similar pricing environments or transaction dynamics with the first entity. For example, the pricing improvements for a distribution business unit with a wide product portfolio can apply to a different product distribution unit in a relatively straightforward way. The analytical techniques, supporting tools, and improvement actions developed initially for one entity can have direct influence therefore on a business that operates in a similar environment but perhaps with a different geography, product, or service focus.

Another form for expected follow-on influence in an organization is from a common executive sponsor. If the entity where pricing improvement is taking place falls under the same direct general manager as another entity, and that general manager is an executive champion of the pricing improvements at the first entity, then rollout of the pricing improvements to the other entity or entities managed by the same executive can be expected. Given the importance of an executive champion to the success of the initial entity's pricing improvement, having the same champion in place at the potential follow-on entities is very advantageous (Liozu et al. 2012). For example, a division president that actively leads the engagement of the shared pricing team at one of his/her business units will be more likely to drive the follow-on implementation of additional pricing improvements at the other business units within the division.

A third form of expected influence is organizational peer pressure. Across a portfolio of businesses, successful pricing actions taken by a "key opinion leader" in the portfolio can pull forward the pricing improvements at other businesses even if the other businesses have different pricing dynamics or corporate managers.

In multi-entity organizations, the separate businesses typically have variable prior exposure to the concepts of strategic and scientific pricing. This differing exposure to pricing sophistication impacts the estimate of second- and third-order effects of an initial pricing improvement initiative. Business units with prior exposure to successful pricing initiatives and concepts will be more likely to accept, implement, and change more quickly. Variations in each business unit's prior exposure to pricing will also affect their historical price realization rates, which in turn has a direct and substantial impact on the business' ability to implement future pricing improvements (Hinterhuber and Liozu 2012). Thus, the expectation should be higher for follow-on influence from businesses with prior pricing exposure and higher historical price realization than for businesses that have had no prior exposure to strategic pricing and lower historical price realization success.

The specific calculation in this second step in the resource allocation process involves a determination of the likelihood of follow-on results by a single business against the PCA process estimated dollar impact for the other businesses. The likelihood measure indicates to what degree the pricing improvements will happen at these other businesses without the specific involvement of the shared pricing team. This probability factor ranges from a high of 100 percent to a low of 0 percent as the likelihood moves from virtual certainty to practical impossibility. This likelihood factor then is multiplied against the PCA first-order impact estimate to reach a probability-weighted overall impact (Figure 11.3).

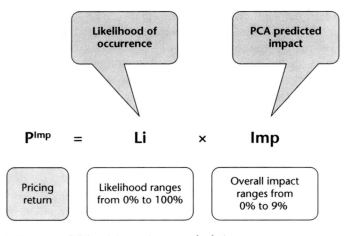

FIGURE 11.3 PCA pricing estimates: calculation

Step 3: Deploy resources

The third step is to actually deploy resources based on the total estimated impact and costs. This step brings together the initial impact estimate from the first step with the potential for follow-on impact determined in the second step. At the end of the second step, the pricing team has a first-order estimate for each entity of the impact of pricing improvements and the pricing team and business resource investments required as well as a probability-weighted estimate of the follow-on impacts of the initial investment.

The team should then deploy its resources in a way that maximizes the estimated ROI by choosing the projects with the greatest return, including first-order and follow-on impacts, from the lowest resource investment. These deployment decisions should be shared broadly with the organization to help build early organizational buy-in for the expected second- and third-order improvement actions.

Step 4: Track actual results

The last step in the suggested allocation approach is to track actual costs and returns to inform where next to deploy the pricing team resources. As pricing implementations are completed, success metrics are paramount to the long-term sustainability of the centralized pricing department. While ROI estimates were used in the initial project selection and resource allocation process, these calculations are refined during the implementation in order to incorporate true project variables like better defined affected sales and actual time allocated. Once these details have been determined, the baseline estimates are compared to actual results.

The baseline accuracy and the rigor used to measure actual outcomes are important since these calculations will have an impact on future resource allocation. Actual performance relative to baseline estimates by different parts of the business and pricing team now becomes an additional variable in the resource allocation process. The potential for a virtuous cycle of improvement is greater for business units that meet or exceed their goals as opposed to those with lower opportunity realization and change management hurdles.

Conclusions

A repeatable resource allocation methodology that incorporates an expansive view of impact from frontline employee buy-in to leadership influence effects is instrumental to the successful operation of a shared pricing function. In order to maximize profitability for the overall business, a central pricing function will need to execute arms-length and rapid PCAs on its multiple entities, assess the potential leverage of investing in a particular business unit, and then deploy resources based on an expansive ROI measurement.

To repeat an important earlier argument, the key to maximizing the ROI of a shared pricing resource is the multi-step engagement sequencing. Pricing teams must look beyond the traditional first-order impact to develop a broader perspective on enterprise-wide returns that encompasses several possible steps along the improvement sequence. Shared pricing teams can utilize this suggested allocation approach in order to improve their ROI measurement, increase their potential impact, and help drive faster pricing transformation across their businesses.

Contribution to the measurement of the impact of pricing

The ROI calculation used for allocating pricing resources across different business entities or companies should in the end include the following factors: expected financial return (revenue and margin expansion), expected investment of resources (FTEs, hours based upon past experiences, and any software/hardware that may be required), soft cost contingencies for organizational obstacles, and the probability-weighted follow-on influence impact estimates.

As outlined in Figure 11.4, the overall ROI for a pricing improvement project takes the first-order financial return from the initial entity and adds the probability-weighted impact of the other entities. This total is divided by the sum of the pricing team's costs, the initial entity's costs, and the follow-on entities' costs of pricing improvement.

The authors' suggested approach for allocating shared pricing resources across a multi-entity business or portfolio enhances the measurement of the impact of pricing in three specific ways. First, this approach expands the definition of return on a pricing investment by explicitly including pricing improvement from other entities that were not immediately included in the initial investment. The impact of the original investment is leveraged in the way that a single business unit's pricing performance can energize, educate, and indirectly incent another business unit to

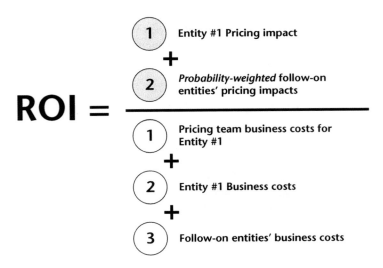

FIGURE 11.4 ROI: calculation

pricing action. The corporate peer pressure on commercial teams and general managers to improve can be a powerful factor in pricing enhancements. By including
these expected second- and even third-order effects of an initial pricing resource
investment, this approach improves the ROI by correctly identifying actions
that only happened as a result of the original investment (Figure 11.5 compared to
Figure 11.1).

Second, this allocation approach permits more selective resource investment.
Just as the expanded definition of return improves the accuracy of the ROI measurement, a more selective investment picture produces a more exact ROI
measurement. The investment included in the measurement of the impact of pricing
is inclusive of all of the first-step activities including the shared pricing team
resources, the business unit dedicated resources, and any supplemental costs for tools
or training. The second-step and beyond impact of the business unit's pricing
improvement on neighboring business units requires no additional incremental
investment of the shared pricing team's time. The ROI measurement of the shared
pricing team is therefore improved by associating a more limited cost lens to the
overall investment and impact calculations.

Finally, this allocation approach directly connects a ROI calculation to the
deployment of a dedicated pricing resource and thereby embeds pricing impact

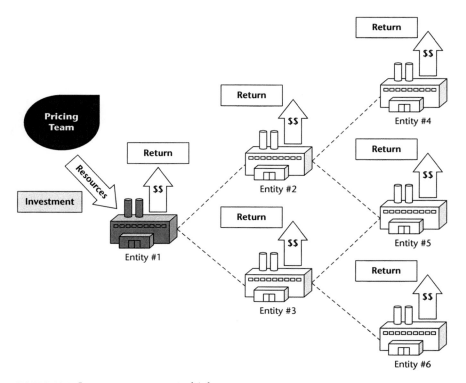

FIGURE 11.5 Impact assessment: multiple-step

measurement within the pricing function itself. This allocation approach in effect makes the impact of pricing improvement the central reason for having a pricing resource in the first place. It fundamentally links the existence of the pricing organization to the financial impact of pricing improvement.

References

Baker, W., Marn, M. and Zawada, C. (2010) *The price advantage* (2nd ed.). Hoboken, NJ: John Wiley & Sons, Inc.

Bower, J. L. (1986) *Managing the resource allocation process*. Boston, MA: Harvard Business School Press.

Coyne, K. (2008) *Enduring ideas: The GE–McKinsey nine-box matrix*. McKinsey & Company, Inc. Retrieved April 2013 from www.mckinseyquarterly.com/Enduring_ideas_The_GE-McKinsey_nine-box_matrix_2198

Dvorin, D., Haedt, J. and Lennon, V. (2013) Pricing due diligence in the mergers and acquisition process. In: Hinterhuber, A. and Liozu, S. (eds) *Innovation in pricing*. New York, NY: Routledge, pp. 197–216.

Henderson, B. D. (1973) *The experience curve – Reviewed IV. The growth share matrix or the product portfolio*. Boston Consulting Group. Retrieved April 2013 from www.bcg.com/documents/file13904.pdf

Hinterhuber, A. and Liozu, S. (2012) Is it time to rethink your pricing strategy? *MIT Sloan Management Review*, 53, pp. 69–77.

Liozu, S. M., Hinterhuber, A., Perelli, S. and Boland, R. (2012) Mindful pricing: Transforming organizations through value-based pricing. *Journal of Strategic Marketing*, 20 (3), pp. 197–209.

Tomkins, C. (1991) *Corporate resource allocation: Financial, strategic and organizational perspectives*. Hoboken, NJ: John Wiley & Sons, Inc.

12

MAKING THE CASE FOR VALUE-BASED PRICING SOFTWARE IN B2B MARKETS

Ed Arnold

Introduction/thesis

For business to business (B2B) companies who choose a value-based pricing strategy, perhaps their biggest organizational challenge is embedding best practices into the actions, decisions and behaviours of their cross-functional teams. Consistent execution is where the 'rubber meets the road'. Otherwise, the significant financial rewards of a successful value-based strategy are missed. One benchmarking study showed that the top 5 per cent firms with a value-based strategy combined with strong executional capabilities outperformed the industry average operating profit by 1.24 times (Hogan 2008).

Yet companies often shrink from systematic implementation of a value-based strategy because of the perception that it is a costly, multi-year change management process (Crouch and Hunsicker 2013; Hinterhuber and Liozu 2012). My experience implementing cloud/software-as-a-service (SaaS) pricing application suggests that need not necessarily be the case. By supporting better collaboration across product, marketing and sales, a company can begin to show positive results in the first year, especially if they possess certain organizational readiness factors. This chapter summarizes the experiences of four large B2B enterprises that have quickly deployed a cloud/SaaS application to support execution of their value-based strategy.

Context: growth of collaborative technology in business enterprises

In recent years there has been an explosion of new consumer technology migrating into the daily operations of B2B enterprises, notably mobile, social, video and cloud. Simultaneously, the dominant corporate computing model has begun to transition from centralized, on-premise applications to third-party SaaS. Findings from a recent study (Csaplar 2013) indicate that 80 per cent of enterprises have adopted at least one cloud/SaaS application, with CRM being the most common.

Cloud/SaaS applications promise better work team collaboration. Professional services firms in particular have taken the lead in deploying this technology because of these specific benefits: better management of dispersed global workforce, knowledge sharing, faster/better decision making, higher degree of on time/on budget project completions and better communication with customers (Castellina 2013). In manufacturing industries, specific benefits include fewer errors, faster response time, increased operational effectiveness and better adoption of standards/best practices (Csaplar 2013). Collaboration therefore is a key competitive differentiator.

True cloud/SaaS applications for pricing are quite limited at this time, both in general and particularly for value-based pricing. For this chapter I focus on one such application to explore the possible impact of technology-enabled collaboration on implementing a value-based pricing strategy. A brief description of this application is as follows: it is used to model and communicate customer value based on the Economic Value Estimation (EVE) methodology as described in the classic book, *The Strategy and Tactics of Pricing* (Nagle et al. 2011). It is important to draw a distinction between this application and other pricing software applications used for price management and transaction analysis. For a deeper description of these pricing software categories see Nagle (2012).

I would submit that the task of value modelling more naturally lends itself to work team collaboration than other types of pricing applications. For example, price management is an operational/control activity; likewise, transaction analysis relies heavily on statistical expertise (often referred to as 'pricing science'). The collaborative aspects of EVE are supported by historical practice in that it has been used by various professional consultancies for nearly 20 years. A recent paper examined the 'conversational' nature of EVE among cross-functional parties both inside and outside an enterprise (Forth 2013). For this reason, I propose that this application is an ideal case study to test my thesis.

Methodology

Since 2009 I have worked with approximately 20 large B2B enterprises in deploying my cloud/SaaS, value-based pricing application. This, combined with several years of collective experience in technology deployment in other contexts, affords me a unique perspective on the potential positive impact of technology on work team collaboration.

To test my hypothesis, I conducted six in-depth, qualitative interviews with respondents at four companies at various stages of deployment (see Figure 12.1, p. 169). Identities are kept anonymous to protect client confidentiality. All of them regard details about their implementation as highly proprietary given their customer base and global competition. Respondents were asked about their company's new product processes, technology deployment experiences, business metrics and related

TABLE 12.1 Key adoption metric (as of April 2013)

Company	Initial date of deployment	Current number of users	Current number of VM/VP*	Usage transactions to date**
A	September 2010	203	370	10,228
B	February 2011	50	71	3,853
C	June 2011	70	110	4,112
D	September 2012	36	42	1,202

* Value Models or Value Propositions
** Includes creation, edits or viewing of Value Models or Value Propositions

topics. The purpose of the interviews was to identify key deployment factors and to provide input to build a pro forma return on investment (ROI). The six interview respondents included a corporate pricing leader, a marketing director, a business development leader, a business unit manager, as well as two pricing managers.

The four companies studied share common characteristics. All are large B2B global enterprises with annual revenues well in excess of $1 billion and deliver above-average financial performance in their respective industries. These companies tend to serve large OEM (Original Equipment Manufacturer) customers with strong purchasing power. They produce a broad range of products including specialty materials, components and technology solutions. Significantly, they all explicitly compete on the basis of innovation, and use a formal new product development (NPD) process. None compete directly with each other. In terms of location, two are US-based, one is European-based and the fourth is a US-business unit of a European parent.

One notable difference among the four companies is the amount of time it has used the cloud/SaaS pricing application. At the time of writing (April 2013), this ranges from six months to over two years. However, in all companies, there exists a significant critical mass of users and content (see Table12.1).

Key findings

All respondents regarded the initial deployment of the cloud/SaaS pricing application as successful as measured in a variety of ways: user feedback, compliance, usage, etc. and that it contributed positively to key business results. Respondents at one particular company were also quite candid about their unique organizational challenges. From the interviews I uncovered five organizational factors that determine deployment success. These are:

1) *Previous experience with value modelling*: Two companies already had a long-established tradition of using EVE models in their NPD process, supported by formal instructor-led training. As one respondent commented, 'this was truly deployment of the tool and not the philosophy . . . We already had that mindset

of value-based pricing.' In other words, a core group of team members understood value-based pricing concepts and had first-hand experience with EVE methodology. The cloud/SaaS application simply provided a common platform for collaboration with others. Yet, even with these experienced teams, the technology deepened their knowledge of value modelling. One respondent explained:

> The old process was just a marketing person at their computer talking with a lot of different people but doing it offline and not really capturing the gist of what it meant . . . but now you can get a bigger group of people together who are subject matter experts in technology, marketing and sales and do this in a couple of hours. So it's fostered a more collaborative process.

At the other two, less-experienced companies, formal training was delivered as part of the cloud/SaaS application deployment. In this situation, even though team members lacked formal EVE training, in many cases they were intuitively inclined towards value-based concepts or had previously built customer ROI models. This is not unusual for companies that explicitly compete on innovation. Also, prior experience with value modelling did not necessarily need to be widespread, but only among the top performers within the product, marketing, pricing or sales functions.

2) *Formal links to the NPD process*: Since the primary goal of a value-based pricing approach is to capture value from product innovation, the need for formal linkage between the corporate NPD process (i.e., Stage Gate) and the cloud/SaaS pricing application seems obvious. At the time of writing, two of the four companies make output from the platform mandatory, whereas at the other two companies the links are less formal or in the process of being established. A respondent described in detail how a formal link works at his company:

> By the time you reach Stage 3, you are expected to have a pretty good idea about the customer value proposition. So if I'm a gatekeeper, I'd be asking a lot of questions about the EVE and what it looks like . . . And when they come back for the next stage I'll ask what have they learned about differential value versus the competitive reference. And if they can't show me that, I'm ready to kill the project. Let's work on something else.

All companies felt the NPD process was the logical first focus for deployment because it is where there is the greatest potential upside for value capture. For a deeper discussion of this topic see Braun (2011).

3) *Proactive and committed program management*: At all companies, a dedicated program manager was tasked with the day-to-day responsibility for establishing

and nurturing the user community for the cloud/SaaS pricing application. One respondent emphasized, 'Somebody has to drive it. Somebody has to keep it alive [by] inviting people to get on, share successes and generate interest. It's essential to have that.' However, there were differences in the level of program management resources dedicated. For example, at one company, a program manager spent up to 25 per cent of time in the first year delivering over 20 workshops with the assistance of another team member. Another company has a team of five pricing managers responsible for deployment. At a third company, the program manager is in the process of implementing an ambitious internal communication program (including incentives such as iPads) to touch upwards of 1,000 product marketing people using events as well as using an internal social media platform.

Patience and discipline are important; one respondent advised: 'I would encourage people to give it a good year to implement [it] and even then it's continuous refining and auditing.' Another: 'You need to have a plan . . . we set milestones and have a monthly schedule and a monitoring system to ensure that users are not going back to whatever they used before.'

4) *Establish a core group of 'power users'*: Two of the four companies have been successful in creating so-called 'power users' early in the process. A power user is someone who is firmly grounded in the concepts of economic value modelling and comfortable enough with cloud/SaaS to serve as a coach to other, less experienced users. In my experience, the conceptual hurdle is more significant than the technology; users become technically competent in about four to eight hours.

Sometimes promising power user candidates need to be initially sold on the advantages of a cloud/SaaS application, since they are often experienced spreadsheet value or ROI model builders. One respondent described a situation where a reluctant power user was concerned about the amount of time he spent creating his first value model on the new application and how quickly that perception got turned around:

> So we went back into the meeting and started a brand new EVE. We took one value driver (which took an hour to build previously) and I said, 'The good news is you already did it, so let's drop it in here.' It literally took less than a minute and then the light bulb went off with this guy. He said, 'I get it now . . . we're going to be able to crank through the rest of these!'

Power users are vital during the initial phases of deployment. Not only do they serve as a valuable 'just-in-time' coaching resource, but they help establish a critical mass of content for others to use as examples. Currently, the number of power users among the four companies ranges from two to ten, or approximately 5 per cent of the general user base. One respondent described using a type of 'tough-love' strategy in establishing the role of power users: 'What I started to say was, "Look, I'm NOT available, why don't you use your fellow colleagues in the region to help you run a session?" Then they started to use each other instead of a third party.'

5)   *Focused, phased deployment*: All companies began with a pilot phase lasting from three to six months and involving three to five cross-functional product teams currently within the NPD process. The choice of product/project team is critical. Obviously it had to be a 'real' situation versus a hypothetical training/ academic exercise. The 'sweet spot' in terms of the product development stage tended to be in the middle to late stages in the process where product functionality is well defined and there is reasonably strong understanding about customer benefits and competitive alternatives. In my experience it is critical to avoid challenging 'edge-case' scenarios, e.g., highly complex offerings, or commodity-like products, or highly competitive bid situations initially.

As for the team itself, a cross-functional group of three to five members across product, pricing and sales functions was best, especially if the team members had decent knowledge of the customer segment (or in some cases a particular customer) and competitive alternatives. Since power users tend to emerge during the pilot, selecting energetic individuals who are comfortable using cloud/SaaS applications is important.

All companies studied limited the scope of the initial roll-out, from pilot through first year to a particular region and/or business unit. Once the user base was in place, then expansion into other regions, business unit and even outside of the NPD process occurred naturally.

Quotes from various respondents describe the journey:

'Now not just [our business unit] but in other businesses throughout [our company] are gaining traction. We showed the [technology] to a number of folks . . . We're getting a lot more demand now than we had in the first year.'

'It's funny; you do the rollout in North America. Then, you do the rollout in Europe and it's the same story: "why do we need this? We have spreadsheets." The same thing happened in Asia. So you have to start all over again, but it's a lot quicker sale in the regions because they can now see what was created in North America. Then they say, "Wow, this is already done. I just need to tweak it and I'm all set."'

'You have to start somewhere. Our somewhere was new products – that was the right place to start. And we have 100% compliance on that. As far as other situations . . . it's not mandated, but as it's needed or requested, it's done. Especially in competitive situations where we lost business or not doing well in the market and you want to understand if you priced it correctly.'

All four companies had strong evidence of at least four of the five factors. Yet the degree of intensity varied – which roughly corresponds to the level of adoption. It seems that these factors appear to reinforce each other. For example, an effective program management effort or previous value modelling experience enables establishment of power users. Likewise, formal links to the NPD process helps solidify a value modelling experience. What this suggests is that the potential for early ROI for a cloud/SaaS pricing application depends on the presence of all five factors in at least some degree and the stronger, the better.

Excluded from the list of factors is executive-level support. All respondents acknowledged its importance, especially if the company has little or no experience with cloud/SaaS applications and where a traditional corporate IT department may push back. I see this situation becoming less frequent because of the trend in corporate adoption of cloud/SaaS applications as mentioned above. I see executive-level support as more of an environmental factor in that it is instrumental for choosing an innovation, value-based business strategy in the first place and ensuring that the organization has the proper processes and program management resources in hand. That is to say, executive-level 'lip service' by itself does not accomplish much.

The greatest challenge to adoption shared by all companies is perceived lack of time. There were universal comments about heavy workloads of team members. At least among this sample of companies, profitable firms do run lean. At one company, overall adoption appeared to be adversely affected due to a large-scale corporate merger. Again, the chief culprit was time, with many integration-related activities distracting managers at all levels. Another company had comparatively minor interruptions because of delays during a parallel implementation of a traditional on-premise pricing system. As one respondent from that company put it, 'I never perceived we had any significant issues with the [cloud/SaaS application] implementation. Compared with other IT projects it was fairly uneventful.' He added, 'And uneventful is a good thing for corporate IT projects.'

Finally, one interesting finding that emerged from the interviews is the definition of three different types of work team collaboration. These are: 1) cross-functional with a business unit, e.g., R&D (Research & Development), pricing and sales; 2) cross-regional within a business unit, e.g., North America to Asia-Pacifica; and 3) cross-division either in the same or across regions. Respondents felt that the first two types of collaboration were significantly enhanced by the cloud/SaaS application. The third type had special challenges in terms of reconciling value within a solution, as well as business rules for revenue and margin sharing.

ROI methodology

My approach to measure the potential ROI for a cloud/SaaS application is Economic Value Estimation (EVE), a methodology first described by Tom Nagle in his classic book, *The Strategy and Tactics of Pricing* (Nagle et al. 2011). Simply stated, EVE quantifies tangible economic value that a customer gains (or loses) by using one product/service offering versus another. The offering is compared to a specific next best competitive alternative (NBCA). The main distinction between EVE and financially based ROIs is that it provides a more direct comparison of the true total costs of ownership (Forth 2013).

In this chapter, I use a version of an ROI formula called the Case ROI Method which is described in a recent article by Beram and Burton (2011). Case ROI presents value in terms of benefits – the revenue gains and cost savings generated by the use of a product or service – net of the value delivered by the next best competitive alternative. The Case ROI formula is: (Total Value − Our Price)/Our Price; or Additional Value/Our Price. The Total Value number comes directly from an EVE model.

To begin, I built a basic EVE model for a hypothetical B2B company, based upon the characteristics of the four studied companies, namely a $1 billion revenue global company (or business unit) with a strategic commitment to innovation in the form of a formal NPD process. Further, I assumed that this company has already adopted a value-based philosophy in order to maximize value capture for new products. Given this context, this particular EVE model quantifies the potential value that a cloud/SaaS application has versus a conventional method NBCA, i.e., discrete, hand-made spreadsheet calculations.

For this EVE model I decided to set the cost of the NBCA at zero. Practical experience has shown that this is the best course of action when the true cost of the NBCA cannot be readily estimated or is not explicitly tracked or budgeted. The cost elements of the conventional methods are essentially time-based – the amount of time employees spent engaging in the value capture activities of the planning process, not to mention the impact of those activities. Rather than be bogged down attempting to quantify these, it is much clearer to reveal them in the value driver calculations, as we will see below.

Building a basic EVE model starts with mapping the offering's features against customer benefits and then to customer economic impacts (value drivers). Figure 12.1 shows the specific differential features of the collaborative technology, e.g., 'common consistent framework', 'reusable standardized logic and data', etc., and how they relate to multiple customer benefits such as 'less time to gather, analyze and act upon strategic data' and so on.

Translating core customer benefits into workable, logic value drivers requires developing a set of viable hypotheses. Inspiration for this came directly from the interviews, samples of which are:

'Previously we didn't use a dynamic tool . . . We could have messed up on something as simple as the competitive price moving up or down 20% and suddenly you may be leaving money on the table, or you aren't closing deals because your solution is overpriced based on the competitive offer.'

'With a spreadsheet you would have been starting all over again and it would have been different depending on who's leading the process . . . What's previously taken them 6–8 hours, they can crank out in an hour.'

Link Features to Benefits

Features \ Benefits	Less time to gather, analyze and act upon strategic data	More up to date analysis to act upon	Reduce downtime because of personnel changes and lost work	More effective knowledge transfers among employees	Increased number of differentiating customer contacts	Better prepared sales teams
Common consistent framework	✓	☐	☐	☐	✓	✓
Reusable standardized logic and data	✓	✓	☐	☐	☐	☐
Easy/automated updates	☐	✓	☐	✓	☐	☐
User/group data access management	✓	☐	✓	☐	☐	☐
Customer friendly output	☐	☐	☐	✓	✓	✓
Cloud-based subscription	☐	☐	☐	☐	☐	☐

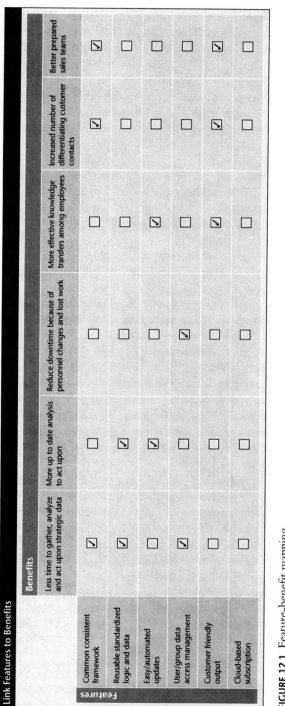

FIGURE 12.1 Feature–benefit mapping

'I got to think we're cutting it [value modelling time] down by 50%. And now [with collaboration technology] it's just a consistent view – across all functions. It has brought a lot of good engagement with folks who weren't as engaged before.'

'We're doing a significantly larger amount [of value modelling] . . . probably 5 to 8 times more because it's so much easier to use the tool, everybody can do it. All of the marketers can do it on their own as opposed to having a facilitator.'

'There's no reason why we shouldn't be able to win more business . . . Last year we won 60–70% of [bids] . . . so we're good when it comes to that. We lose because we're not the cheapest company. We win on technical performance – so why don't we win on [value] pricing?'

'Overall we estimate a 2–4% increase in gross margin on all new projects/ offers dealt with.'

From this I constructed three distinct positive value drivers: 1) better new product pricing decisions; 2) improved new product sales success rate; and 3) reduced time for new product planning. In addition, one negative value driver in terms of additional cost was identified: Program Management Costs. See Table 12.2 for a detailed description of value drivers and Table 12.3 for variable driver assumptions.

The final EVE model is shown in Figure 12.2. Despite using somewhat conservative data assumptions, the model suggests a very high ROI for deploying technology to support stronger collaboration around creating and executing a value-based strategy within the first year. I need to stress that this result does not represent the actual experiences of the four companies studied. This is only a theoretical estimation of possible impacts.

It is also important to bear in mind that over 95 per cent of the quantified differential value comes from two hypothetical revenue value drivers – and that actual results may vary significantly. In my experience, revenue drivers tend to have a much more dramatic impact on value than do incremental cost drivers. Nonetheless, even with much more modest sales performance projections, ROI estimates will continue to be very positive. Although it is fair to look very sceptically at the data, the underlying logic of the value drivers appears solid.

Certainly further company case studies would refine the value drivers and the overall model. It would also be worthwhile to do a multi-year version of this model to show the impact of adoption in future years.

Conclusion

The findings suggest that a cloud-based/SaaS pricing application can accelerate execution of a value-based strategy for companies that compete on the basis of

TABLE 12.2 Value driver definition

Value driver	Logic	Key variables
Better new product pricing decisions	By providing a consistent framework, product teams can make better new product pricing decisions that capture more differential value across a broader set of products.	• Total company revenue per year • Percent new product revenue • Increase in gross margin for new products • Percent adoption first year
Improved new product sales success rate	By providing customer-facing employees with better information to support communicating the value of new products, they can more successfully negotiate higher than average pricing with customers.	• Total company revenue per year • Percent new product revenue • Increase in win rate for new product sales • Percent successful opportunities in first year
Reduced time for new product planning	By providing cloud-based data and user management, product teams avoid lost productivity because of lost work, change of personnel, inconsistent formats and can share best practices.	• Number of employees involved in new product planning pricing • Average hours spent on pricing (per year, per employee) • Average hourly cost per employee (fully loaded) • Percent reduction in new product pricing planning
Program Management Costs	An additional cost in the first year to keep the program vibrant.	• Average management salary (fully loaded) • Percent of time focused on program management (first year)

innovation. Taking into account the deployment experiences of our four company case studies, this technology enables more productive team discussions and decisions around pricing and reduces the amount of non-productive time caused by personnel changes and lost data. Further, it can facilitate a higher degree of knowledge transfer, cross-functionally as well as from more seasoned employees to newcomers.

Admittedly, the ROI estimates of this chapter are speculative and should be considered directional at best. No doubt these findings should be validated with a more rigorous study of employee time spent on planning, and by tracking the commercialization results of new products in terms of value captured. On the latter point, collecting and reporting value capture data has a formidable constraint; more than one respondent noted that doing so would actually undermine their already tough negotiating positions with their large customers. For these customers at least, value capture is a success best enjoyed discreetly.

TABLE 12.3 Variable driver assumptions

Key variable	Data	Source and notes
Total company revenue per year	$1 billion	Assumption based on profile companies.
Percent new product revenue	15%	According to a 2012 Product Development Institute Study, new product sales account for 30% in sales. We took a more conservative estimate.
Increase in gross margin for new products	2%	From customer interviews (see quote above).
Percent adoption first year	20%	Assumption based on author experience.
Increase in win rate for new product sales	5%	Various studies cited in Customer Experience Matrix blog cites multiple Forrester CSO Insight studies that show 5–8% increase in win rates because of marketing automation.
Percent successful opportunities in first year	20%	According to a 2008 study by Alinean, typically 20% of sales deals use tools.
Number of employees involved in new product planning pricing	100	Assumption based on profile companies.
Average hours spent on pricing (per year, per employee)	16	From customer interviews.
Average hourly cost per employee (fully loaded)	$72	Based on salary.com search of fully loaded product management salary divided by 240 (eight-hour) working days.
Percent reduction in new product	50%	From customer interviews.

One of the great advantages of cloud/SaaS applications is the relative ease of technical deployment. Therefore, the main challenge is human, i.e., organizational adoption. The data presented in this chapter suggest that the rate of adoption is related to five organizational readiness factors. These factors are: 1) previous experience with value modelling, 2) formal links to the NPD process, 3) proactive and committed program management, 4) establish a core group of 'power users' and 5) focused, phased deployment. As discussed above, there is a correlation between the level of adoption and strength along these five factors. The rate of adoption can also be judged according to the healthy amount of usage (see Table 12.1) of the collaborative technology itself, which continues to grow monthly. These usage transactions can be interpreted as evidence of collaboration. In my view, human resistance to using collaboration technology itself is not an issue as much as other competing organizational priorities.

Economic Value Estimation of cloud-based, collaborative technology for value-based pricing for a $1B+ global B2B company versus conventional methods

ROI summary
Cost: $72,000
Total value: $2,083,400
ROI: 2,794%

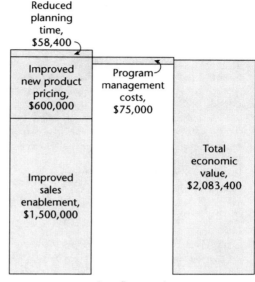

Reduced planning time, $58,400

Improved new product pricing, $600,000

Program management costs, $75,000

Improved sales enablement, $1,500,000

Total economic value, $2,083,400

(per first year)

FIGURE 12.2 Economic Value Estimation and ROI

I certainly expect that the major shift in B2B corporate computing to cloud-based/SaaS applications will continue unabated. Further, the business applications that run on them will undoubtedly become more social as well as mobile. This will have profound effects on the way teams collaborate on strategizing and executing value. In a world where Gangnam Style can get over a billion viewers on YouTube within months, just imagine how far an innovative organization can go by leveraging cloud/SaaS to capture more of its differential value.

Contribution to the calculation of pricing ROI

In this chapter I demonstrate that it is possible to measure the positive impact that collaboration technology has on the execution of a value-based pricing strategy within a company. By using the EVE methodology, it is relatively easy to expose the hidden costs of an inefficient, manual process. Even more significant are the potential gains in making better pricing decisions and developing effective marketing and sales tools for communicating value directly to customers. Deploying technology therefore does not need to be a multi-year leap of faith, but rather a program that can be planned, tracked and adjusted on a near-term basis.

References

Beram, A. and Burton, M. (2011) The case ROI method: Versatile sales. *The Journal of Professional Pricing*, 20 (4), pp. 26–29.

Braun, R. A. (2011) *Improving the value proposition for new products.* Cambridge, MA: LeveragePoint Innovations.

Castellina, N. (2013) *Professional services automation in the cloud: Maximizing employee value.* Boston, MA: Aberdeen Group.

Crouch, M. W. and Hunsicker, G. (2013) The journey to pricing excellence. In: A. Hinterhuber and S. Liozu (Eds) *Innovation in pricing: Contemporary theories and best practices.* New York, NY: Routledge, pp. 178–182.

Csaplar, D. (2013) *The growing importance of SaaS as an application deployment model.* Boston, MA: Aberdeen Group.

Forth, S. (2013) Cross-functional collaboration in value based pricing. In: A. Hinterhuber and S. Liozu (Eds) *Innovation in pricing: Contemporary theories and best practices.* New York, NY: Routledge, pp. 298–309.

Hinterhuber, A. and Liozu, S. (2012) Is it time to rethink your pricing strategy? *MIT Sloan Management Review,* 53 (4), pp. 69–77.

Hogan, J. (2008) *Building a world class pricing capability.* Cambridge, MA: Monitor Group.

Nagle, T. (2012) *Price versus value management – Know the difference.* Cambridge, MA: LeveragePoint Innovations.

Nagle, T., Hogan, J. and Zale, J. (2011) *The strategy and tactics of pricing: A guide to profitable decision making* (5th ed.). Englewood Cliffs, NJ: Prentice-Hall.

13

TRANSLATING PRICING-SOFTWARE-ENABLED CAPABILITIES TO MEANINGFUL FINANCIAL IMPACTS

A holistic approach

Craig Zawada, Jeffery Collins and Doug Fuehne

Introduction

Pricing software is a key enabler to any company's pricing strategy. However, pricing software investments are sometimes presented based on a 'leap of faith' business case that they will generate sufficient Return on Investment. The result is that many companies delay or defer these important investments. However, the impact from pricing from pricing software is very measureable, but takes thought, creativity and pre-planning. This chapter provides specific guidance on which metrics a manager should choose to bring tangibility to its software investments. Managers will increase the probability that pricing projects will get approved, and will increase their ability to move their company to truly world-class pricing performance.

While this chapter deals specifically with pricing software investments, we believe that the guidance on Key Performance Indicators (KPIs) can also be used to measure the impact from any pricing improvement initiative. Most importantly, the creation and reporting of metrics to measure the impact of a pricing software investment is the key step to developing a robust Pricing Performance Management System (see Figure 13.1).

KPIs in context

Constructing an effective Pricing Performance Management System is based on the identification and quantification of KPIs that accurately measure pricing activities and that resonate with key stakeholders. Development of metrics that are mathematically sound and easily defensible is essential to stakeholder acceptance. This implies situations arise where a trade-off must be made between mathematical accuracy and stakeholder acceptance.

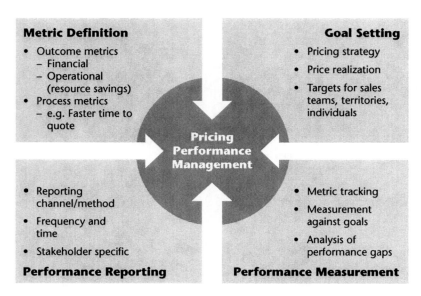

FIGURE 13.1 Pricing Performance Management System

Well-defined metrics empower the ability to manage towards goals – goals that are well accepted because they directly reflect outcomes from stakeholder pricing activities. Finally, the method and frequency of reporting KPIs also drives the acceptance of the metrics.

Measuring the financial impact of pricing software is particularly challenging for a variety of reasons. First, pricing software typically addresses a number of pricing pains; therefore no one metric is sufficient to capture the total benefit. Next, it is difficult to isolate the impact of pricing decisions in general, much less those that have been enabled with pricing software. This poses significant challenges when defining metric calculations and defending conclusions. Finally, some benefits such as efficiency gains are typically considered 'soft' by many companies and although attributable to the software, do not directly impact the Profit and Loss statement. This chapter details specific metrics related to the following categories of benefits reported by companies that have invested in pricing software:

- Pricing Improvement
- Sales Effectiveness
- Pricing Efficiency
- Implementation Success

By identifying a set of metrics and defining robust and defensible calculation methods for each, companies investing in pricing software can create estimates of value that are readily accepted by stakeholders and that accurately reflect the impact of the investment on the business.

Pricing Improvement

Pricing Improvement metrics are designed to measure the impact of better pricing decisions on financial performance. Metrics are typically reported as a change relative to a benchmark value over time. The units are typically sales, revenue and/or margin dollars, but can be reported as percentage improvement depending on the metric being utilized.

The key difficulty in quantifying Pricing Improvement is controlling for other factors that could also impact changes in sales, revenue or margin dollars over time. For example, the following are typically controlled for when quantifying the benefit of software informed pricing decisions:

- Variation in costs of goods sold
- Changes in product mix
- Changes in customer mix
- Changes in volume
- Changes in foreign exchange rates

While not exhaustive, the above factors must be addressed to avoid either overstating or understating the effect of better pricing decisions on key financial metrics.

Finally, the optimal method for estimating the impact of Pricing Improvement from an investment in pricing software is to conduct a well-constructed A/B comparison. This is obviously only possible if the software capabilities are rolled out incrementally regionally, by customer group, or by product line. To ensure a meaningful comparison, it is critical that a representative control group be chosen. Failure to choose a representative control group against which to compare the pricing performance of the test group will lead to spurious conclusions. Table 13.1 details metrics typically used to measure the impact of a software investment on Pricing Improvement.

Sales Effectiveness

Of the functional groups affected by pricing software, the greatest impact is often experienced by the sales organization. Pricing software capabilities can result in more efficient use of time, better pricing decisions leading to higher average margins and increased business. Specifically, pricing software enables greater understanding of the drivers of customer profitability, empowers informed negotiation, allows the tracking of changes in customer behaviour and profitability over time and alerts sales to previously unseen opportunities. For example, pricing software can provide analytics such as customer level pricing waterfalls that enable sales to identify areas of margin leakage or, by comparing a customer to a segment of their peers, differences in product mix that could be leveraged to increase wallet share and customer profitability.

TABLE 13.1 Pricing Improvement KPIs

Metric	Calculation	Insight	When applicable
Pilot region success	Pocket price (adjusted for product mix) improvement in regions adopting tool versus comparable regions not yet using tool	Improvement in price compared to benchmarks – ability to isolate other factors	When rollout is sequential by region or product line
Pocket price premium versus market prices	Pocket price trend compared to industry benchmark prices (i.e., as measured by third parties, or as reported in competitor public filings)	Price premium compared to market prices	When industry price benchmarks exist
Price realization (mix adjusted)	Contribution of P to change in revenue over time (controlling for contribution of mix, volume and change in Cost of Goods Sold (COGS))	Measures the effectiveness of segmentation and process improvements on realization of price changes	Always
Improve product mix	Change in percentage of total revenue from identified high margin products	Shows financial impact of cross-selling. Could also be used to measure the impact of targeted rebate or promotion programmes	When product mix improvement is a key objective
Reduced price variance	Normalized variance of invoice price (coefficient of variation)	Shows increased price discipline within a segment	When reduction in price variance within a segment is a key objective
List price yield %	(List Price − Pocket Price)/List Price – absolute, and trend over time	Improved price realization from list price changes	When company uses list price changes to drive price increases but had historical difficulty in getting actual pocket price improvement
Reduction in price waterfall elements	Period over period improvement in specific price waterfall items	Shows improvement in key areas of discount reduction focus for the company (e.g., Days Sales Outstanding, Freight, etc.)	When there are objectives for better control over specific elements of the price waterfall
Price trend versus historical price levels	Broad measure of pricing – not adjusted for product mix (could be invoice price, gross margins or contribution margins)	Overall improvement in margins and pricing	When product mix is relatively stable

Metrics designed to measure the impact of pricing software on Sales Effectiveness reflect the range of ways in which sales are impacted by software enabled capabilities. Typical metrics used to quantify the impact of software capabilities on Sales Effectiveness include:

- Per cent change in volume sold
- Percentage of salespeople meeting quota
- Change in per cent of quoted deals won
- Change in customer attrition rate
- Volume compliance

Per cent change in volume sold

This metric is relatively general and can be used to capture the impact of a number of software enabled capabilities. As mentioned, improved analytics delivered to sales allow for identification of up-sell opportunities. Moreover, faster quote generation can improve win rates leading to increased sales volume. Finally, win rate can be improved by improving the quality of prices quoted. Specifically, pricing software can increase the probability of winning at the time of quoting by delivering prices that are based on understanding of peer segments and scientifically derived customer willingness-to-pay.

Percentage of salespeople meeting quota

Increased win rate obviously improves the probability of sales meeting pre-established sales quotas. Where quotas are based on revenue or volume, better prices (i.e. prices close to or equal to a customer's willingness-to-pay) and more efficient quoting can increase sales from existing customers as well as increase market penetration, further driving volume. Where sales quota has a margin component, the ability to translate existing data to scientifically derived prices based on customer willingness-to-pay and deliver those prices at the point of sale significantly improves the ability to make quota.

Change in per cent of quoted deals won

This metric provides a more specific measure of Sales Effectiveness when quoting business. However, while more specific in terms of what is being measured, the metric employed without additional context could lead to erroneous conclusions. Sales performance measured purely by per cent of quotes won could encourage strategic behaviour on the part of sales, buying business at the expense of margin. Therefore it is critical that additional metrics that report the quality of deals won also be included in an overall analysis of sales performance.

Change in customer attrition rate

This metric is designed to quantify the reduction in customer attrition through better prices delivered faster by sales to existing customers. As with the previous metric, reporting simply reduced attrition could mask strategic behaviour on the part of sales. A key advantage to pricing software that delivers the ability to compare like customers based on a data driven segmentation is the identification of customers who are at risk based on pricing they receive relative to their peers.

Volume compliance

Pricing software provides actionable insights into customer behaviour including adherence to volume commitments. The metric is used to measure the ability of salespeople to translate the information provided into improved customer performance. Specifically, to empower sales to have a data driven conversation regarding failure to meet volume commitments and either increase sales to forecast levels or adjust price (Table 13.2).

Pricing Efficiency

As mentioned in the introduction, Pricing Efficiency gains are typically considered 'soft' by many companies – more 'indirect' benefits rather than real dollars that hit the profit line. However, the gains from best practice use of pricing software almost always leverage Pricing Efficiency. Without these gains, pricing and sales analysts cannot spend the required time on improving strategy or improved analysis – they are still mired in the day to day grind.

KPIs to monitor the improvement of Pricing Efficiency include:

- Improved time to generate list prices
- Reduction in costs to generate list prices
- Reduction in cycle time to quote
- Percentage of quotes auto-approved
- Reduction in costs associated with review and quoting of deals

Improved time to generate list prices

One of the main efficiency value benefits the authors find is simply generating list prices faster. In one case study, a services customer using a cost-plus strategy had statutory labour costs that increased at unpredictable intervals. While the 'cost' – the pay rate – was required to be immediately implemented, this customer had an extended period where the increased costs were not passed on to their customers via price increases. The result was lost margin for a period of time. Simply improving the speed at which the company could publish prices based on these costs significantly reduced the margin leakage.

TABLE 13.2 Sales Effectiveness KPIs

Metric	Calculation	Insight	When applicable
Per cent change in volume sold	(Current volume − Historical volume)/ Historical volume = % change over time	Impact on sales volume	Always
Percentage of salespeople meeting quota	Number that meet or exceed/ Total number of salespeople − absolute, and compared to prior periods	Quota attainment	Always
Change in per cent of quoted deals won	Current win rate − Historical win rate = Change in win rate	Indicates improved competitiveness of offer-impact of better pricing on win rate and therefore increased revenues	When good win/loss information is available
Change in customer attrition rate (number or revenues)	Current attrition rate − Historical attrition rate = Change in attrition rate	Indicates effect use of price to manage customer churn. Must be balanced against strategic goals regarding penetration and customer quality	When customer attrition is an important metric and easy to measure
Volume compliance	Per cent of committed deal volume ordered	Customer adherence to volume commitments	When customers agree to purchase a specific volume level in exchange for price or other considerations

While these benefits were 'direct', the 'indirect' benefits of increasing price list speed generally involve freeing up time for pricing analysts to be more strategic.

Reduction in costs to generate list prices

Another case study had a customer with a diverse set of list prices being updated quarterly. Prior to pricing software, the analysts created the new pricing (in Excel) using their multitude of leader–follower relationships and strategies for the various markets. The IT team then used 30 staffers (sometimes hiring contractors) and took just under six weeks to load these price files into the Enterprise Resource Planning system to become available for negotiating and invoicing. Following the implementation of pricing software, with automated interfaces into the Enterprise Resource Planning system, the cost to load prices was essentially zero following the pricing analysts work.

Reduction in cycle time to quote

Salespeople often say 'time kills deals'. In several scenarios the authors are familiar with, the customers saw an increase in win rate that led to direct benefits. While win rate is addressed in the Sales Effectiveness section, it is important to note that anecdotal evidence suggests that the same deal offered faster can increase win rate.

If salespeople can get quotes out faster, they can get more quotes out and drive higher revenue for the same unit sales time.

Percentage of quotes auto-approved

Having quotes auto-approved based on the pricing and terms scenarios in the quote contributes greatly to the overall reduction in cycle time to quote.

Reduction in costs associated with review and quoting of deals

As in the case study for automating the creation of price lists, companies who use extensive labour to review and approve quotes often times can put the labour to higher value use (Table 13.3).

Implementation Success

While implementing pricing software packages brings great ease and efficiency to the user, it can be complex to implement. This is due to the number of different business processes it touches as well as the disparity of data that can be required for creating the most effective pricing strategies.

Measuring Implementation Success is important both during selection of a vendor as well as during the project itself. The authors have found that several KPIs are critical to measuring vendor success as well as for measuring your project success.

TABLE 13.3 Pricing Efficiency KPIs

Metric	Calculation	Insight	When applicable
Improved time to generate list prices	Difference between total hours spent to generate new list prices before and after solution	Indicates improved pricing processes	When reduction in time to create a price list is a key improvement area
Reduction in costs to generate list prices	Difference in hours required to generate list prices pre and post solution multiplied by the average loaded hourly rate of pricing resources	Monetized impact of improved list price generation. Valued at the cost of resources employed to review, update and disseminate list prices	When reduction in resources required to create a price list is a key improvement area
Reduction in cycle time to quote	Time2/quote − Time1/quote = Net change	Indicates improved pricing processes	When reduction in time to quote is a key improvement area
Percentage of quotes auto-approved	Auto2/Quotes2 − Auto1/Quotes1 = Change in % of auto-approved deals	Measure of improved pricing processes, reduction in pricing resources dedicated to review and approval of deals. Can be monetized by translating into time and multiplying by the average loaded hourly cost of pricing resources used to review quotes	When reduction in resources required to quote deals is a key improvement area
Reduction in costs associated with review and quoting of deals	Net change in hours dedicated to review and quoting of deals multiplied by the average loaded hourly rate of pricing resources	Monetized impact of improved quoting processes. Valued at the cost of resources employed to review and approve deal quotes	When reduction in resources required to quote deals is a key improvement area

The KPIs are listed and described below, and outlined more fully in Table 13.4 at the end of this section:

- Adoption rate
- Time to go live
- Percentage of users trained
- Deal compliance rate
- Pricing maturity progression

Adoption rate

No matter how good the pricing software is, the value eventually obtained from it will be zero if no one uses the software. The best way to ensure high adoption of the software is following a good change management plan. John Kotter's (1996) eight stage change process provides some good 'leading indicator' KPIs for anticipating adoption rate. Measuring the number and timing of communication pieces, the number and dollar value of quick wins generated and the amount of executive involvement in the project are all suggested ways to ensure that adoption will happen.

Once the software goes live, measuring which users are using the software and publishing those metrics will be a self-fulfilling metric. Also, anecdotal evidence of users making better decisions should be communicated out and will help others get on board.

Time to go live

At the project kickoff, Kotter (1996) would also suggest to establish a sense of urgency with the project team. The value delivered from pricing software is typically so large that any delays can cost millions of dollars in lost opportunity. Phasing your project to realize even small dollars as early as possible generates the quick wins, gains momentum and can even pay for later stages of your project. Closely monitor the target go-live date throughout the project against the planned date, and measure both actual days and percentage deviation from this target. These time-to-go-live metrics should also be evaluated during the vendor selection process, as they can be quite different across the various vendors.

Percentage of users trained

This metric is relatively straightforward, and a good indicator of eventual adoption as well. Your training plan, along with the communications plan, should be one of the main outputs of your change management strategy.

Deal compliance rate

The ultimate metric of adoption is the number of deals or quotes that are complying with pricing strategies published by the pricing team via the software. When sales management can quickly see which sales reps are using published guidance and which are not, and can compare the margin and revenue performance of those two groups, the value of the pricing software can quickly be seen by all. Frequently publishing a list of the top adopting reps, and the lowest adopting reps, engages the competitive side of the sales team and has been proven to be an effective adoption aid.

To help with long-term adoption by sales, including the sales teams as part of the implementation team is critical. The right sales super-users will have great insight into what makes a tool 'adoptable' by your company.

Pricing maturity progression

The prerequisite for this metric is an evaluation of the current state of pricing maturity. Following the implementation of the pricing software, and at agreed-upon intervals such as every six months for two years, another check is performed. Measuring progress against agreed-upon best practices ensures the original intent of the pricing software is preserved.

Any number of maturity profile tools is available for use in base-lining and measuring this KPI. The best tools consider multiple dimensions, such as organizational development, process maturity, strategy development, as well as these KPIs themselves. Typically this KPI set is used only when companies are relatively early on their journey to pricing excellence.

Each of the above metrics should be used as part of a holistic plan to ensure the pricing software is utilized to the fullest and the ultimate metric, total dollar benefit to the company, is realized with the highest likelihood.

Benchmarking and reporting

Once the appropriate metrics have been identified as well as the associated calculations it is critical that past performance be quantified using the defined calculation methodology. The resulting benchmark level of performance serves as a reference point from which current performance is measured. There are essentially two method types of benchmarks that can be used to measure the impact of pricing software against a control or peer group which is representative of the group with access to the software capabilities or against historical performance (see Figures 13.2 and 13.3).

Finally, even well-constructed pricing performance KPIs are subject to some level of white noise or random variation in the data. This requires developing statistical tests to identify what is and what isn't attributable to pricing actions. Obviously, the greater the level of noise within the data, the more difficult it is to identify the impact of pricing actions.

TABLE 13.4 Implementation Success KPIs

Metric	Calculation	Insight	When applicable
Adoption rate	Users/potential users, per cent of deals completed using pricing tool	Tool usage	Always
Time to go live	Go-live date versus plan	Implementation compared to agreed-upon targets	Always
Percentage of users trained	Trained users/users	Skill progression	Always
Deal compliance rate	Per cent of deals at various guidance levels (e.g. below floor, floor to target, target to stretch)	Sales acceptance rate for guidance	Whenever a deal management tool or quoting tool is deployed
Pricing maturity progression	Company completes pricing maturity survey before and after implementation	Company progression along the best practice continuum	When company is starting out at a relatively low level of pricing maturity

Pricing benchmarks

Against past performance	Against peer performance

• Need to control for:
  – Costs
  – Mix
    • Product
    • Customer
  – Exchange rate
  – Seasonality
• Product life-cycle
	• Sequential pricing actions
	• Product or customer
	• Representative peer group
	  – Can use segmentation to define peers
	• Beware of spurious correlations

FIGURE 13.2 Pricing benchmarks

Measuring significant test results

• Test vs. Control
  – Peer
  – Forecast

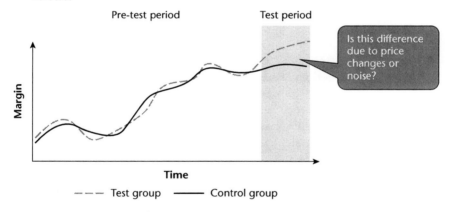

FIGURE 13.3 Measuring results

To become world-class at pricing, companies need to have an investment mindset – wherein there is a continual push to invest and reinvest based on the prospect for additional sales and profits. Pricing software can play a key role in achieving world-class pricing capabilities and should be approached with this same lens. These investments do not need to be a 'leap of faith' business case. The metrics outlined in this chapter will hopefully help you pre-plan your software investments, helping convince senior management that these investments are measurable. After implementation, they will help you ensure that the value is being recognized, and will help with further investments in your pricing capabilities.

Integrating it all together to calculate Return on Investment

In the four categories discussed above, potential KPIs have been laid out with calculations, insights and recommendations on when to use each. When determining the Return on Investment of your pricing endeavour, you need to bring together all of these into one calculation. Here are the steps to take to accomplish this:

1) Pick the appropriate KPI you will monitor and use for your specific situation from the above lists based on your business goals.
2) Categorize the benefits from each one as 'direct', 'indirect/soft' and 'avoided risk'
    - Typically, we see companies calculate two separate Return on Investment – one for direct only, and one for direct + indirect. The risks avoided are always held out separately.
3) Measure the current baseline of each metric.
4) Set targets for improvement in the metrics and the timeframes in which these improvements will be realized.
5) Calculate the dollar value of improvement for each KPI based on the calculations herein and the improvement in the metric from the baseline.
6) Reflect these dollar improvements on a timeline based on Step 4.
7) Calculate the cost of the investment to obtain each improvement and reflect these costs as 'negative cash flows' on the timeline.
8) Aggregate the cash flow streams and calculate a net present value over this timeline.
9) This represents your total benefit number. This can be expressed in terms of net present value, Return on Investment (% positive cash flows by time period divided by negative cash flows), or payback period (time when total cash flow on your timeline = zero)
    - As noted in Step 2, we often see Return on Investment expressed as direct only, direct plus indirect, and a separate category of risks avoided that is not cash flow based.

Contribution to the measurement of the Return on Investment of pricing

Measuring the Return on Investment from any pricing initiative, including pricing software, has historically been a challenge for managers – yet it is absolutely necessary when deciding to invest scarce time and money to investments in advanced capabilities.

This chapter has provided the following contributions to the discipline around Return on Investment measurement:

- Provides a holistic framework to provide measurement of Return on Investment from various lenses including margin, sales, usage and implementation metrics.

- Details an exhaustive list of specific measures along each of these categories and guidance on when each measure is applicable – given different pricing and go-to-market models.
- Provides specific ideas on how to isolate the impact from the pricing initiative in light of external market and economic factors.

The greatest limitation to effectively measuring the performance of pricing initiatives generally, and pricing software investments specifically, is usually not the ability to construct meaningful metrics but the availability and quality of data. To that end, a significant but unintended benefit of any investment in pricing software is often the improvement in availability and quality of data. The Return on Investment of the investment in total – that is in data quality, software and the associated costs of implementation – must be balanced against the transformation of pricing from tactical and reactionary to strategic and empowering business strategy.

Reference

Kotter, J. P. (1996) *Leading change*. Cambridge, MA: Harvard Business School Press.

14

INTERVIEW WITH A PRICING LEADER

Robert Smith, Director of Corporate Pricing for Eastman Chemical

Stephan Liozu: **You have seen me write a lot about getting more attention for pricing in the C-Suite and I wanted to get your thoughts on that. What do you think of such a low level of pricing awareness in the C-Suite or of the low attention paid to pricing in general?**

Robert Smith: I feel like we have done pretty well with that at Eastman. For many companies there is a failure to understand the study from McKinsey which shows the impact of the 1 percent change in pricing, fixed costs, variable costs, and volume, and the substantially higher benefit derived from working on pricing versus the other three areas. People fail to understand the leverage that exists with improved pricing.

That is such a powerful notion from my perspective and so compelling to make it easy to justify investment. Yet I do not know whether people in other companies just do not believe that or whether they are too busy with other priorities.

Stephan Liozu: **When I show that 1 percent chart from McKinsey, I do get a lot of push back from people in general. You do have to make a statement that, all things equal, if you increase price 1 percent, EBIT goes up 10 percent. But then people respond that nothing ever stays the same.**

Robert Smith: Well, that is true. Nothing stays the same. That is one of the challenges, as there are many factors in play all the time. Nevertheless, in a short-term timeframe, one is able to see the impact if a price increase is implemented in an appropriate way in the marketplace. When you implement that price increase and see it stick, and then you'll see immediate financial benefits or results from it. Other factors may have an impact, but on a short-term basis, this is hard to argue with it, from my perspective.

There are a lot of different factors in play out there. If we use that argument, we can say we should not do anything about anything because every factor is moving around. Taking no action is not an acceptable answer.

At some point, we have to take action and when we go back to the McKinsey study, we can see how much impact pricing can have. I have had the opportunity to see enough of it to understand the impact and to see it play out. I think our executives have as well. They understand that we can really make a difference in the business if we are focused on pricing and get serious about supporting it.

Stephan Liozu: **You have had a long career in pricing and you probably were not as mature and sophisticated as you are today. What were the hard lessons for you when you were faced with the justification of pricing ROI? What makes it so complicated to calculate and communicate, in your opinion?**

Robert Smith: First of all, for many folks, attempting to justify pricing ROI is new territory. We may have been involved in justifying capital investments for manufacturing or maintenance, but justifying an investment in pricing in the beginning was a venture into uncharted waters. Companies often possess a victim mentality in pricing as they feel others are to blame for the state of their pricing. Candidates for causing this victim mentality are "dumb competitors," poor industry structure, and the economy, among others. Once a company believes it can make a difference in business performance by taking concrete actions in spite of these factors, then progress in pricing ROI determination can be made.

In addition, since there are many hands involved in the implementation and management of pricing, taking or giving credit must be managed carefully and judiciously. Pricing, sales, business management, marketing, finance, and other supporting groups can all play a prominent role in pricing success, and it's important to share the credit with all. If one mentions that the pricing organization drove the overall improvements, immediately the sales people will raise their hands and say: "wait a minute; we helped out; we had to actually go out there and do it; you guys were just thinking about it." Then somebody in business management may say the same thing: "we saw some consolidation in the marketplace; instead of having five competitors, we have three and that's what really made it happen."

All these things work together, so we have to be very careful in talking about pricing ROI. It is critical to avoid stepping on people's toes or to take credit for what somebody else may feel they have responsibility for. It is better to share and frame it from a team perspective.

Stephan Liozu: **The reality is that you have a very mature pricing organization and you have been doing this for a long time. If you look at early stages of pricing transformation when companies try to get into pricing and require investments, they do compete internally with other capital investment requests right?**

Robert Smith: Yes they do. In the early days, we framed the pricing improvement projects in the same or similar terms as some of the other improvement projects that are being looked at for IT spend. We would review the level of return expected for some manufacturing investment requests and use these as a minimum threshold for pricing projects. Can we deliver that? If we believe we have a valid business case to do that, then that is the basis on which we can try to justify and conduct the pricing implementation.

The bottom line is that what you have to do is work effectively and document the wins that you have. I found that to be particularly challenging because people will claim that they are too busy to do so. We might hear "yes, I'm getting a benefit. I used this tool or process, and it helped me. But every time I have a win at a specific account, I just have a hard time remembering to document the benefits." You have to really drive a higher level of accountability on benefit realization with your team.

One of the things recommended is to define annual commitment contracts that staff should set and should commit to specific goals for a certain level of earnings or contribution margin capture as a result of the pricing actions that they have taken. And if you put this process in place, people tend to start documenting and you can validate your business case that way. It allows you to show a benefit for the collective effort, as well as giving the individuals on your team an opportunity to develop major accomplishments of their own.

Stephan Liozu: **So in essence what I hear you say is that you may want to break down your larger investments into smaller chunks and then force accountability of documented wins? Then you justify by showing wins and you justify larger investments?**

Robert Smith: Yes. You could choose to have a broad company-wide initiative or you could choose to do it in smaller, more-focused efforts. And I am pretty heavily biased towards the smaller, more-focused efforts. I think those are more sustainable efforts because they give you a better chance to win the hearts and minds of people that are involved with them. They see and believe what happens and it is a lot easier to build a supporting structure that will last once the initial project has been completed.

I have talked to people who were trying to do broad initiatives across large enterprises using either a team of internal consultants or a team of external consultants that would work for several months and then would leave. The concern I have with that approach is the sustainability of the efforts. What is left behind when they leave? You may have a short-term victory but a year later are you still going to see everything in place that worked?

In the smaller, more-focused initiatives, it is easier to have a higher degree of success and a higher degree of accountability. Once you get those wins, it is pretty easy to take that success story over to another business and show the case study. So you show what the business did, how hard they worked, and the risks they took. You ask other business leaders: "does that seem like it would make sense for you?" In many cases the answer will be "yes" and then it becomes possible to go and get the next increment. For some people, that is too slow. It could take a few years to do that. But the alternative is to run the risk of doing a "big bang" that looks interesting at the beginning but may not win the hearts and minds of everybody. You may see a short-term uptick but in the long term you really have not gotten any traction or gotten it to stick as well as it could have.

Stephan Liozu: **I also think it is easier to create and justify small chunks of investments. But it does get complicated when you have to justify investments in methodology, tools, training programs, coaching initiatives or other investment in softer things. Have you ever done justification for these—like a pricing training or a pricing council—or do you imbed that into all the programs?**

Robert Smith: We have tried to build budgets in our Corporate Pricing organization to help with that. This was a challenge in the beginning because we started our team at the end of 2008 and the beginning of 2009 when budgets were tight. Every year after that we would just have to look for incremental opportunities to improve our budget and to build and improve skills through effective training and coaching. The best case that can be made for expenditures on some of these softer activities is when businesses are experiencing pain. I find that most leaders are not highly motivated to work on pricing unless they are experiencing some form of earnings enhancement need in their business. We also find that businesses that have new hires who might not fully know their new roles are much more interested in spending on training and making investments at that particular point in time.

The other thing that we have seen from a training perspective is that when we change our systems or processes in some way, it creates an opportunity for us to come back in and train on some details of the functionalities that have changed. We need to help people understand how our tools or processes might be working differently. Sometimes we have capitalized on those opportunities to do some training on pricing concepts so that we help pricers think and act differently. In some cases we have been able to use other training delivery methodologies, and a good example of one we've used recently is Adobe Captivate, where you essentially build training with voice and PowerPoint slides in a way that works automatically. We can make it available to people 24/7 and if somebody is having difficulty performing a specific function, they have got a help site they can go to and get access to without having to call somebody or having to have a training class. That has been a fairly low cost investment we have been able to make and it has not been hard to persuade the businesses to support that. So in the end, it is kind of a similar story to the software investments: if we can have some success stories on a smaller scale, it makes it easier for us to sell a bigger investment at a later time.

Stephan Liozu: **Please allow me to come back to my original question, do you think the difficulty in the measurement of the impact of pricing is more on the scoping side, on the measurement side, or on the communication side? What do you think?**

Robert Smith: Well, it is a tough question because there are difficulties on all sides. The measurement side is a challenging one, and the difficulty is getting people to document gains, as we discussed previously. Documentation is critical, because major investments in pricing capabilities are made over many years and investment money is secured through robust value propositions. We must demonstrate the value capture or we do not deserve to get any more money. So we go to each project team and tell them that their job is not finished until they have completed sufficient value capture to deliver the value we promised when we began the effort.

Our pricing team partners with our business teams to leverage these new capabilities to get the value capture. We jointly start documenting with an interesting accountability approach that may help answer your question. The Pricing Council is the body that is governing pricing investments. Our Corporate Pricing organization helps generate ideas for investments and they bring them to the Pricing Council, which has representatives from each business unit. The Pricing Council determines whether the business units are willing to support the ideas and relevant investments. One of the things that we are doing in the Pricing Council is to review an impact matrix that we show every time we meet. We review investments, benefits business units are getting, and the overall benefit realization rate. So there is accountability in the Pricing Council because the people sitting on the Council represent organizations having made investments in pricing and they are looking for a payoff. So we have created a strong accountability loop there for pricing investments, and it is training people to start documenting value capture better to make sure we are getting back the returns that we are expecting. That loop of feedback and accountability is focused on checking that each investment is tracked and that we are getting the expected payback.

Stephan Liozu: **In essence, before you ask for pricing investment money, you have to show that you can deliver the payback which is typically what other functions have to do anyway. I mean unless it is a business critical investment but the burden of proof for pricing is even higher?**

Robert Smith: Yes the burden of proof for pricing investments is high. Each project is getting scrutinized carefully. You need to have a track record of success and have the discipline in the process to build accountability and credibility.

Stephan Liozu: **Thank you Robert. What would be your top three recommendations for pricing practitioners to make pricing investment justification better or easier?**

Robert Smith: Focus on quickly measurable items. First, you look at other benchmarks in your company of how they have justified ROI and see how they did it so that you can do the same. Second, start measuring easily quantifiable activities such as the impact of an individual price increase. That's a powerful one. How much contribution margin did you have before the increase and how much did you have after it? Third, build a price waterfall to identify opportunities to stop price leakage. That's probably the most important one as you see immediate impact and it creates a very revealing picture of customer profitability.

Stephan Liozu: **Now you have heard me say many times that one of the reasons why the pricing profession is not advancing as much as others is because we, as a profession, have a tough time measuring, capturing**

all these impacts, and selling it to the C-suite. Would you agree with this?

Robert Smith: Yes, I see that in other companies. I am astounded when I hear people in other companies tell me that they cannot get their management excited about working in pricing or about making investments to support pricing. I do not understand that. Some pricing practitioners talk to the top leaders of companies and tell them what improved pricing capabilities, processes, and systems will do. These top leaders say they understand the impact, they believe the numbers, but they are not willing to make these investments. I see companies go back to the same old formula over and over again. Let us get the purchasing guys out and let us work the suppliers over and reduce variable costs. Or, let us go out and let us get more sales volume in an effort to fix everything. Finally, let us cut fixed costs. At some point, you get to where you lose your ability to function as a viable supplier because you've cut so much.

Stephan Liozu: **So would you agree that it is still very difficult to get businesses to jump on the change train when times are good, which is the best time to invest in pricing as well, because you have the money and the cash flow?**

Robert Smith: Yes, I agree with that, Stephan. Typically businesses that are most willing to invest in pricing and the most willing to change are the ones that experience the most pain due to poor profitability. Additionally, there are many outstanding investment alternatives within our businesses, including necessary and appropriate emphases on growth and new product development. The point I would make to our management is that we can and should work on all of these.

Stephan Liozu: **Do you think pricing has a place in the growth story especially when times are good?**

Robert Smith: Absolutely. Pricing is part of the growth story. Every new product will need a well-developed pricing strategy and customer value proposition to ensure the product price reflects appropriate recognition and capture of value. In cases of inorganic growth, it's important to ensure best practices in pricing are being appropriately leveraged in new acquisitions and that our pricing processes and tools enable the new organization to perform at its best in the area of pricing. Also, there are always opportunities in our existing businesses for profit growth through effective pricing. The market continues to change over time and this always creates opportunities for further improvement.

Stephan Liozu: **Thanks. Have you ever calculated the cost of doing nothing in pricing?**

Robert Smith: The way we've looked at this is to show what we are going to miss if we do not launch specific pricing initiatives or we fail to leverage their benefits. In other words, we would focus on lost opportunities. We have also had enough experience with various types of pricing organizational structures in our business units to see the cost of failing to focus efforts on sustaining good pricing practice.

Stephan Liozu: **What is in your view the one most critical dimension for the measurement of the impact of pricing?**

Robert Smith: Accountability in the measurement of the value capture and impact of pricing initiatives.

Stephan Liozu: **Thanks for your time Robert.**

Robert Smith: You are welcome.

15

ROI AND THE IMPACT OF PRICING

The state of the profession

Stephan M. Liozu

Introduction

Measuring the impact of pricing has become a priority for many pricing teams who compete for investments and management's attention with other functions and processes. Pricing professionals understand the need to make the case for these pricing investments and to justify their existence. There are many discussions, but in practice the calculations are difficult.

Whether it is a lack of science or knowledge related to the ROI of pricing calculations or a general lack of skills in the area, the pricing profession does not compete well with manufacturing and R&D (Research & Development), which traditionally have greater experience in securing investments and in getting management attention. My experience shows that a $100,000 investment in manufacturing assets might fall into the discretionary investment budget, while the same investment in a pricing software might require far more convincing and sweat equity.

The purpose of this chapter is to introduce the current state of knowledge about what the impact of pricing is reported to be, to show the results of a dedicated survey on the ROI of pricing, and to lay the foundation for future discussions and research. By conducting this dedicated survey, we wanted to capture what is being done in the field, what difficulties are encountered in the calculations, and what types of investments are measured for ROI and payback.

Impact of pricing: the anecdotal evidence

There is plenty of anecdotal evidence in the marketplace about the impact of pricing. In fact, the positive impact of pricing has been documented by some of the most reputable pricing consulting companies, as shown in Table 15.1. These firms survey their client base and evaluate the ROI and the payback of a large number of projects. While their approach lacks rigor and representativeness of the entirety of pricing, it does provide some interesting data points that may trigger the interest of top executives.

As a pricing practitioner, you might disagree with some of these impact numbers. In fact, in our discussions with them, they are giving us a rule of thumb of a 1 percent

TABLE 15.1 Reported impact of pricing

Source	Impact	Description	Year
Simon-Kucher & Partners	35%	Increase in EBITDA (Earnings Before Interest, Taxes, Depreciation, and Amortization) for firms with higher pricing power.	2012
Deloitte	3.2%	Average operating margin increase of 3.2% for pricing initiatives after 18 to 24 months of implementation.	2012
Deloitte	26%	Companies that are pricing leaders are 26% better at managing true profitability.	2012
Gardner	2–4%	Pricing optimization software leads to average total revenue improvement of between 2% and 4% and a payback of under two years.	2012
Innovation Insights	15%	By 2015, best-in-industry enterprises will increase revenue by up to 3% and profits by up to 15%, due to improvements made using price optimization technologies.	2012
Simon-Kucher & Partners	14%	Companies with a dedicated pricing organization are 14% more likely to expect a (strong) increase in EBITDA in the next three years.	2012
McKinsey & Co	15–25%	Well-executed pricing-improvement program often yields price increases of two to four percentage point or more, sustaining a long-term price advantage may represent roughly 15–25% of a typical company's total profits.	2010
Monitor Group	8%	Firms adopting non-value-based strategies earn 8% less in EBITDA versus their peers.	2008
Monitor Group	30%	Together, the right strategy with an empowered organization can deliver a powerful payoff—operating profits 30% higher than those of low performing firms.	2008
McKinsey & Co	2–7%	Committee leadership on pricing strategy improves a company's operating profit margin by between 2% and 7%.	2002
McKinsey & Co	8.7%	1% point improvement in average price of goods and services leads to an 8.7% increase in operating profits for the typical Global 1200 company.	2001

return to the bottom line as well as a ratio of investment to payback of 7 to 10. So for every dollar invested in pricing, a firm should expect a return of $7 to $10.

The reality is that this is all we have at this time because of the lack of transparent measurement at the profession level. So, in essence, the process for any company is to take these anecdotal numbers and benchmark their potential ROI and payback numbers against them. That helps with a potential guidance on payback but could also create some issues with high expectations inside the firm. Each pricing project is different, and benchmarking could have a reverse effect.

The reality is that we need to measure that impact and start the transformational pricing work. We still face extraordinary circumstances in the economic environment. It is a combination of flat growth, increased cost pressure, and an increase in competitive pressure. So it is not surprising to see many companies announcing mixed results on Wall Street as well as launching another round of cost-cutting efforts. In fact, we have seen the Dow and S&P reach new highs as traded companies make quarterly announcements of expected profitability results. While all companies are facing flat sales or barely increasing volumes, we see a mixed bag in financial results! Companies that announce poor profit results typically seem to blame those results on lack of demand and on commodity pricing pressure in their market space. Leaders are increasingly forced to react to competitive price wars in the market. In fact, 46 percent of executives report being in a price war, and 83 percent blame competition for starting it, as reported by a Simon-Kucher pricing research study (2011). My view is that it is not reasonable to only blame tough market conditions and commodity prices for poor business performance. One of the major differences between firms that are doing well and those that are doing poorly is pricing power and how much attention firms pay to value and pricing management programs. I would venture to say that profit outperformers on Wall Street manage pricing and value management programs with a vengeance. Others simply surrender their pricing power to the market and focus on maintaining market share and capturing volume to maintain sales revenue levels. It is, in the end, a question of culture and focus at the C-suite level.

Survey methods

We designed a cross-sectional self-administered survey to achieve the objectives associated with the current gap in the field of practice. Pricing professionals and leaders involved in managing pricing activities for their firms constituted our population. The survey was emailed to a commercial list of 2,000 such pricing professionals in November 2012. Responses were returned over a six-week period. There were 313 surveys returned partially or fully completed, for a response rate of 15.7 percent. A series of procedures shown to enhance survey response rates of managers were undertaken: 1) all respondents were assured of individual and organizational anonymity; 2) a cover letter explaining the practitioner and academic nature of the research project was included with the survey; 3) two further waves of the survey were sent at two-week intervals, reminding members to respond;

TABLE 15.2 Sample descriptions

Nature of firm		HQ location	
Manufacturing firm	48%	North America	40%
Service organization	36%	Latin America	2%
Retail/distribution	16%	Europe/Middle East	52%
		Asia/Pacific	6%
Number of employees		**Respondent location**	
Less than 500	20%	North America	32%
500 to 1,000	8%	Latin America	3%
1,000 to 5,000	19%	Europe/Middle East	54%
More than 5,000	53%	Asia/Pacific	11%
Firm primary orientation			
B2B	82%	**Total respondents = 313**	
B2C	18%		

and 4) members were offered access to survey results upon completion of the study and were incentivized with a raffle prize. Characteristics of the respondents are provided in Table 15.2.

Survey findings

Our first objective was to evaluate how many of these respondents had a formal process for measuring the ROI of pricing (ROIP). A vast majority (53 percent) do not have such a process, and 14 percent are not sure, as shown in Figure 15.1. There is clearly a need for more adoption of the ROIP methodology presented earlier in this book.

Although they declared that they did not have such a formal process, 69 percent of our respondents agree that it is important or very important to formally measure

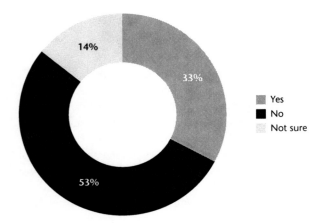

FIGURE 15.1 Existence of formal ROIP measurement process (n=313)

the ROIP and the impact of pricing, as shown in Figure 15.2. Only 4 percent reported that it was not important or not important at all to make these calculations.

We then asked our pricing professionals to evaluate the success of their ROIP calculation on a scale of 1 to 7 (with 1 representing *poorly* and 7 *very good*) for four different types of measurements.

The results shown in Table 15.3 indicate that pricing practitioners struggle across the board and do not qualify their process as successful, with scores between 3.5 and 4. They seem to do a better job of measuring ROIP for their specific pricing initiatives and projects versus pricing systems or overall transformational projects. Pricing professionals in B2C firms seem to have slightly more success in calculating their overall pricing function, with an average score of 4.1.

When asked about their measurement objectives for ROIP, respondents focused on measuring the impact and ROIP of pilot projects for pricing programs (39 percent), as shown in Figure 15.3. Generally speaking, management will ask for proof of the impact of the pricing project by recommending a pilot program be run. Second on the list is the measurement of the comprehensive corporate pricing program, which is, in my experience, the most complex ROIP calculation to make.

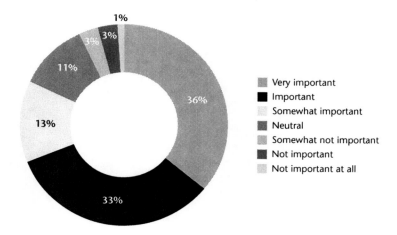

FIGURE 15.2 Declared importance of measuring ROIP (n=203)

TABLE 15.3 Success in measuring ROI (n=313)

	Total	*B2B*	*B2C*
Pricing initiatives and projects	3.93	3.9	4.0
Pricing function	3.60	**3.5**	**4.1**
Pricing systems	3.53	3.5	3.7
Overall pricing transformation	3.53	3.5	3.7

Note: Numbers in bold are significantly different at 95% confidence.

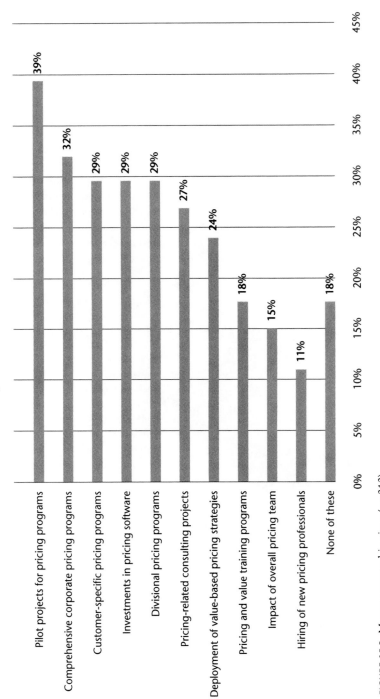

What do you measure ROI for?

Category	Percentage
Pilot projects for pricing programs	39%
Comprehensive corporate pricing programs	32%
Customer-specific pricing programs	29%
Investments in pricing software	29%
Divisional pricing programs	29%
Pricing-related consulting projects	27%
Deployment of value-based pricing strategies	24%
Pricing and value training programs	18%
Impact of overall pricing team	15%
Hiring of new pricing professionals	11%
None of these	18%

FIGURE 15.3 Measurement objectives (n=313)

It is interesting to point out that the human-resources-related dimensions of pricing investments are not frequently measured. Only 11 percent of respondents measure the ROI of hiring pricing professionals, 15 percent measure the impact of the overall pricing team, and 18 percent measure the ROI for training programs.

Most of the ROIP calculations and impact measurements are conducted by internal pricing analysts, as shown in Figure 15.4. Financial staff and business analysts also seem to get involved.

The difference between the involvement levels of management consultants (48 percent) and pricing consultants (10 percent) is quite staggering. That seems to indicate that pricing consulting firms may lack the proper tools and skills to assist pricing practitioners with these calculations.

One of the critical elements of a progressive ROIP measurement process is to be able to extract the incremental impact of pricing to the P&L (Profit & Loss). This is where many discussions typically happen. First, the extraction is complicated. Second, it is difficult to isolate the pricing effect. When asked about the focus on their ROIP measurement, a majority of respondents declare that they track the incremental gross margin from pricing (59 percent) or increase in sales revenues due to pricing (57 percent), as shown in Figure 15.5.

Few track the pricing power in the marketplace (19 percent) or the impact of new products (27 percent). It is also remarkable that only 36 percent of respondents are able to track the incremental operating profit margin from pricing. This may be due to the difficulty of isolating the incremental effect of pricing all the way down to the operating profit line.

This is probably why respondents rated the estimation of the isolated effect of pricing as the most difficult thing to measure the impact of the overall pricing function, as shown in Figure 15.6 (scale of 1 to 7, with 1 being *very simple* to 7 being *very difficult*). This isolation mechanism is critical to measuring the impact and ROI of pricing but also to being able to respond to other functions' objections, who typically take credit for the improvement in the top or bottom line. This has to be

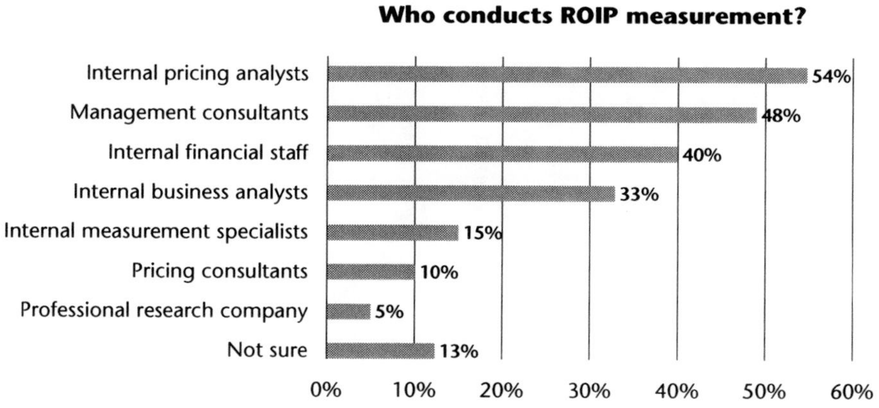

Who conducts ROIP measurement?

FIGURE 15.4 Measurement responsibility (n=313)

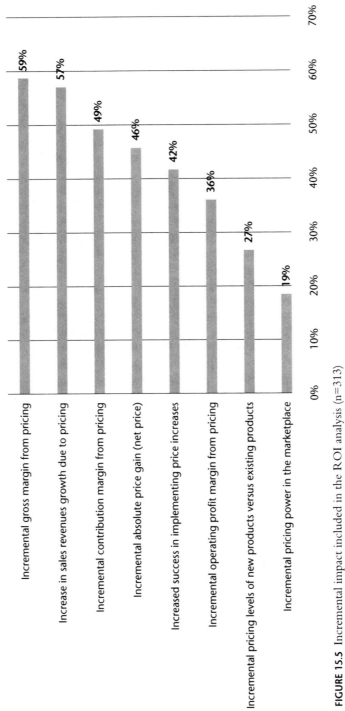

FIGURE 15.5 Incremental impact included in the ROI analysis (n=313)

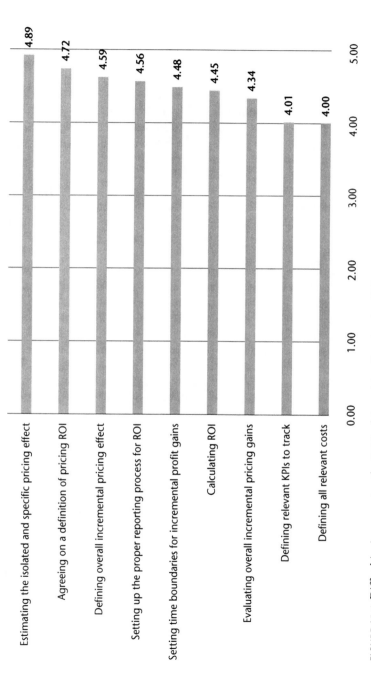

FIGURE 15.6 Difficulties in measuring the ROI of the pricing function (n=204)

TABLE 15.4 Trends in pricing

In 2012 versus 2011, your _____ has/is . . .?	Increased	About the same	Decreased
Use of pricing tools	47%	47%	6%
Investments in pricing	39%	48%	13%
Pricing headcount	24%	64%	12%

an area of focus for the profession if they want to increase their level of sophistication in this exercise. There are methodologies available for isolating the incremental impact. One of them is the Six Sigma process. Another one is the design of controlled experiments. Chapter 6 by Ruggiero and Haedt proposes statistical methods for tracking and measuring the increased effect.

The ratings of the difficulties in measuring the ROI of the pricing function listed in Figure 15.6 clearly show that nothing is simple when it comes to ROIP. Because pricing actions and activities are conducted in a very dynamic environment, it is difficult to isolate the moving parts so as to be able to apply the ROIP formula. Pricing professionals also seem to struggle with defining relevant key performance indicators to track.

When asked the same question but with respect to specific pricing activities, respondents also rated defining the overall incremental pricing effect as the most difficult element to track, as shown in Figure 15.7. Equally difficult is establishing a proper reporting process for ROI and agreeing on a definition of pricing ROI. We hope this book will assist with the latter.

Because of the narrower nature of pricing activities, respondents seem to consider the definition of relevant costs and of the initiative scope to be a bit simpler.

Finally, we asked our survey informants to rate the trend in their use of pricing tools, their investments in pricing, and their intention to hire pricing professionals, as shown in Table 15.4.

Contribution to the measurement of the impact of pricing and ROIP

The objectives of this chapter were to share with practitioners the state of the art associated with the measurement of ROIP. The profession needs to pay close attention to ROIP and needs to develop the proper tools to help practitioners justify their existence. Our review of the impact of pricing revealed fragmented information on the impact of pricing offered by pricing consulting firms. Our survey results support our view that the profession needs to provide more science and data to measure the impact of pricing and to formally measure ROIP.

Our contribution is also intended to reassure pricing practitioners that they are not alone in the struggle for ROIP calculation. Our findings show that the profession seems to have difficulties in measuring ROIP and is not overly successful at it. The same can be said about the calculation of the return on marketing

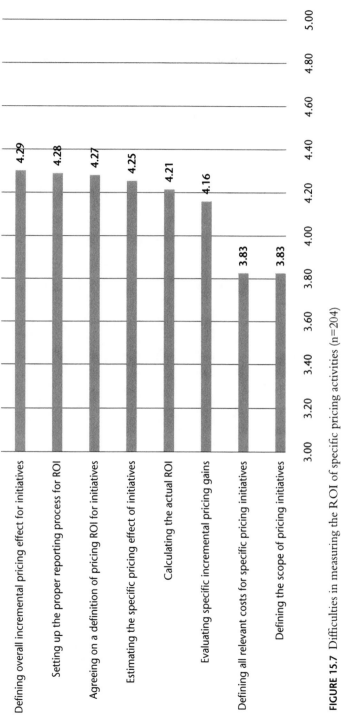

FIGURE 15.7 Difficulties in measuring the ROI of specific pricing activities (n=204)

investments and the calculation of the ROI of social media. This is a much bigger issue than just pricing. But we need to take a proactive approach to better justify pricing investments so that we can get the deserved attention in front of the C-suite.

Finally, we provide pricing professionals with condensed anecdotal evidence on the impact of pricing as researched by some of the best pricing consulting firms. These data points can be used when making the case about pricing inside the organization.

16

CLOSING THOUGHTS

Kevin Mitchell

Pricing is evolving as a business and management discipline. Right now we are in the midst of a golden age of pricing literature; more people than ever have interest in and access to books such as this one. In addition to books and other publications, there is an ever-increasing wealth of knowledge available via various electronic methods – social media groups centred on pricing issues, content expert-led web-based content, networking groups based on geography or industry, and online training venues.

Compare the resources available and strategic importance placed upon pricing now with what would have been available to a proto-pricer from a couple of generations ago. Of course, there were always people who performed pricing functions in business, but they likely would have been very confused by any of the now commonplace terms we would use today to describe how to determine the amount asked for in return for provided goods and/or services.

Our proto-pricer's job may have been a set of clerical duties without all of the arts and sciences involved with pricing careers today. Perhaps he or she created and maintained price lists – with actual prices coming from a business owner's 'gut' decision. Limited status and gravitas could mean that any number of other business functions could override predetermined prices without a second thought – there may be no other repercussions.

The next step in pricing's evolution would have been toward tactical jobs and duties, perhaps taking figures from cost accountants, estimators, the finance department, or product groups and adding a margin percentage to come up with base prices with limited delineations between customer types, or order types and done with little or no regard for competitive forces at hand. Again, exceptions to base prices would have been rampant – perhaps more of the norm than exceptions given potential business pressures that could come from other more established, more highly regarded, more senior positions or departments.

Now there is a different story in many leading organizations. Pricing is gaining more attention from various aspects, including but not limited to:

- Stock market analysts are more likely to incorporate pricing and margin performance into their company reviews
- Colleges, universities, and business schools are offering more classes (and in some cases even majors and concentrations) in pricing
- Senior management and chief level officers are more likely to have strategic pricing initiatives in place[1]
- Pricing salaries are increasing[1]
- There are many more training opportunities within the pricing discipline[2]
- There are more pricing software packages available
- There is much more thought leadership in pricing emanating from consultancies, large and small, academics, and management theorists.

Although pricing is certainly evolving, our discipline still lags behind other business functions with regards to data analysis, advanced training, networking opportunities, and career options. Given pricing's stance as the biggest lever to company profitability,[3] our field is still limited and trailing when compared to others in these areas.

Pricing people have become skilled at certain tactics and analytics (elasticities, market segmentations, determining willingness to pay, waterfalls, volume break-even, etc.) but we have not yet become skilled at measuring the impact of pricing and pricing training within our companies. For example, there have been studies that have shown positive correlation between senior management focus on pricing, strategic pricing initiatives, and company profitability[4] but is there quantitative information showing the value of a skilled, dedicated, centralized, or centre-led, well-trained pricing department? What happens to company margins when pricing departments do a good job of 'managing up', selling ideas to senior leaders, and forging better connections with other departments? Are pricers being professionally trained and if so, then what is the value of training?

It's very easy for corporations to cut training budgets during difficult, recessionary times, but this is often a short-term fix that ignores long-term issues and opportunities. It is penny wise, but pound foolish to forego equipping your teams with the information and skill sets necessary to move your most important lever for various reasons:

- Marketing and competition are really changing quickly now – with new dynamic strategies, new pricing tools, complex marketing channels, and smarter, better connected buyers. Pricers need training on tactics, analysis, negotiation skills, and strategies to keep up.
- Pricing is one of the most important functions for a firm, yet it is often neglected when it comes to formal professional education.

- What is the value of networking amongst ourselves? What about connections to thought leaders, consulting experts, and leading technological solution providers? What is the ROI of attending a pricing conference, getting a Certified Pricing Professional designation, or advanced online training?
- Is your organization taking advantage of lower-cost options available such as the numerous online training forums, Webinars, white papers, blogs, and social media discussion groups that are available?

Another step in pricing's evolution has been the development of the Certified Pricing Professional (CPP) designation, created in conjunction with several leading academics, pricing thought leaders, and leading minds from pricing consultancies and software companies.

At the time of writing (second quarter of 2013), over 2,500 pricers worldwide have earned credits toward the CPP and over 500 of these have completed the Final Exam. According to company leaders who have sent teams to earn the CPP, the top benefits of the certification are:

- Best Practices from Top Pricing Experts – The CPP faculty represents the top minds in business and academia. All of our course materials are based on industry best practices, extensive applied experience, and practitioner success stories.
- Comprehensive Pricing Training – Some courses cover broader fundamental pricing strategies, while others provide in-depth study of more advanced pricing topics. All CPP materials are designed to equip your department with the tools and concepts that will improve profitability.
- The Ability to Develop an Internal Pricing Culture – You can quickly orient your employees to best pricing practices and help instil a structured approach to pricing within your company, creating a powerful internal culture of like-minded pricing experts for your firm.
- Rigorous Certification Process – In addition to earning credits by successfully completing workshops and/or online courses, participants go through a rigorous certification process including an extensive 300-page study guide, covering 14 essential pricing areas and online preparation sessions. For final certification, participants must pass a comprehensive four-hour CPP Accreditation Exam – one of the many reasons why the CPP is the most respected pricing credential in the world.
- You Can Bring Your Pricing Function In-House – Your firm knows its products, services, and strategies better than any external consultant. Empower your own organization with the knowledge needed to improve profits and minimize revenue leaks, while saving on outside fees.

Of course, pricing training also greatly benefits the individual undergoing the advanced learning in addition to benefits gained by their employers. According to those who have earned the CPP designation, some of the greatest benefits include:

- The opportunity for immersion in pricing best practices and marketing methods
- Access to the solid study materials, excellent reference articles, and the CPP workbooks
- The professional networking opportunities with other pricers who are pursuing the CPP
- Systematic instruction for increasing your knowledge whether you are experienced or new to the field
- The relevance of the subject matters covered
- The expertise of the workshop instructors
- The knowledge and ability needed to employ a more structured approach to pricing within your organization
- Salary increase and promotion
- Opportunities to develop and manage new pricing departments within their organizations
- Increased respect and focus from supervisors, colleagues, and employees
- Learning strategies and tactics to improve your organization's profitability
- Establishing yourself as an expert practitioner in the field
- Joining an exclusive group who excel in virtually every aspect of pricing
- Personally standing out as a candidate for firms who seek to employ the best executives in pricing
- Being on the leadership track to advance one's career.

Stephan Liozu, Andreas Hinterhuber, and many of the others included in this book share a common goal of increasing pricing's stature to a level equal to its importance as a business function, margin driver, and profitability lever. It is my charge to you to lead, manage, recruit, train, and motivate the pricers within your companies, as I believe that investments in our currently underrepresented discipline will prove to be most fruitful for you and your organization. This book is another step in the right direction. It is providing key insights on how to justify our existence and our efforts. I strongly encourage you to discover these techniques and to experiment. Let's bring the real story of the impact of pricing in organizations.

Notes

1   Professional Pricing Society – year end salary and demographics surveys (2007, 2008, 2010, 2011, 2012).
2   The organization that I am lucky enough to be a part of, the Professional Pricing Society currently offers large conferences on three continents and has over two dozen online pricing workshops.
3   Marn et al. (2004) and many others.
4   Our lead author Stephan Liozu's study and recent studies by the firm Simon-Kucher & Partners are recent examples.

Reference

Marn, M. V., Roegner, E. V. and Zawada, C. C. (2004) *The price advantage*. Hoboken, NJ: Wiley.

INDEX

Word order is letter by letter; page numbers for figures and tables are in *italics* and the letter 'n' refers to an end note.